Teaching: The Book

Instructional Skills and Strategies for the Experienced and the Novice Teacher

Jean T. Anastasio
David J. Perry
Timothy J. Sharer

APL Associates

SECOND EDITION • VERSION 1

Published by
APL ASSOCIATES
PO Box 250
Camillus, NY 13031
Telephone/Fax: (315) 672-5668
aplassociates@twcny.rr.com

Copies of this book may be obtained by contacting:

APL ASSOCIATES
PO Box 250
Camillus, NY 13031
Telephone/Fax: (315) 672-5668
aplassociates@twcny.rr.com

Discounts are available for bulk quantity purchases to corporations, professional associations, and other organizations. Contact the publisher for details.

ISBN 1-4276-1321-4

LCCN TXu-329-152

FIRST EDITION

Printed On-Demand by
MORROW GRAPHICS, INC.
901 James Street
Syracuse, NY 13203
315.425.0051 Phone
315.426.9663 Fax
www.morrowgraphics.com

Cover Art by

CORBIN SHARER
420 West 12th Street
Wayne, NE 68787
sharer@huntel.net

TABLE OF CONTENTS

Section Four: The End of Class 131

Section Five: Parents and Teachers 157

Section Six: Closing Thoughts 183

Section Seven: About the Authors 185

Section Eight: Appendices 189

Section Nine: Index of Subjects 235

Acknowledgements

The production of this book would not have been possible without the contributions of many who through the years have been of great assistance in making APL Associates successful in achieving our goals for this organization and for the profession of teaching. The collaboration that resulted in the publication of this book about their shared passion for effective teaching and learning was truly a "labor of love."

Jean, David and Tim would like to thank their families for their encouragement and support which have been important motivations in undertaking and completing this project.

In addition, they would like to thank:

- **Krista Schoch** who keeps APL Associates on track and running like clockwork.
- **John Zalonis** for his continuing contributions to the success and reputation of APL Associates.
- **Corbin Sharer** for creating, designing and producing the cover art.
- **Holly Anastasio** for editing this edition and contributing the sketches throughout the book.

Introduction

What's in this book?

In the course of our work with pre-service and in-service educators, we've witnessed teaching and learning orchestrated by competent teachers who (either intuitively or because of professional development) employ strategies which are learner-friendly, highly effective, and which challenge learners to excel in the achievement of the learning outcomes. In fact, we would go so far as to say, "Great teachers make teaching look incredibly easy." However, what you see a great teacher doing on the surface only minimally represents the multi-faceted responsibilities of teaching. We have written this book in order to more formally examine many of those multi-faceted responsibilities. Whether you read this book from cover to cover, or use it as a resource, you will find researched-based strategies designed to assist teachers in the improvement of classroom instruction, classroom organization and classroom management.

We have lived and worked under the axiom, **"If you want it – teach it!"** From our collective experience, we believe that in order for certain classroom practices and procedures to be in place (how to hand in homework, how to behave in the lunch line, how to respond to asked questions, etc.), those practices and procedures must be taught to students in a manner similar to the teaching of academic content or skills that students need to know to be successful inside and outside of school. Teachers must stop assuming that students know how to do routine school tasks because many students do not. Teachers must design and teach lessons on any specific behavioral, organizational, or managerial components relative to their classroom that are necessary for each student to be successful, including such fundamental school practices as getting students to participate, giving clear directions, effectively organizing lessons and lesson materials, getting students to complete and hand-in homework and other tasks essential to student and teacher success. We do not mean to imply that students know nothing about school processes, because students bring a great deal of prior knowledge into the classroom setting. That being said, we also believe that educators have specific methods they use to be both effective and efficient in their classrooms. Your students likewise deserve to know what those methods are, and how and when to successfully use each method in that particular classroom. It is on that premise that the idea for this book was initiated.

The book is divided into nine sections that relate to specific teacher needs at important junctures within the teaching and learning environment. While some of this information is common knowledge and widely known in the field of education, we have found that these ideas are infrequently and inconsistently utilized in everyday teaching. The predictable results of inconsistent or infrequent use of effective strategies are decreased productivity, frequent reteaching and review, and minimized achievement for most students.

Section One addresses effective strategies for **Before Class or the Day** such as positive teacher attributes, teacher goal setting, becoming the teacher you want to be, the four basic learner outcomes of instruction, motivation, the classroom success ladder, lesson outcomes, classroom conditions, serial positioning, providing an exit, feeling tone, level of concern, the components of the successful student behavior management process, the five steps in successfully teaching a behavior, shaping, behavior management and teaming and building level behaviors. Section Two explains teaching strategies to use at the **Beginning of Class** such as setting the stage, greeting students, using agendas, communicating the "what" and "how," bell ringers, and going over homework. In Section Three, we explain what should happen in the **Middle of the Class**. Strategies addressed are anticipatory set, active participation, wait-time, wait-time extended, interaction sequence, checking for understanding, clear directions and information, chaining, checking for understanding of directions, note taking, managing time to facilitate learning, the monitoring map, knowledge of results, modeling, interest and group work. Section Four contains information about the **End of Class** such as closure, practice, homework, work orders, reflecting on the day and planning for tomorrow. In Section Five we address strategies concerning **Parents and Teachers**. These strategies include managing and keeping school a priority, parent conference process, assisting children with homework, managing behaviors at home, and dealing with bullying at school. Section Six contains some **Closing Thoughts** about teacher and learner effectiveness. In Section Seven there is information **About the Authors** and how to contact us. Section Eight contains the **Appendices** including a table of the Instructional Skills covered in this book with a glossary of terms, the four basic learner outcomes of instruction, sample lesson plans for teaching behaviors, a table of differential reinforcement strategies, information from the *Public Agenda Survey of High School Students*, a Course Goals Setting Framework, an APL approach for designing and planning effective lessons, and a list of references that were influential in the formation of this book. The final section of the book is an index of the subjects referenced throughout the book.

Why is this book beneficial?

As we begin a closer examination of teaching and learning, two key questions are often asked of us by beginning and veteran teachers. The first is, "How can I do a better job of teaching my students?" And the second is, "How can I do a better job of managing student behavior?" In the book, we address those questions specifically to assist you at the beginning, middle and end of the day and class with the selection of strategies to use for teaching and the management of your classroom. The answers to these two questions are associated with the need for teachers to think carefully about the "what," the "how" and the "why" of effective teaching leading to effective learning. We've asked ourselves what we think are the key elements of effective teaching. After years of examining the phenomenon of teaching, we've arrived at what we call the **three power words for teaching: organization, consistency and specificity**. Educators and other experts agree that the single most important factor in the learning of a child is the overall competence of the child's teacher (Darling-Hammond 2002; Goldhaber and Brewer 1999; Hanushek, Kain and Rivkin 1999). In order to improve the outcomes of learning, we must strive to improve the skills and instructional effectiveness of teachers. While no one book can answer all questions or solve all problems related to teaching and learning, this book offers practical and usable instructional, organizational and managerial ideas that are proven effective in assisting teachers to be **organized, consistent** and **specific** in the "real world" of teaching.

For whom is this book beneficial?

While this book is written with the classroom teacher as its primary audience, we also offer some **advice to parents** in Section Five. Some of that advice consists of how to help your children with homework, how to be successful in parent teacher conferences, how to keep school a priority for your child and you, and how to teach home behaviors to your children. In the course of our work, we have taught thousands of parents in our Parent Workshops these specific strategies. Parents across the country have responded back with testimonials of the overwhelmingly successful results from their application of these ideas in their own lives and families. We encourage parents to venture beyond Section Five and to get better acquainted with the many ways their child's teacher is working to ensure that their child is successful in school and in life.

A word of caution is necessary here. Each of the authors has read widely in the areas of instruction, organization and management. As with any "how to" book, these ideas have worked extremely well in consistent practice for the authors. But as with any advice on how to improve one's teaching, there is no "magic" formula or prescription which takes the place of good practice built on techniques proven while working with children, adolescents and adult learners. We trust that you will find some new ideas within this book and that you will have some of your own ideas about teaching and managing a classroom confirmed. *This book is about encouraging positive change to achieve positive results.* Teachers must be experts in two key areas. They must be **experts in the content they teach**, and they must be **experts in how teaching works** (effective instructional strategies). Remember the old adage that: "If you always do what you've always done, you'll always get what you always got." Here's hoping that you are getting the results you want from teaching as well as the satisfaction of knowing that you are doing what is effective and efficient for each one of your students.

[For additional reading please refer to the Reference Section of the book beginning on page 201.]

Section One: Before Class or the Day

In this section, topics related to before class or the day will be addressed. Before teaching and learning can begin, time must be taken to acknowledge, think through and decide on the main features of your teaching philosophy, professional goals, classroom organization and management, implementation of instructional strategies and creating a learning environment that promotes success.

Positive Teacher Attributes

In order for teachers to become and remain effective, they must develop positive attributes that contribute to student success. Here are seven basic positive attributes we believe will contribute to the successes in your classroom and life.

1. Positive teachers must become **relationship experts**. Good teachers know that being honest, respectful and positive are the keys to building effective relationships resulting in successful classroom productivity. You must give respect to get respect and be mature enough to admit when you're wrong. In essence, we are saying what William Glasser (1998) is saying: Relationships are more important than anything else.
2. Positive teachers must become **content experts**. Good teachers view their main responsibility as teaching. This requires teachers to be experts in their content area(s). An organized regimen of professional reading and advanced studies is integral to achieving this goal.
3. Positive teachers must become **learning theory experts** (Sousa 2006). Good teachers understand the importance of using developmentally appropriate practices and of knowing how people learn. Effective teachers rely on diagnosis (analyzing the tasks and identifying prior learner knowledge), remediation (filling in the gaps in the learners' knowledge through practice) and enrichment (increasing rate and degree of learning) as key aspects of successful teaching.
4. Positive teachers must become **critical thinkers and teach problem solving** (Sousa 2006). Good teachers expect some difficulties in helping all students learn, but are prepared to provide the appropriate follow-up instructions that will

help students be more successful. Guiding students toward metacognition and autonomy in learning should be a priority for teachers. Metacognition is thinking about thinking, knowing "what we know" and "what we don't know." A thinker's job is to manage his/her thinking using the basic metacognitive strategies of connecting new information to former knowledge, selecting thinking strategies deliberately, and planning, monitoring, and evaluating thinking processes (Dirkes 1985).

5. Positive teachers must **set and maintain appropriate standards of behavior**. Good teachers expect all students to meet at least the minimum specified behavior objectives. Be organized, specific and consistent in your expectations for dealing with the students. *Remember: "Fair does not necessarily mean the same."*
6. Positive teachers must **use labels sparingly** and **make sure those labels are mindful**. Good teachers expect to deal with individuals [mindful labels], not groups or stereotypes [mindless labels] (Savage, McLaughlin, Powell & Zehm 1998). All teachers must use labels during evaluation. Mindful labels not only have the intent of assisting the student, but in fact do make learning more purposeful and successful. Providing students with labels that positively affect their intellectual and social growth is a necessary ingredient for success in your classroom and in life.
7. Positive teachers must **know their audience**. Good teachers build a stimulating classroom environment that makes learning enjoyable for all students, not just for the high ability group. Challenge yourself to work diligently to enter the "quality worlds" (Glasser 1997) of each one of your students.

Developing these seven attributes may encompass a more formal program of study such as a graduate degree program, workshops or clinics on any or all of these topics, or less formal methods of reading and discussion with colleagues of articles or books or websites devoted to the development and growth of these noteworthy attributes. Whatever method is chosen, it is necessary to undertake it with regularity and to extend what one learns by applying it in the classroom. One caution is necessary, however. We've seen many teachers read and/or hear about new instructional or managerial techniques that are guaranteed by the author/speaker to revolutionize education. As with any tool, you must have the right one for the job or you may indeed create more work for yourself by using the wrong one. Careful consideration of what it is, how you will use it, when you will use it and with whom, and the expected outcomes of its use are crucial to influencing the level and consistency of success you desire for your students.

Teacher Goal Setting

The job of teaching requires much time, a commitment to the altruistic values of education and job-specific knowledge. We frequently hear people refer to the mistaken axiom, "Those who can't, teach." Nothing, however, could be further from the truth. While many people believe that anyone can teach, it is profoundly apparent that not everyone can teach effectively. Therefore, it is vitally important that each of us who has chosen teaching as our profession remain vigilant regarding our ongoing needs to develop our knowledge and skills about teaching to the fullest extent possible. The desire to further develop as a teacher can be strategized in a more efficacious way to help us meet those goals.

The following strategy is recommended as one effective means of improving teaching. This simple ten-step process should be used in an organized and consistent manner to achieve maximum results.

Ten Steps to Enhancing Teaching Effectiveness

1. Teacher must answer these two questions: First, what do I want the students to "walk out the door with" at the end of the lesson? And second, what will students do to exhibit that they have mastered the content or the skill?
2. Once you have determined the answers to those two questions, then choose the instructional strategies you want to immediately implement in your classroom. You may want to refer to **Appendix A** in Section Eight as a quick reference for the basic instructional skills and which outcome each achieves. (Example strategies: communicating the "what" and "how"; using agendas; frequent checking for understanding; and running a closure)
3. Next, review each strategy for the following information:
    a. What is the definition of this strategy?

   b. Which outcome of learning does it meet?
   c. What are the steps in this strategy necessary to be successful?
   d. What is the best time during instruction to use this strategy?
   e. How frequently should one use this strategy during a lesson (class)?
   f. How will I know if I used the strategy correctly?
   g. How will I know if the strategy achieved the outcome I desired?
   h. What evidence do I have that the strategy was effective?
4. Repeat this process for each of your chosen strategies.
5. Make a commitment to use these strategies faithfully, consistently and correctly for one month.
6. At the end of the month, accurately assess the results. Videotaping and/or peer observation/assessment are both effective strategies to produce useful feedback. After the observation of the lesson, conference with your peer assessor (if you have one).
7. Begin the conference by indicating what you think went well, and then what you believe you could have done in a more effective way. Then, your peer assessor should indicate what he/she saw you do that was effective, and what he/she saw you do that needs improvement. Together you should brainstorm what adjustments are necessary for you to make to enhance your use of these strategies.
8. Next, select two new strategies to study and use during the next month. Make arrangements for additional observations to assess your use of the new strategies. Continue to practice and use your original strategies as you implement the two additional instructional skills.
9. Continue this process over time to more fully develop your repertoire of effective instructional strategies.
10. Don't be afraid to ask your students for feedback. Good teachers do not fear but welcome feedback from students in an effort to improve their teaching and communication skills.

One of the best methods we've seen in place is one used by an elementary school in the Midwest. In this school, the teachers and para-educators have identified three strategies at the beginning of the school year that they are all going to use consistently and correctly during the school year with the intent of adding three more new strategies each month until all the basic instructional strategies are in place. This process does not limit teachers initially to using only those three skills, but rather it demonstrates a commitment from the teachers to be more organized, specific and consistent for the sake of all the students in that building. Teachers may not use all of the basic strategies in every lesson they teach, but when more of them are consciously used, more active and productive learning occurs. That elementary school was guided by the **three power words for teaching** that were examined in the introduction to the book: **organization, specificity and consistency**. We commend the teachers, para-educators and administrators of that school for adhering to that recommendation.

Becoming the Teacher You Want to Be

For the purpose of assessing teacher effectiveness, let's classify teachers into the following four categories: **Super Stars, Rising Stars, Middle Stars,** and **Falling Stars**. It is helpful when setting professional goals to know where one stands along this professional continuum. It is essential that when you make personal and professional assessments of your teaching efforts and results, that you do so as objectively as possible. Without the objectivity we may fail to recognize accurately our current status. Let's take a closer look at each of these four categories. We have divided each category into two sets of characteristics. The first set is **personal** characteristics; the second is **organizational** and **professional** characteristics. Each set is broken down into checklists to make it easier to run a self-assessment on your own characteristics, and we encourage you to check off those that you believe identify your teaching efforts and results. We'll start with the category **Super Stars** and move through each in turn. As you read the characteristics within each category, consider placing a check in the box next to the characteristics you already possess and exhibit with regularity. Be honest in your examination so that you accurately represent your professional self.

Super Stars are teachers who possess the following characteristics:

Personal

- ☐ Has a positive attitude
- ☐ Is enthusiastic / energetic
- ☐ Is willing (has a "can do" mentality)
- ☐ Is loyal
- ☐ Is willing to work with others
- ☐ Is reliable
- ☐ Takes initiative
- ☐ Is reflective

Organizational / Professional

- ☐ Sets goals
- ☐ Consistently meets expectations of the organization
- ☐ Consistently follows established rules
- ☐ Is a team player
- ☐ Is involved
- ☐ Has a strong grasp of instructional delivery skills and strategies and implements them
- ☐ Has a well defined and appropriate student behavior management approach
- ☐ Is an expert in his/her area(s) of content / curriculum
- ☐ Knows, understands, and incorporates standards
- ☐ Has consistently high student performance results
- ☐ Is highly regarded by students, parents and staff
- ☐ Welcomes feedback
- ☐ Seeks opportunities to grow and improve

Rising Stars are teachers who possess the following characteristics:

Personal

- ☐ Exhibits many (60-85%) of the Super Star characteristics in this category
- ☐ Is loyal
- ☐ Is reflective

Organizational / Professional

- ☐ Exhibits many (60-85%) of the Super Star characteristics in this category

Middle Stars are teachers who possess the following characteristics:

Personal

- ☐ Exhibits a few (40-60%) of the Super Star characteristics in this category
- ☐ Is not as open to feedback
- ☐ Is moderately reflective
- ☐ Will move if pushed or prodded

Organizational / Professional

- ☐ Exhibits a few (40-60%) of the Super Star characteristics in this category
- ☐ Does an "OK" job
- ☐ Is satisfied with his/her overall student performance
- ☐ Does not often seek opportunities to grow and improve
- ☐ Is easily swayed or led by some in the Falling Star category
- ☐ Cuts corners

Falling Stars are teachers who possess the following characteristics:

Personal

- ☐ Exhibits less than 40% of the Super Star characteristics in this category
- ☐ Tends to be cynical (sarcastic)
- ☐ Focuses on the negative (why things won't work or why things can't be done)
- ☐ Is inflexible
- ☐ Frequently complains
- ☐ Blames others for problems or failures (students, parents, administrations, state, standards, etc.)

Organizational / Professional

- ☐ Exhibits less than 40% of the Super Star characteristics in this category
- ☐ Has a lukewarm or negative classroom climate
- ☐ Is often inconsistent (with behaviors, rules, procedures, instructional delivery)
- ☐ Has mediocre to poor student performance results
- ☐ May often have student behavior management concerns
- ☐ Requires significant monitoring and maintenance
- ☐ Is not positively viewed by others (students, staff, parents, etc.)
- ☐ Cuts corners
- ☐ Tends to stir things up (not a team player)
- ☐ Will actively work to block organization initiatives (resistive)
- ☐ Can be disloyal
- ☐ May breach confidentiality (inappropriate sharing or discussing of confidential information about students, staff, parents, etc.)
- ☐ Is not readily open to feedback

As you check off the boxes (characteristics) in the table below (Table 1), the degree of teacher effort and results will be reflected by the number of checks and under which of the four teacher types those checks reside. Constant vigilance is necessary if one is to become and remain a **Super Star**. No one is relegated to remain in a particular category, but can (and probably should) make choices to improve based on which area(s) may need attention. The process of reshaping one's personal and/or professional characteristics is not simple, but it can be accomplished with commitment and the implementation of a plan for improvement.

Table 1. Categories of Teacher Characteristics

Category	Personal Characteristics	Organizational/Professional Characteristics
Super Stars are teachers who possess the following characteristics:	☐ Has a positive attitude ☐ Is enthusiastic / energetic ☐ Is willing (has a "can do" mentality) ☐ Is loyal ☐ Is willing to work with others ☐ Is reliable ☐ Takes initiative ☐ Is reflective	☐ Sets goals ☐ Consistently meets expectations of the organization ☐ Consistently follows established rules ☐ Is a team player ☐ Is involved ☐ Has a strong grasp of instructional delivery skills and strategies and implements them ☐ Has a well defined and appropriate student behavior management approach ☐ Is an expert in his/her area(s) of content / curriculum ☐ Knows, understands, and incorporates standards ☐ Has consistently high student performance results ☐ Is highly regarded by students, parents and staff ☐ Welcomes feedback ☐ Seeks opportunities to grow and improve
Rising Stars are teachers who possess the following characteristics:	☐ Exhibits many (60-85%) of the Super Star characteristics in this category ☐ Is loyal ☐ Is reflective	☐ Exhibits many (60-85%) of the Super Star characteristics in this category
Middle Stars are teachers who possess the following characteristics:	☐ Exhibits a few (40-60%) of the Super Star characteristics in this category ☐ Is not as open to feedback ☐ Is moderately reflective ☐ Will move if pushed or prodded	☐ Exhibits a few (40-60%) of the Super Star characteristics in this category ☐ Does an "OK" job ☐ Is satisfied with his/her overall student performance ☐ Does not often seek opportunities to grow and improve ☐ Is easily swayed or led by some in the Falling Star category ☐ Cuts corners

Table 1. Categories of Teacher Characteristics (continued)

Category	Personal Characteristics	Organizational/Professional Characteristics
Falling Stars are teachers who possess the following characteristics:	☐ Exhibits less than 40% of the Super Star characteristics in this category ☐ Tends to be cynical (sarcastic) ☐ Focuses on the negative (why things won't work or why things can't be done) ☐ Is inflexible ☐ Frequently complains ☐ Blames others for problems or failures (students, parents, administrations, state, standards, etc.)	☐ Exhibits less than 40% of the Super Star characteristics in this category ☐ Has a lukewarm or negative classroom climate ☐ Is often inconsistent (with behaviors, rules, procedures, instructional delivery) ☐ Has mediocre to poor student performance results ☐ May often have student behavior management concerns ☐ Requires significant monitoring and maintenance ☐ Is not positively viewed by others (students, staff, parents, etc.) ☐ Cuts corners ☐ Tends to stir things up (not a team player) ☐ Will actively work to block organization initiatives (resistive) ☐ Can be disloyal ☐ May breach confidentiality (inappropriate sharing or discussing of confidential information about students, staff, parents, etc.) ☐ Is not readily open to feedback

The Four Basic Learner Outcomes of Instruction

The four basic learner outcomes of all instruction are **focus**, **rate and degree of learning**, **retention**, and **transfer**. When we achieve ***focus,*** students are attending to the main idea, concept, or skill that is the essence of that lesson activity. In our efforts to achieve student focus, we may use several key instructional strategies: a lesson agenda, a bell ringer, sharing the instructional objectives, an anticipatory set, a transition phrase, on-the-clock, even a check for understanding. All these instructional cues are intended to help students focus on the main idea and to avoid having them lost in less important information which may be supportive but not always highly essential to the main concept. If the teacher does not actively design lessons that have focus strategies, each student is then required to create his/her own focus strategy. Some students are quite capable of focusing without teacher cues. However, as you can imagine many students struggle with identifying the main idea of a lesson when left to fend for themselves. It is always better to not leave student focus to chance, but to purposefully and frequently embed focus strategies into every lesson to promote student success. We've all been in a class, or a meeting and had our attention drift to what we're going to have for dinner, or what bills we need to pay, or how we are going to get all those essays graded by 8:00 a.m. tomorrow, only to find upon returning to reality that the instructor or chair has proceeded to a different topic and we've been left behind. Our students face the same barriers to maintaining focus. When we deliberately address the issue of focus by using strategies to acquire and maintain student focus during the lesson we greatly improve our students' achievement of the outcomes of the lesson.

The second essential outcome of instruction is ***rate and degree of learning***. Rate and degree of learning refer to the pace (rate) at which students learn a concept or skill and depth (degree) also to which the students learn a concept or skill. It is of vital importance that we know our students well enough to match the speed at which we cover a concept and the overall depth (how well) our students can manage in grasping all the parts of the concept. In striving for rate and degree, we must analyze the content we intend to teach by breaking it down into its components (task analysis), ordering those components into a sequence that makes sense, teaching each component in that rational sequence, and, in between each component, checking for student understanding of what has just been taught and learned before moving on to the next component. It is of essential importance that we constantly monitor the rate and degree of our students' learning. When we do, we are assured of what they have learned, if what they have learned is accurate, and to what degree they have learned it. Through this monitoring process, we are able to ascertain if (and when) students have sufficiently achieved the lesson objectives. If the objective is satisfactorily achieved, then we may move on to the next objective in the sequence. By using focus, active participation, and frequently checking for student understanding, we are serving two significant purposes. First, we will know with greater accuracy where students are on the continuum of achieving that objective. Second, by using focus, active participation and frequent checking for understanding, we are actually able to increase both the rate and degree of student learning because these instructional strategies provide for more effectual time-on-task. Rather than just telling students, we are coaching, demonstrating, modeling, listening, asking questions, guiding practice, keeping students active and all the while holding students accountable for their own learning. *Knowing* instead of *guessing* that students have achieved the objective allows the students and the teacher to move on to additional learning confidently and with a significantly higher achievement overall. This is where the science of teaching influences the outcomes of the processes of teaching and learning without stifling the art of teaching (being creative and responsive to teachable moments).

The third essential outcome of instruction is ***retention***. When we teach for retention, we are using strategies that assist students in building long-term memory schemata that will not only be more easily and reliably recalled for later uses, but will serve as the foundational network for additional conceptual and procedural knowledge that will be offered in future lessons and experiences. Retention is influenced by several instructional strategies. The first is **checking for understanding** (CFU) with deliberate frequency. The information we receive during CFU assists us in the instructional decisions to move on, review, or re-teach depending on the results of the CFU. Second is using **closure** consistently at the end of teaching episodes and major concluding points such as the end of units, or semesters. Third, we influence retention through the deliberate use of **practice** (both guided and independent) and strategically using homework guidelines that provide students with opportunities to practice new information, recent past information and distant past information. With those three focus points in mind (new, recent, distant) we can ordain greater encoding of information, and we can connect that information to existing schemata, making it more easily recalled and more deeply retained in memory. In Section Three we will discuss the **forgetting curve**. The forgetting curve provides us with information resulting from memory research that assists us in ascertaining how to more effectively use CFU and practice to achieve the desired retention results. More about these ideas will be explained in subsequent sections.

The fourth and final essential outcome of instruction is ***transfer***. Transfer is teaching students to use knowledge, skills and attitudes in new contexts. Transfer gives students opportunities to generalize information beyond the immediate context where it was learned. There are several important features to be gained from teaching for transfer. First, students begin to see how knowledge is contextual, but not necessarily relegated to only one context (place). Too often students come to believe that there is "school knowledge" and there is "knowledge we can really use." Teaching for transfer allows us to help students overcome that misconception about knowledge and skills by helping them assign **meaning**. Second, by seeing knowledge and skills in other settings we provide a broader background for students to remember the information more deeply. This concurrently enhances ***rate and degree of learning*** and ***retention*** as well as the outcome of ***transfer***. If we want our students to become problem solvers who use higher-order thinking skills in alternate and novel contexts, teaching for transfer provides precisely the venue for building those much needed and highly respected life skills. Let's take a look at an instructional strategy that has significant impact on all four of these essential outcomes of learning.

Motivation

Motivation is defined as the mental process, function or instinct that produces and sustains incentive or drive in humans. Motivation helps us achieve the intended instructional outcomes of ***focus, rate and degree, retention*** *and* ***transfer***. Motivation can assist humans in becoming accountable for the outcomes of a task. It can assist students in becoming accountable for their own learning and behavior management. Motivation is a key element in helping students achieve success. **Success** may be defined as the feeling that a student experiences that results from genuine achievement. **Genuine achievement** may be defined as the outcomes based on work or effort which gives you a good feeling. *It is important to note that the most effective motivator is success.*

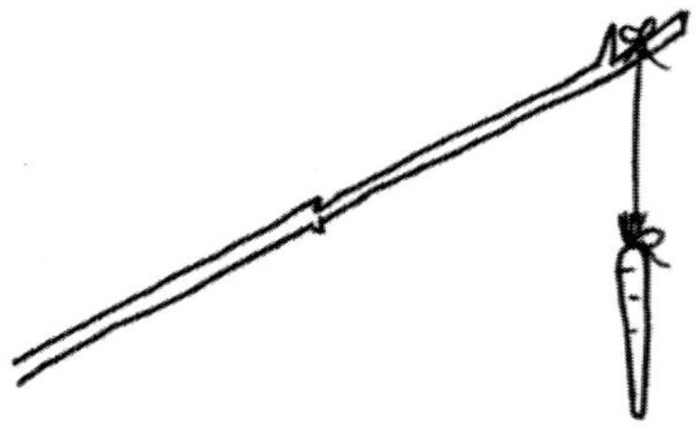

Motivation takes two primary forms: **intrinsic motivation** and **extrinsic motivation**. Intrinsic motivation is the most powerful because it originates from within the learner. Extrinsic motivation is also quite powerful, but it is dependent on stimuli that reside outside the learner.

Intrinsic motivation may be better defined by two key characteristics:

- ☐ Process: I like the process.
- ☐ Product: I like (or enjoy) the product.

Extrinsic motivation may likewise be better defined by two key characteristics:

- ☐ Process: I do not like the process.
- ☐ Product: But, I like (or enjoy) the product.

An example of extrinsic motivation would be: "I don't like lawn mowing, but I like the way a mowed lawn looks." An example of intrinsic motivation would be: "I like reading professional journals because I enjoy being in the know about relevant topics."

It is important to keep in mind **two key points about motivation.** First, don't get hung up on whether a student is extrinsic about a task. And second, extrinsic motivation is often changeable to intrinsic motivation.

There are two other key factors that assist in the motivating of students. First, we must endeavor to help students make **sense** of the learning so that it is linked, connected, and matched to what the students already know and to what the students need to know and be able to do to be successful. Second, we should strive to make the learning **meaningful** which helps to provide use, value and relevance to what is being taught/learned for the students.

Motivation is even further complicated when we consider that it is significantly impacted by what students believe about their ability to learn or not learn. **Students who struggle** with school frequently attribute the few successes they have on an assignment to good luck, the task being easy, the teacher liking or feeling sorry for them, or a combination of the three. Likewise, **students who usually succeed** with school assignments often attribute their successes to effort and ability. **Students who are most at-risk** with respect to school achievement may attribute their lack of achievement to bad luck, the task being too difficult, or possibly the teacher doesn't like them or want them to succeed. This last group believes that no matter how much effort they expend, there is no possibility that they will achieve the standard, be able to complete the work or earn a passing grade. Success seems impossible for group three. Motivation is linked in many critical ways to both effort and ability. That being said, it takes more than encouragement and praise, more than one, two or even several successes, and more than debunking the myth of luck, degree of difficulty, or being liked by the teacher. When motivating students who struggle, we must look into their past school histories to see how and why they became strugglers. We must listen to what they say to us in order to find out what interests them. We must be led by those ideas when we design activities and assignments so that those assignments and activities create interest and will better foster honest success. We must also help all our students discover that **effort** is one of the key components of a successful person that can be directly controlled and that does directly impact the outcome of any pursuit. Our students must also learn that **“failure is not a terminal condition – but an opportunity”** -- an opportunity that provides for additional learning and that reveals our true character.

When we are successful at something we feel good intrinsically about the process and about ourselves. Therefore, we are more inclined to want to repeat that process and to “feel” successful again. Being successful does more than just motivate us. It also provides a higher level of confidence whereby we are more willing to take the risks required to continue learning. As teachers we may try every conceivable strategy we know to motivate a student, but if that student has not previously experienced success, or does not see the possibility of experiencing success with whatever it is we want him/her to do, no amount of encouragement will do what it takes to motivate him/her. The Amish have a saying that was once a more widely held belief: “True self-worth comes from feeling capable.” We must endeavor with all our resources to help all children become capable. Therein lies the essence of the axiom, “**success must come before motivation**.”

Classroom Success Ladder

Classroom success is dependent on teaching, learning, motivating, and successful student performance on the given tasks and assessments. The sequence of these events, particularly where and when motivation is introduced, has an impact on how successful our students become. The ultimate **goal** in any classroom is that students learn the material at the established level of acceptable performance and subsequently become interested in furthering those successes with similar experiences. Along the way we apply strategies to motivate students as we work with them in moving closer and closer to the goal. In order to ultimately rely on the students’ intrinsic motivation, we must start at the beginning and follow a sequence that moves students toward classroom success. We call this specific sequence the **classroom success ladder**. Figure 1 (page 20) illustrates the concept of the classroom success ladder. As with any ladder, we start at the bottom and in application it works as follows:

- ☐ First, teachers must understand and use **instructional strategies** in ways that positively affect the learners. The premise of this book is to identify and illustrate specifically those strategies that will assist in accomplishing those positive effects and why those strategies result in success.
- ☐ Second, teachers must design instruction so that kids can attain some level of immediate **success**. Admittedly, one must take risks to learn, and the biggest risk for many students is the fear of failing. Encouraging your students and providing a safe environment where learning risks are minimized begins the process of motivating students extrinsically and assists in moving students in a positive learning direction.
- ☐ Third, to make **extrinsic motivation** productive, teachers must know their students well enough to be able to identify effective ways to extrinsically motivate each student which encourages them to take the necessary risks to learn. The outcomes of successfully using extrinsic motivation are seen as students relish the successes they achieve and, in turn, become excited to continue their learning process.
- ☐ Fourth, part of students achieving success must include students making meaningful connections between what they already know and what they are currently learning. Assigning **meaning** to new content and skills enhances success. When **meaning** is achieved, students have been able to successfully understand the intent and the significance of the new material. This step is crucial if we are to achieve the fifth step in the process.
- ☐ **Successful learning** is the fifth step and is the goal for all learning experiences. Successful learning results when meaning is assigned which encourages future student successes in the learning processes. Remember, to be able to assign accurate meaning, students must understand both the **sense** and the **meaning** of the new concepts they are learning. This "intellectual wrestling" is crucial in the cognitive processes.
- ☐ Step six is the place in the process where **intrinsic motivation** occurs and where student curiosity is further fueled by the desire for more feelings of success. Abraham Maslow would call this the state of Self-Actualization, where a human

being is tapping into his/her capabilities and engaging his/her talents as he/she enjoys both the processes and results of learning. Students will seek additional experiences when they become intrinsically motivated by their successes and by understanding how the new information is relevant to their lives and connected to what they already know. This further illustrates our premise that *success comes before motivation.*

Figure 1. Classroom Success Ladder

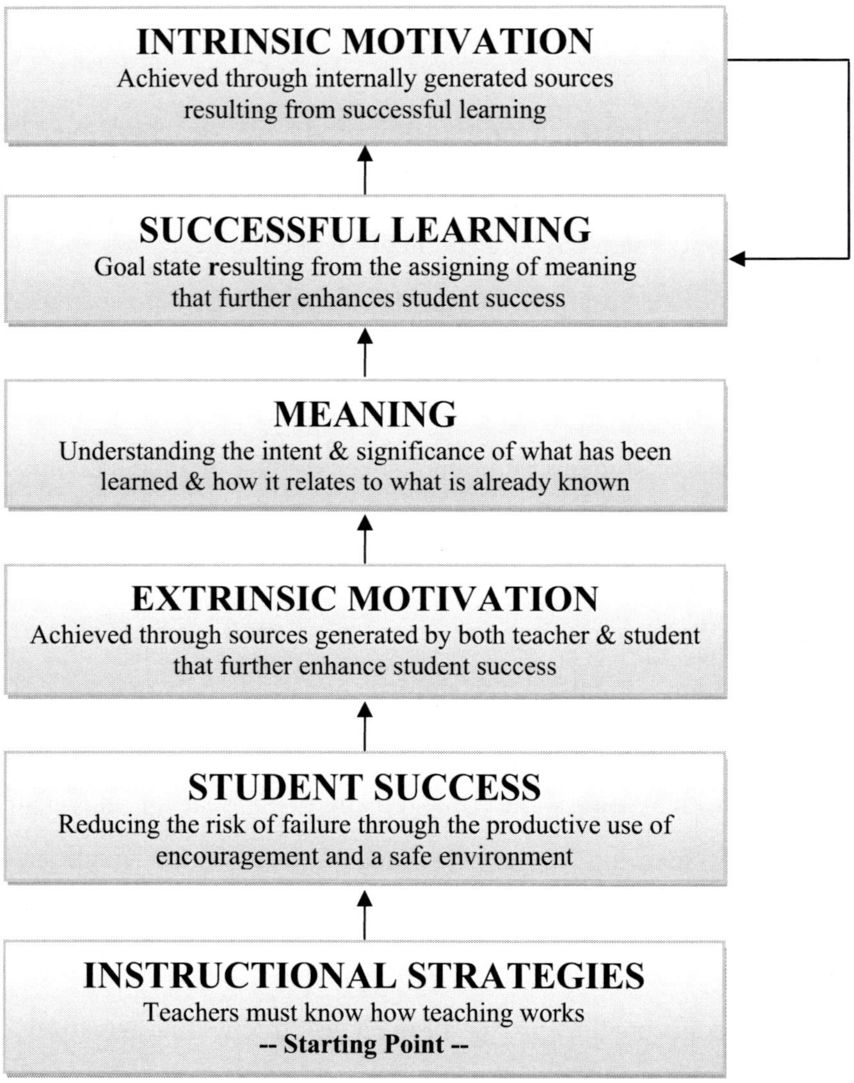

Lesson Outcomes

Instructional Objectives: The "What" and "How"

The "**what**" of instruction could be nicknamed the "right stuff." It is what we want students to know (content, skill or attitude) when the lesson is completed. The "**how**" is the specific action students will take to prove to us that they have accomplished the "**what**" of the lesson. In educational terms we call this the **instructional objective**. We can break the objective down into two essential parts. The first ("**what**") is the **content,** or what it is that you want the students to "walk out the door with." The content is the meat of the subject, the information needed and/or the skills to be acquired. That information must be specific in order to provide focus. That information must also reveal what students **need to know** (basic or essential content) and what would be **nice to know** (enriched content).

The second ("**how**") is the **behavior**. This is what students will need to do to show you that they have accomplished that specific content; to exhibit that they have "mastered the content or skill." In other words, how will students do this? Will they write it, say it, demonstrate it, take a test, or (best) teach it to someone else (which is the most powerful demonstration of their degree of mastery)?

While these two components of instructional objectives are the most significant, there are other supportive components that help to identify the "**what**" and the "**how**." Let's examine the other components.

The four components of instructional objectives are the conditions, the content, the behavior and the performance. The **conditions** of an objective deal with the "givens" within the lesson plan or delivery system such as directions, time components, materials, and the activities undertaken in the lesson. The **performance** indicates to what degree students need to be able to show or know this content or skill. For instance, if given ten problems to solve, your declared level of competent performance could be getting nine of ten correct. Within each lesson, each child could have a different degree of performance based on that child's specific needs to demonstrate growth as well as mastery. There are significant reasons and benefits that result from sharing your objectives with your students at the beginning of the lesson.

In the next part of this section, we will discuss several important components of classroom conditions. Taking each component into consideration before students enter the classroom or begin an activity can greatly assist you in more successfully achieving the lesson outcomes.

Classroom Conditions

Classroom conditions are factors that we manage within the physical environment that impact instruction and learning. Classroom conditions contribute to both student focus and to the students' level of comfort within the learning environment. There are two areas of classroom conditions. The first area encompasses those factors within the classroom that can't be directly managed by the teacher. The second area addresses those factors that can be directly managed. Let's begin with a look at the first area.

Classroom Fixtures

Those factors within the classroom that are static and not easily changed include heating and cooling processes, lighting, windows, flooring, paint color, position of fixed furnishings such as chalkboards, bulletin boards, projection screens and the like. The main strategy for teachers in dealing with these fixed components is to know where each of them is, how each of them affects students, and how to account for each of them positively within the classroom set up and within the teaching and learning processes. After examining and accounting for the "fixtures" of the classroom, we can turn our attention to working more effectively with those factors that can be managed to facilitate the processes in the classroom.

Classroom Walls

Consider how you might use the walls in your classroom. A good percentage of the side walls should be devoted to the displaying of student work. Displaying student work helps the students feel at home. The back wall of the classroom could be a place to post reminders for yourself and the students. This could include names of instructional strategies you want to use as a reminder to include them in your instruction. Other items for the back wall could be another copy of the agenda to see as you face the students, the lesson objectives, an anticipatory set idea, announcement reminders for the close of the morning session or the end of the day, and any long-term assignment due dates to serve as reminders for you (to periodically remind students) and for the students to have a consistent place to find that type of information.

The front wall of the classroom should have one identified section that the students always focus on during the teaching and learning processes. Having a specific section provides consistency, organization and predictability so students are not confused about where to focus during instruction.

Teacher's Desk

The location of the teacher's desk is another important component of classroom conditions. Our advice is: don't place the desk in the front and center, but off to the side or in the rear of the classroom. Our reasons for recommending this are as follows. First, it's a distraction whether it's messy or neat. Second, teachers must be **on their feet, not on their seats**. Teachers need to manage the classroom by walking around using proximal behaviors and noticing what students are doing throughout the course of instruction, during student seatwork time, during group work, etc. Third, an inanimate object between students and teachers can create an adversarial climate. It is better to be immediately and consistently accessible for your students. Eliminating the physical barriers in the classroom is one means to achieving the goal of accessibility.

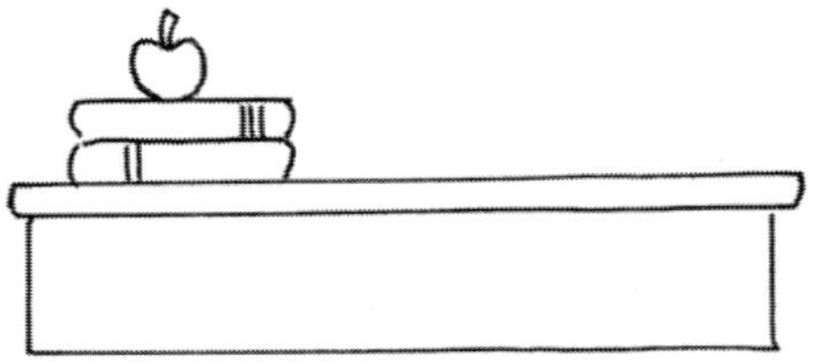

Live Plants

Live plants in your classroom can make a wonderful contribution to the classroom environment. Well-cared-for plants help create a comfortable climate. Plants also assist as an oxygen rejuvenator. Plants give you an opportunity to employ student help in caring for the plants. One proven method is to create a helper chart assigning specific jobs to students to teach responsibility. It is important that you outline specifically the steps of each job; that you teach and model those steps specifically for the students; give them time to practice the steps with your coaching; assign them the jobs in some organized rotation so every student gets to eventually perform and learn all the tasks. For more information on this strategy, see **teaching a behavior process** later in this section.

Animals

Animals in your classroom present other kinds of challenges for several reasons. The type of animal you choose to have as a class pet represents a very important decision about the climate in your classroom. For example, most people are very uncomfortable with snakes and mice even if they are under lock and key. So keep in mind that while you may enjoy all types of animals, your students, other teachers, the custodians, administrators and parents may feel much differently. Another factor to consider about class pets is what happens to the animals during school vacations. If you expect students to alternate taking the class pet home and caring for it over a weekend you may find that parents are not receptive to that type of situation. Additionally, in some circumstances, a student's home situation may not be conducive for animal habitation. Besides these concerns, should the class pet expire while in the care (or neglect) of a student, that student's reputation in your classroom may be seriously and irreparably damaged. Unless you are prepared to care for the animal at your home, or return to school daily during vacations to provide that care, it would be better to reconsider your idea of having a class pet. One other item bears mentioning as well. When choosing to have a class pet, it is important to consider the reproductive system and cycle of animals. Two gerbils could quite easily turn into ten within a few weeks. Then your class pet responsibilities have become significantly enlarged. While a class pet can enliven the environment of your classroom, you must weigh the daily responsibilities against the gains before making the decision to purchase or accept as a gift a class pet.

Effective Room Arrangements

The way your classroom is arranged can also make a contribution to the outcome of ***focus***. Room arrangements refer to factors that we manage within the physical environment that impact instruction and learning. Let's look at three components relative to room arrangements.

Seating Arrangements

When determining the seating arrangement in the classroom, you must answer this question: what do you want to accomplish through this seating arrangement? Do you want as few people as possible between a student and you? Are you going to use pair-sharing with the instructional strategy of **wait-time extended**? If so, you must consider which seating arrangement will most effectively enhance the use of those teaching strategies. In addition, you must identify where you tend to stand when you are standing still. Make yourself the apex of a triangle. If there are students you suspect may need close proximity to you, position them near the front of the room at the other two corners of the triangle. It is important that you teach seating as a behavior. In other words, what students should do with their feet, seat, hands, arms, legs, etc.

It is most beneficial to alter the seating arrangement to meet the needs of each specific lesson. If you are teaching in a classroom where the chairs are attached to the floor, consider what other options are available to you to most effectively engage the students in learning. For maximum student-teacher interaction, we prefer to use a "U" shape or three-sided square, with the teacher standing in the opening of the "U" or the square.

As you consider the "U" shaped configuration there are a variety of options as follows:

The Basic "U":

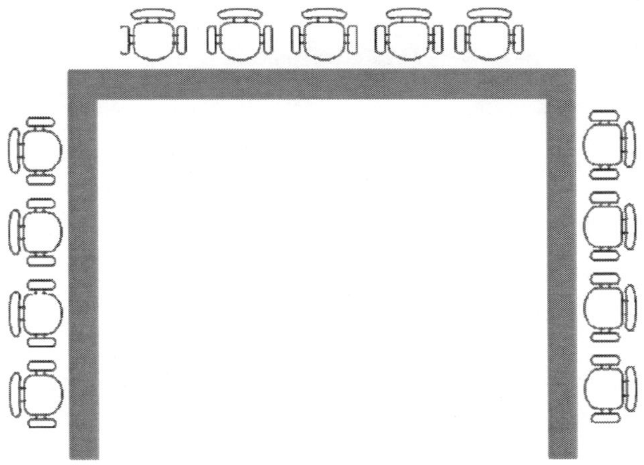

The "U" Within the "U":

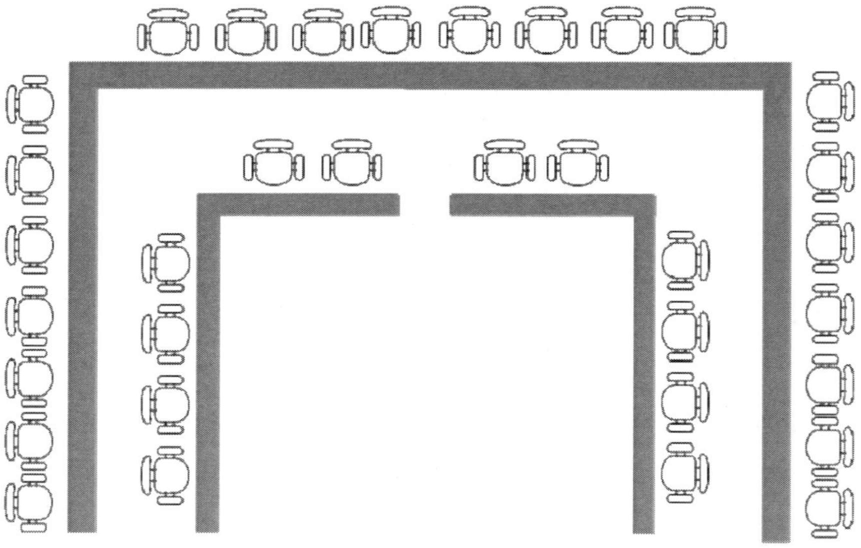

Some considerations in this format:

1. *Points of access from inside the "U" to allow easy monitoring to the outside "U".*
2. *Room size or total number of students may be criteria to consider in choosing the arrangement.*

The Modified "U":

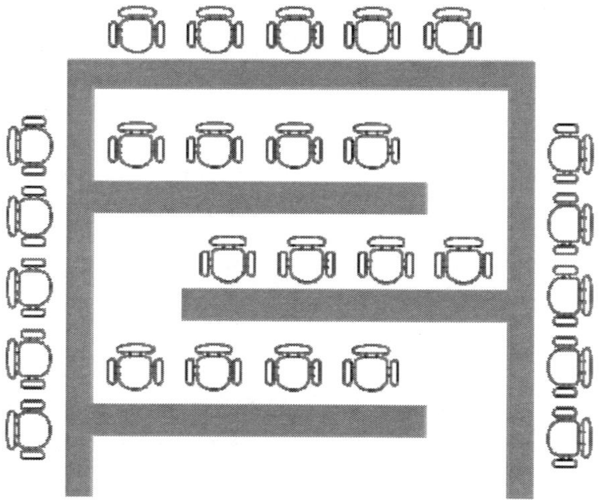

Some considerations in this format:

1. *Allows for easy access to all students for monitoring and control purposes.*
2. *Room size or total number of students may be criteria to consider in choosing the arrangement.*

SECTION ONE

The Chevron:

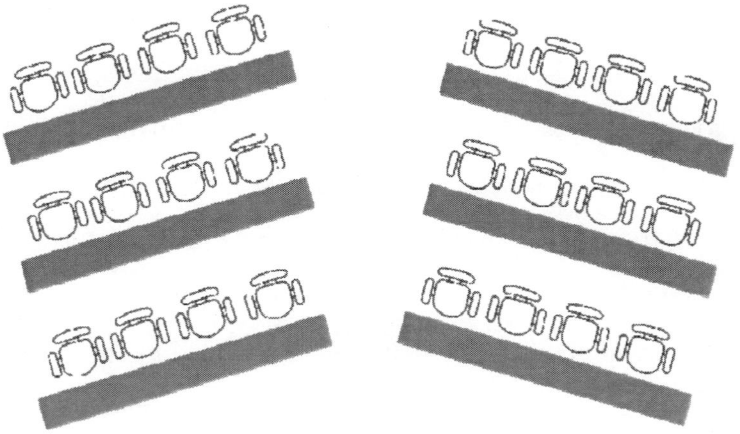

One consideration in this format:

1. *An effective arrangement when dealing with very large numbers of participants or students.*

The Pod:

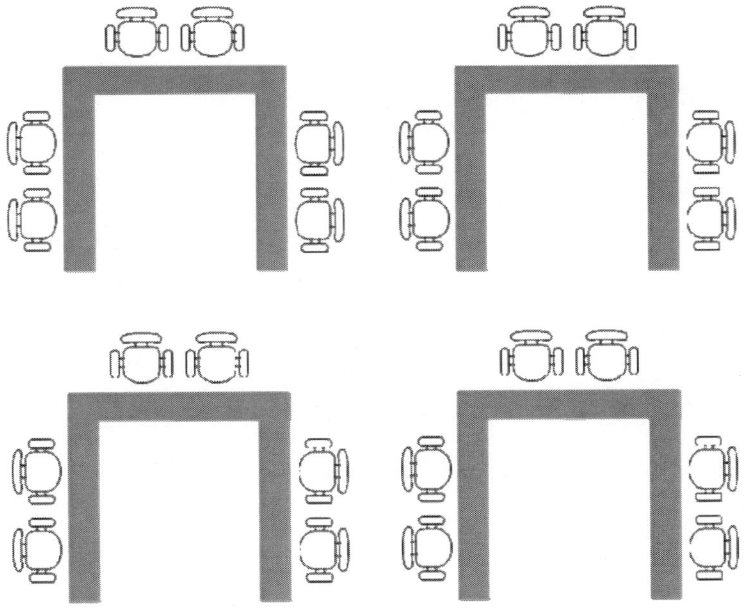

Some considerations in this format:

1. *Can create several small "U" shaped configurations.*
2. *Can vary in size from four to six students.*
3. *Facilitates group work and projects as well as whole group instruction.*

Seating for Quizzes and Tests

It is important that you consider how and where you want students to sit during the taking of quizzes and tests. When taking quizzes and, in particular, tests, it is important that students are able to concentrate, remain undistracted, have sufficient lighting, do not have to worry about other students viewing their work, and are not tempted themselves to look at the work of others. If the room arrangement must be altered for test taking, please do not say to your students that they're having a special seating arrangement for the test because you are concerned about the students being tempted to cheat. If the temptation is a legitimate concern, then you may want to consider composing and handing out two forms of the test alternated by student (i.e. student 1 has test form A and student 2 has test form B, student 3 test form A, etc.). This eliminates the temptation which then minimizes the need to discipline students later for cheating.

Equipment

When using any type of instructional equipment it is important that when you are finished using it, you move it out of the way. For example, when you finish using the overhead projector, move it back and off to the side so it is not a physical or visual barrier between you and the students, or between students. Turn the equipment off when you're not using it. A running, unused overhead projector (or other equipment) is a waste of energy, and a potential distraction for students. Additionally, it is important that when you are finished using a map or the projection screen, put it up to avoid having it become or remain a conflicting focal point for students. Keep in mind that if equipment is of no use, you should get rid of it; otherwise it is clutter in the classroom, particularly if it may impede movement into, out of, or around the classroom.

Teacher

The teacher is the most important factor in classroom conditions. Not only is the teacher personally significant in contributing to the classroom environment, but other characteristics that you bring into the classroom also have important influences. The choices you make as to how you dress say much about you as a professional. We think teachers should establish a type of "uniform" that they wear when teaching and or meeting with parents. In today's schools, there is a variety of acceptable modes of dress, but we consistently find that teachers who dress professionally are taken more seriously by students, colleagues, administrators, parents and the public. Often, achieving and maintaining respect from others as a teacher is an uphill battle. Some teachers, however, have contributed to the reduced respect the profession has received by how they dress at work and how they conduct themselves both on and off the job. While different districts have different expectations about how teachers dress, we recognize from our study of multiple sources including ***New Dress for Success*** by John T. Molloy, that how one dresses has a tremendous impact on at least two areas: the first impression he/she makes (and remember: there is only one chance to make a good first impression), and all of his/her non-verbal communication. Therefore, we recommend female teachers wear dress slacks or skirts, dress blouses or sweaters, or dresses, comfortable but good looking shoes, and have neat grooming with respect to hair and hygiene. For male teachers we recommend wearing dress slacks, dress shirts and ties or dress sweaters, comfortable but good looking shoes, and maintain neat grooming with respect to hair, whiskers and hygiene. One can be fashionable without appearing overly casual or trying to dress like the students you are teaching. Teachers need to be neat, clean, and free of body odor and bad breath. Keep in mind that you are a role model, and as such, everything you do, say, and what you look like is teaching someone something. In addition, you are a representative of a professional group. We feel compelled here to mention a few exceptions. If you teach physical education, you will need to wear attire that is compatible with your need to be physically active and able to participate with your students. Other teaching roles that may require special clothing are industrial technology teachers, family and consumer science teachers, and science teachers. When working with food, chemicals and other hazardous materials, and with power equipment, a teacher must consider safety along with the need to be professional. With that last idea in mind, we want to offer one final thought about teacher dress. Most professions have some code of dress whether explicit or implicit. We ask you to consider the messages you may be sending by the way you dress. Does your mode of dress communicate that you are a person who is confident and serious about the work you do, or does it communicate a less serious and potentially unprofessional message?

Serial Positioning

As we look to the act of teaching it is essential that some thought be given to the overall organizational scheme that teachers adopt and implement on a consistent day-to-day basis. This scheme (model) serves as a template within which information, activities, and interaction are generated. The general blueprint for operation can flex from day-to-day and from lesson-to-lesson. Each lesson consists of three major parts. Part one is the beginning of the lesson which we will call, "**A**." The middle part of the lesson is part "**B**," and the ending part of the lesson is part "**C**." Each part of the lesson serves a specific function.
(Please refer to Appendix G for greater detail.)

Here is the blueprint for this lesson:

A	B	C
Beginning Block: ***Prime Time 1***	**Middle Block**	**Ending Block:** ***Prime Time 2***
☐ Bell ringers ☐ Sharing the agenda ☐ Sharing the objectives ☐ Going over homework	☐ Sharing 1st objective ☐ Anticipatory set ☐ Input for objective 1 ☐ CFU for objective 1 using 5-1 & 10-2 rules ☐ Practice with feedback ☐ Repeat for each objective	☐ Closure ☐ Assigning homework ☐ Getting the homework started

The "meat" of the lesson will occur during the middle block. This is when you will be sharing the new information with the students. It is a given that all three parts are important, but the two most important time blocks within every lesson are the beginning and the ending. Beginnings and endings have a tremendous influence on what students remember about the lesson. We call these two blocks of time **prime time. Prime time** is **the first 7 to 10** and **the last 7 to 10 minutes of a class**. The first block is powerful in that what you do and what students experience in the opening 7 to 10 minutes of class sets the tone for the rest of that lesson. The second block is powerful in that what you do and what students experience during the last 7 to 10 minutes of a lesson tremendously influences what they remember and value about that experience. These are the optimum times for practice to occur since people tend to remember more of what they see and hear first (**primacy**) and what they see and hear last (**recency**). Research on human memory has identified this significant feature of remembering. Ausubel and Yousef (1965), and Gay (1973), reported that spaced reviews increase retention more than mere repetition. Let's take a look at an example of this phenomenon.

Remember a time when you attended a movie, a concert, or a live theater production or just finished reading a book. After it was over you probably found yourself thinking about and remembering what you experienced, and possibly even sharing it with others. Exactly what did you remember about the experience? Again, research into human cognition has identified what you **remember best** is what you experienced first (**primacy**) and what you **remember second best** is what you experienced last (**recency**). When giving a synopsis of that book or movie or concert, you find yourself covering predominantly the beginning and the ending. Make no mistake about this, the phenomenon of primacy and recency is very powerful. Primacy-recency is discussed more fully in the next part of this section.

The term **serial positioning** is used to describe a teaching strategy that takes maximum advantage of these two very important blocks of time. The overall organizational approach we are recommending is based upon the concept of **serial positioning** which suggests that student focus, and thus learning, can be facilitated and maximized through the effective design and management of multiple beginnings and endings within an instructional block. The key questions to address in this regard are:

- ☐ How will the teacher both manage and organize the *first* 7-10 minutes of class? **(Prime time 1)**
- ☐ How will the teacher both manage and organize the *last* 7-10 minutes of class? **(Prime time 2)**
- ☐ How will the teacher both manage and organize that larger middle instructional block of time?

Keep these three questions in mind as you consider the organizational patterns you are using to structure your lesson. The descriptions of instructional skills and strategies that are included in this book will serve as answers to these three questions.

Block One: Prime Time 1

Setting the stage is essential in any lesson or instructional block. Therefore starting class on time and in an organized fashion will, to a large degree, dictate the direction and focus of the remainder of the lesson. The following are some strategies that teachers can use to maximize the first block of time during a lesson:

- ☐ Involving the students in a short reinforcement and review activity such as a **bell ringer**.
- ☐ Posting a timed, topical or combination agenda which would represent a breakdown of key items such as skills, information, concepts and activities or events. During this initial block of time the teacher should review the agenda with the students.
- ☐ Going over the homework that is due today in class.
- ☐ Posting of the intended learning outcomes (objectives). Again the teacher should review the objectives with the class.

We should manage and organize the first 7-10 minutes of class by getting started in a focused, organized and efficient manner. By doing so, we are very positively dictating the general climate for the remainder of the lesson. Besides bell ringers and agendas, sharing the objectives can also be a powerful focusing device that helps to pull students into the content of the lesson by activating their past memories and prior knowledge.

Block Two: Prime Time 2

The question of how we should manage and organize the last 7-10 minutes of class connects to the **second block of time** in the serial positioning sequence. This second block is the portion of the lesson that allows students an opportunity to perform two behaviors significant to the learning process. The first behavior during **prime time 2** is to review and reinforce what has been learned in that portion of the lesson. To do so requires rehearsal or practice. This is best facilitated by using **closure**. Remember: the key feature for this instructional strategy is that **students must do the summarizing**. By rewording your instructional objectives into questions, you can guide students in the reviewing and reinforcing processes. To do so is to teach for remembering by giving students additional opportunities to practice the information and/or skills that they have been experiencing. We practice at the beginning of class (prime time 1) by using **bell ringers**. We practice at the end of class (prime time 2) by using **closure**. We practice throughout the lesson by using **checking for understanding.** In using these retention systems, we provide for the multiple and spaced repetitions of the correct answer which is the most effective form of emphasis (Jersild 1928; Mayer 1983).

The second behavior during prime time 2 is getting homework started. We increase and extend practice time through the use of **homework**. Before we examine the second behavior in the final segment of class wherein we explain the use of serial positioning in **homework**, let's review the concepts of **prime time** and **serial positioning.**

In order to take full advantage of the concepts of primacy and recency, we use a strategy called serial positioning. In Serial Positioning we use more beginnings and endings during a class in order to build on this idea of primacy and recency. In this structure, instead of teaching a 30-, 50- or 90-minute class, we break these larger time blocks down into several smaller increments of time (somewhere from 5 to 10 minutes). Instead of one beginning and ending, we have multiple beginnings and endings within one larger block of time. For example, with younger students, we may teach for 5 to 7 minutes and then check for understanding for 1 to 2 minutes. So within a 30-minute lesson, we will have five to six beginnings and endings. With older students, we may teach for 8 to 10 minutes and then check for understanding for 2 minutes. So within a 50-minute class, we will again have five to six beginnings and endings. We call these the **5-1** and **10-2 Rules**. It seems most reasonable that to make practice most effective, teachers should make use of serial positioning strategy (more beginnings & endings) during lessons to give students multiple opportunities to encounter primacy-recency which significantly affects memory (Buzan 1989; Thomas 1972).

Homework and Serial Positioning

Now, let's take a look at how the idea of serial positioning affects homework and getting homework started. Homework is really both primacy and recency. Homework is **primacy** when we go over it at the beginning of class and when we begin the homework process before students are dismissed from the class or for the day. Homework is **recency** when it is the last thing students do before they leave the class or for the day. If we believe the research results on primacy and recency, then we should make every effort on a consistent basis to begin homework in class and to have that activity last until dismissal time. By getting homework started in class (primacy), our students are more apt to finish the homework because they have had your support to begin the work and even more importantly, your support to begin the work correctly. By making homework the final activity for the lesson (recency), we are giving a powerful edge to the remembering of the experience, and we are modeling good time management instead of time wasting and/or procrastination. While the practice of turning the last few minutes of class over to students to do whatever they want is all too common in schools, it could be considered a form of teaching malpractice, but at the least it is teaching time wasted.

Here are some final thoughts about serial positioning. The first 7-10 minutes of class and the last 7-10 minutes of class are the **prime time** for practice. Those times are key because of the concept of primacy-recency**.** Remember, **primacy-recency** is a phenomenon best defined by saying that people tend to remember best what they see and hear first, and what they see and hear last. With that phenomenon in mind, we should also note that **Mondays** (primacy) and **Fridays** (recency) should not be considered "throw-away days" but are equal to Tuesdays, Wednesdays and Thursdays as excellent days of the week for learning and teaching. In the beginning of this book, we stated that **organization, specificity and consistency** are the **three power words for teaching**. Using the strategies outlined above on a daily basis will be of tremendous service in the ensuring that your students see organization, specificity and consistency throughout the structure of your lessons and that students get ample opportunities to increase retention and reduce forgetting.

Providing an Exit

Providing an exit is a strategy designed to facilitate the human needs of youngsters in a structured instructional environment. The intended instructional outcome is ***focus.***
This strategy may also be called the **pass option** or the **exit option.**

This "temporary exit" provides the opportunity for a student, who may have unintentionally been "put on the spot," in front of his/her peers and does not feel she/he can contribute at the moment, **to pass**. The pass option is most effective when the teacher returns to the student who passed for confirmation/clarity on an answer given by another student or the instructor. Thus, this "temporary exit" allows time for the students to gather their thoughts and composure and then be able to re-engage and contribute to the class or activity.

The purpose of this strategy is to promote increased student involvement in a less threatening educational environment. The following **guidelines** outline the process of the pass option and thus provide examples of how this procedure is most effectively used in the classroom.

- ☐ Prior to implementing the pass option, the teacher should:
  - ☐ Explain why it is being implemented.
  - ☐ Teach what it should sound like or look like if it is a non-verbal signal.
  - ☐ Clearly communicate that it is temporary, not permanent.
- ☐ Do not limit its use. It is recommended that the number of passes per student not be limited in a given lesson or class period. Limiting the pass contradicts the concept. In addition it creates a record keeping chore for the teacher which may result in an equity problem. It further does not facilitate managing anxiety for which it is intended.
- ☐ The teacher should come immediately back to the student who passed once having gotten the appropriate answer from another student following the pass. In other words, student A passes. The teacher then goes to student B who answers correctly. The teacher shifts back to student A and says, "Tell me one thing you heard student B say."
- ☐ If students are routinely misusing the pass option, the teacher can retrain the offending students on their own valued time. The goal here is to assist students in maintaining their focus while maintaining an appropriate comfort level, as well as using it appropriately.

Some important reasons why your students may use the **pass option** include:

- ☐ The student lacks confidence in his/her answer.
- ☐ The student doesn't know the answer.
- ☐ The student has misunderstood or didn't hear the question.
- ☐ The student has personal problems and wasn't engaged.
- ☐ The student is ill and is having trouble concentrating.
- ☐ The student may have been daydreaming and didn't hear the question.

An important student benefit for using the **pass option** with students is that it takes the student temporarily "off the hook," but it doesn't leave them "off the hook." After calling on another student, you must go back to the student who passed and ask him or her to tell you one thing that (the other student) said.

The pass option facilitates the important feature of feeling tone. It allows us to re-focus a student, reduce anxiety and maintain student dignity. The issue isn't why the student passed; we only want to be sure the student has the correct information before we go on to the next topic.

Feeling Tone

Feeling tone is the psychological climate that the teacher creates in the classroom. It facilitates the achieving of the outcome of ***focus***. The emotional state of mind of the learner, whether female or male, older or younger, is an essential variable to manage as we address instructional delivery with the end goal of providing a successful experience for each student. Emotions often take precedence during cerebral processing and can impede or assist cognitive learning (Sousa 2006). That is why emotional climate is so important. Students have identified the following teacher characteristics as essential in defining a "good teacher": enthusiasm, likes kids, knows how to interact with kids, and is consistent (which is essential to a "good" classroom and a positive classroom climate). These student opinions and attitudes are additionally supported by numerous studies such as *Public Agenda: What American Teenagers Think about Their Schools* (1996) [see Appendix E.].

In detailing various strategies or procedures that contribute to this positive emotional classroom climate (setting the stage, sharing agendas, classroom conditions, learning objectives, bell ringers, exit option, etc.) it is important to emphasize that when teachers take advantage of those classroom elements that they can directly control, it significantly enhances the predictability of student behavior and correspondingly the more successful achievement of the lesson outcomes.

Much has been written about school climate and the teacher's role in establishing a climate conducive to student learning. The research on class size demonstrates that up to a point, reducing class size is one way to improve student performance (Darling-Hammond 1996; Bracey 1999). An equally interesting conclusion in this report identified the teacher as the most compelling variable when looking at student performance and that the teacher's overall affect (student to teacher relations skills), organization and management plan or model, and instructional delivery system contributed most to the positive impact that we as professionals have on student performance. This overall sense of safeness and comfort has come to be known as **feeling tone**. To add to our definition above, feeling tone is the psychological climate that is created as a part of the aura that teachers generate through their verbal and non-verbal actions and systems.

The classroom guidelines listed below promote a system for the effective management of feeling tone and for creating a positive climate based on two-way communication in a non-threatening environment. This positive interaction promotes increased self-esteem and self-confidence by helping students become capable (Fay & Funk 1997), resulting in a sense of overall success for all students.

Knowing All of Your Students by Name

Two significant factors in building quality relationships within the classroom involve two seemingly easy tasks that both have significant impact on rapport and positive working relationships. The first is learning the names of your students and calling them by name each time you interact with them. A person's name is an essential part of his/her identity. In most cases, a person enjoys hearing his/her name used, especially with relation to a positive outcome. Using students' names contributes to a welcoming classroom environment. At the elementary level, this is not a major item as most elementary teachers have much close and constant contact with each of their students. However, knowing students becomes more difficult when student-to-teacher ratios increase. In the elementary school setting, music, art, physical education, and computer teachers, as well as media specialists, guidance counselors and administrators have a much more daunting task when learning the names of several hundred students. It is reasonable to assume that in many middle level and secondary school settings teachers could see well over 100 students per day. Ted Sizer stated (Minton 1999) that, "We cannot teach students well if we do not know them well." For each student, the questions, "Do you know my name?" and, "Am I a person in your eyes?" are most poignant.

There are various methods for learning student names such as name tags on the students' desks, name badges to wear, photographs with name captions, videotaping students saying their names, name games and songs, school yearbooks, permanent records folders and the like. The bottom line is that knowing each student by name and face takes a lot of rehearsal and practice consistently over time. One method we recommend is to have students take a 5 x 8 index card and fold it in half lengthwise. Students should legibly print their first and last names on both sides of the card. Elementary students can leave their cards on their desks most of the time. When not in use, the card should be stored in the desk. Middle level and secondary students can be instructed to bring their cards to class daily; each student should place it on the front edge of his/her desk or table. This is done for the first five weeks of school. While this can be an effective strategy, we still recommend learning (by rote) the names and faces of your students for those venues outside the classroom where you will inevitably meet. Lastly, do not assume that the students all know each other. The use of name cards facilitates the building of student relationships as well.

Greeting Students

The second factor involves taking the time and opportunity to greet each student individually and directly, particularly at the beginning of the day or class. Teachers should be monitoring each student's attitude throughout the teaching and learning processes. A teacher who can sense when students are having difficulty, be it social, emotional, physical or intellectual, is said to possess "withitness." This term, coined by

Jacob Kounin, refers to teachers who know what is going on in all parts of the room at all times. It is the proverbial "eyes in the back of your head." (Charles 1999). Greeting students and frequently interacting with students individually helps you create a warmer and friendlier classroom climate. Our recommendation is to be at the door each morning, or at the beginning of each class. Offering the students a handshake, pat on the back, high-five, or other symbol of friendship helps to break the ice and warm up the climate significantly. Many organizations such as churches, restaurants, and retail stores have practiced this technique for decades.

Showing Enthusiasm

In the survey of secondary students (*Public Agenda: What American Teenagers Think about Their Schools,* 1996 – Appendix E), **showing enthusiasm** was identified as one of the most desirable and memorable teacher traits. Greeting students (and others) in a genuinely enthusiastic and sincere manner has a very positive effect. Being somewhat upbeat, energetic, positive and, yes, even moderately excited about the lesson's objectives and activities communicates a powerful feeling contributing to the feeling tone and the level of student interest in and for the learning session.

Teaching Relationships

Teaching is relationships and is about relationships. Establishing that professional yet positive relationship is critical when setting the appropriate feeling tone. The strategies outlined in this book will assist and support you to this end. If you remember that everything you do, think and say depends on the quality of the relationships you have in your personal and professional life, it should motivate you to continue to work diligently, vigilantly and enthusiastically to create the best working and living relationships possible. William Glasser in his book ***Choice Theory*** (1998) describes at length how relationships permeate every aspect of our lives, including family, school, work and marriage. When we stop to consider that effective relationships are built on mutual respect, giving, caring and nurturing, being other-centered, giving up control over the other person, being honest, and yes, love, we come to understand that each important relationship in our lives continues to develop and continues to need to be nurtured. Successful relationships are built by what we give, not by what we expect.

Making Students Look Good

Making students look good, especially in front of an audience of peers, is crucial to building a productive classroom environment. Catching a student doing well, or being right at something, drives individuals to continue to expend additional effort. Again, it's the processes or systems that the teacher consistently has in place that facilitates these outcomes. Here are some proven strategies to help make students look good:

- □ Using the **interaction sequence** - particularly the interviewing or conferencing segment.
- □ **Wait-time and wait-time extended** - the time to process and share thoughts with others before having to perform.
- □ **Homework partners** - the comfort in working things through with support from another person.

These strategies help to create a physically comfortable and thus welcoming environment for students. "Students in respectful classrooms all feel physically and emotionally safe and valued." (Wessler 2003)

Level of Concern

Level of concern is defined as managing the emotional climate of the classroom to heighten student focus in order to increase participation in a classroom activity. The intended instructional outcome is ***focus***. As previously noted, managing student anxiety through the conscious development of a positive and productive feeling tone is highly recommended. To this end, we are coupling feeling tone development with level of concern management.

Level of concern refers to those activities or approaches that the teacher uses to further manage student anxiety in the classroom. The strategies included in this section provide a guideline for creating an environment conducive to student learning without promoting unnecessary anxiety. Level of concern supports the concept that an appropriate level of anxiety promotes task completion and improves the quality of work. It also serves as a positive motivator and sets parameters or guidelines within which students can work, focus, and be productive and successful.

Uncontrolled anxiety promotes defocus. It can cause some students to rush to complete activities without concern for the quality of the work. It can also cause a student who struggles to complete tasks to give up. Teachers often misdiagnose a student who may be anxious about an activity as being unwilling, unmotivated or uncooperative.

We can all think of situations in our classroom past where our anxiety was raised to such a fever pitch that we wished to be transported to a distant safer location. On the other hand, we can also recall situations in our own classroom past where anxiety was so low as to be nonexistent. Therefore, we were unable to effectively focus in both instances. The skillful management of anxiety within an acceptable range for all is the ideal. We don't want it too high so as to cause almost measurable pain. Likewise, we don't want it too low as to cause students to not find the need to focus.

The following **guidelines** provide strategies to use when establishing a positive level of concern while promoting an environment conducive to learning for all students.

The guidelines are as follows:

1. Set reasonable standards and encourage students to be reasonable risk takers. Be reasonable in what you expect regarding student behavior. Set limits on homework. Break things down into manageable blocks. Do not overwhelm the students.
2. Be specific about the amount of time allotted to complete the required work. Again, be reasonable. Here is a **formula to use when determining the amount of time it takes to complete a task**. First, complete the task yourself. Next, use this formula to help you determine how much time to give the capable student to complete the work. For grades K-6 it will commonly take the student 4 to 5 times the number of minutes it takes you to complete the task (N x 4 or 5, with N being the number of minutes it took you to complete the task). For grades 6-12 it will commonly take the student 3 to 4 times the number of minutes it takes you to complete the task (N x 3 or 4). When grade 6 is in an elementary setting, use the 4 to 5 times formula. When grade 6 is in a middle level departmentalized setting use the 3 to 4 times rule. This presupposes that you **do the work first to**

ascertain these time allotments. If you aren't willing to do the work yourself, should you really be assigning it to your students? Finally, ask yourself the following questions: *Is this task doable as a result? Are there any "glitches," or any misleading or conflicting items?*

3. Use proximity to raise or lower anxiety. How you move around the room is a critical consideration. In most cases when you increase the distance between you and the student, you lower the student's anxiety. When you decrease the distance between you and the student, you raise the student's anxiety. <u>There are exceptions, however</u>. For example, when Student A is being bothered by Student B and therefore can't work, your proximity can lower Student A's level of anxiety (and allow him/her to return to the task) as it raises Student B's level of anxiety (to cease bothering Student A and get back to work).
4. Be aware of the power of the messages you send through your body language. Make sure students understand your non-verbal communication signals. These non-verbal indicators are extremely powerful in raising or lowering anxiety. Smiles, a wink, a scowl, eye contact, hand gestures, body positioning, or stance are examples of very communicative non-verbals. One final tip: it is very important that your non-verbal communication match the verbal. If conflicts occur within your use of these two modes of communication, your students will become and remain confused. **Remember**: 60% of what students assign as meaning with respect to what you say comes from your non-verbals (Gollnick & Chinn 2005).
5. **Be on your feet, not on your seat.** Change the positioning from which you teach with regularity during the learning session. Don't just pace around, but use consistent, focused and planned movement about the room. That type of thoughtful and strategic use of proximity and positioning is helpful in monitoring student engagement and progress and keeping a well-balanced level of concern in the students.
6. Shift the dependency for learning to the students. Pairing students may lower anxiety for some while raising it for others. The teacher may need to be a surrogate or temporary partner for a student who does not feel comfortable

working with another student (such as during the **interaction sequence**). The teacher should make the grouping, partnering or pairing decisions. Leaving this to student choice will result in loss of control of outcomes and may result in some students being hurt when not chosen by a peer. Keep in mind, however, that teaching students how to effectively work in pairs or groups together is also part of your job as a teacher. When encountering students who are reluctant to partner with peers, you need to ascertain why they are reluctant and design effective strategies to help those students overcome their reluctance and learn to work cooperatively and successfully with others.

7. Provide **glow comments** first, and **grow comments** second. This is in reference to **knowledge of results**. When providing feedback to students always be specific. Always start with a **glow comment** (some things that you wish to highlight or compliment the student for) then shift to the **grow comments** (things that you would like to see improve). We will deal with the characteristics of **immediacy** and **specificity** when we discuss knowledge of results more fully in Section Three.
8. Activities and materials may serve to raise or lower anxiety with students. Be specific with directions and reasonable with expectations. Are the materials legible? Are the materials designed for the students' developmental level? Do the materials match the curriculum and standards? Can the activity be broken down into logical chunks so as not to overwhelm the learners?
9. Develop a system or process designed to reduce anxiety on the part of the students when asked to respond to a question or comment. We call our system the **pass** or **exit option**. We discussed the pass option in more detail earlier in this section.
10. Be predictable and consistent with your behavior, your procedures, and your methods, strategies and systems. Doing so creates an appropriate comfort level and working rhythm for both the learner and the teacher, and it encompasses the three power words for teaching: **organization, specificity and consistency**.

Components in the Process of Successful Student Behavior Management

In their excellent book *The First Days of School*, Harry and Rosemary Wong (1998) say "Most behavior problems in the classroom are caused by the teacher's failure to teach students how to follow procedures." We cannot place too much emphasis on how you identify, teach, model and manage classroom procedures in order to ensure organization, order and predictability in your classroom. This section offers effective strategies for teaching your students responsibility and responsiveness.

Successfully managing student behavior on a consistent basis is a nagging concern for all teachers and administrators regardless of experience. As we move further into the 21st century, student performance has increased as a major focus. *A Nation At Risk* and *No Child Left Behind* are but two indicators of the increasing public and political concerns for education. Much has been written and spoken about the various approaches to achieving the goals of *No Child Left Behind* and thus overall improvement of student performance. It is generally agreed that in the area of curriculum development and alignment with standards, we are doing a good job and are continuing to refine and improve the process. In the area of assessment we have experienced some rough going at times but, again, we are getting better. Instructional delivery, which is the primary focus of this book, is seen as a critical variable in achieving a greater degree of student success for all. As some have suggested, "delivery is everything." As part of instructional delivery there is increased focus and attention being given to student behavior management. Many highly competent books have been written on this topic, particularly with respect to behavioral theories and general approaches to student behavior management. Most lack the key component of application, particularly as it affects the classroom environment and the teaching and learning processes, or while containing key application pieces, their scope is limited to a specific concern such as conflict resolution. This increased focus is centering on the fact that if students are consistently exhibiting unacceptable or uncooperative behaviors, the negative impact on the overall success of the organization, as reflected in student performance, is significant. To be more specific, time becomes a major casualty, student defocus can outweigh student focus, the emotional impact on both students and staff can be debilitating, and the creative energy and resiliency of the organization can be seriously drained. The safe environment that is essential to student success comes into question and can be seriously jeopardized.

When reviewing student behavior management approaches it is becoming increasingly clear that those that are the most successful are those that are based upon a teaching or training model. In the private sector, heavy emphasis is placed on ongoing training of staff or personnel. These organizations invest significant time, energy, and money in their people. School organizations and classroom teachers too can build training programs or models that are geared toward developing students' skills in specific areas of student behavior. For example, at the building level, behaviors such as hallway, cafeteria, assembly, study hall, language, dress, bus, etc. could be a part of training for a student success program. At the classroom level, behaviors such as coming prepared, listening, labs, group work, learning centers, library, note taking, and independent work are all samples of in-class training for student success.

What follows here is a detailed description of the process to pursue when "training" or "teaching" students how to be successful.

Teaching a Behavior Process

It is very important that any behaviors having an effect on all who work and learn in a building be considered when determining the principles for managing a school building. While it is more desirable to be **proactive** with our management strategies, we frequently encounter schools whose intent is to be proactive, but whose practice is very **reactive.** In an attempt to encourage you and your colleagues to be **proactive instead of reactive**, we want to suggest a team approach in developing the principles and strategies for managing behaviors at the building level. We call this principle **front loading**. Front loading is **teaching kids the behaviors** we need for our class and school to run efficiently and safely right away and **not merely telling kids** about their behavior. Remember, the very same benefits result when sharing your behavioral objectives with students as are realized when sharing your instructional objectives.

The teaching of a behavior process can be applied to individuals, small groups, classes, or the entire student body of a school. The decision as to group size will be arrived at based upon need and circumstance. For example, you might teach an individual how to work independently. You may want to teach an entire class about classroom procedures, class participation, hand raising or how to work with a substitute teacher. You might need to teach the entire student body the correct procedures for cafeteria, hallway, or assembly behavior. In each instance, the process remains the same. It is important that we make no assumptions when teaching procedures or behaviors. We should not assume the students know nothing and conversely, we should not assume that the students know how to correctly exhibit the effective and efficient behaviors necessary for everyone to be successful in the classroom. We call this process, "**If you want it – teach it!**" The intended instructional outcome is ***focus***. We further define these ideas as a process designed to assist students to be successful by substituting self-control in place of teacher control. Let's look at the five steps to teaching a behavior.

The Five Steps in Successfully Teaching a Behavior

Step #1 Brainstorm the Behaviors or Expectations and Determine and Teach the Content

To initiate the behavior teaching process, you will need to brainstorm a list of specific behaviors or expectations that you wish to see exhibited by your students that are essential to the successful operation of your class or building. For example: how to enter a room, how to line up, class participation, working with substitutes, how to walk in the hall, assembly behavior, cafeteria procedures and behavior, study hall, how to come prepared to class, fire drill, open display of affection in the halls, and a myriad of other essential behaviors which when used make the school more orderly, safe and efficient. Once you have brainstormed the appropriate or expected behavior you will then need to decide which of these should be taught first and an approximate timeline by which others will also be taught and implemented. Consider teaching no more than two or three behaviors the first week of school and then add two more per week until your list of essential behaviors have all been taught. The exception is kindergarten where behaviors are taught non-stop for months. Some additional thought will need to be given as to how many behaviors should be taught in a given lesson or class period. Size of group, grade level and ability level are some factors to consider when making that decision.

After identifying the desired behavior to be taught (i.e. coming prepared to class) you will need to list all the items of information you can identify that students need to know about this behavior. This list will be the content for the lesson for teaching that identified behavior or expectation. Your brainstormed list will then need to be reordered to reflect the order or sequence in which items are to be taught. You will also need to identify your **expected outcomes** that result from the correct and consistent use of the behavior.

After completing the brainstorming part of Step # 1, you will need to teach your procedure (example: coming prepared to class) to the students. During the teaching session, first share the learning objective for the session and the rationale as to why this behavior is important for class organization, order, and efficiency. Second, share your determined sequence of the steps of the behavior and other relevant information with the students as part of what you are teaching them. Third, we recommend that you also share your expected outcomes when students use this behavior. In other words, what will be the resulting effects in our classroom when we all use this behavior correctly and consistently? Finally, following this information sharing, we recommend that you **check for student understanding** of the content and correct sequence for this behavior to ensure accuracy before moving on to Step # 2. Don't forget to use the **5-1 or 10-2 checking for understanding rules**.

Step #2 Model the Behavior

As you pursue the steps in teaching the identified behavior, each item will need to be modeled (demonstrated) so that each student will have a clear picture of what is expected (i.e. how the behavior looks and sounds). The model must be 100% accurate. As a result, choose carefully the individuals (other adults or students) who might assist in the modeling process. Because of the importance of accuracy during modeling, teachers should seriously consider doing the modeling themselves first.

Depending upon class make-up, you may find it necessary to model the various elements of the behavior that you are teaching in chunks of three to four items. This will be determined for the most part by the ability and, in some instances, the ages of the students with whom you are working. Remember, you want them to be successful in reproducing the behavior. Don't give them more than they can handle in any one modeling session.

Step #3 Practice the Behavior

This is the key element in the teaching of a behavior process, if you desire the behavior to be consistently exhibited. In the practice session, following your modeling of the behavior, you can monitor and make appropriate adjustments. The students, as a group, can practice a single element, a group of elements, or the whole process or behavior. How much practice is again a teacher decision based on ability, age and maturity. Throughout the practice sessions, students must receive specific and immediate **knowledge of results** (feedback) in some positive way.

If the students have failed in the practice session to produce the behavior as you described and modeled, you need to indicate that the behavior is not quite what you want. Provide specific points as to where the behavior broke down and then ask students to watch and listen as you go through it again, emphasizing that you know that they can do it this time.

Step #4 Reinforce the Behavior

Reinforcement is a procedure using consequences to strengthen a desired behavior. The intended instructional outcome is ***rate and degree***. Reinforcement is a powerful motivator and has the potential to promote self-actualized individuals (Maslow). If used with consistency and specificity, it builds interpersonal relationships and increases the likelihood of the occurrence of a desired behavior. There are generally three specific types of reinforcement.

Type one is **positive reinforcement**. Positive reinforcement is anything that happens in conjunction with an act that tends to increase the likelihood that the act will occur again. Positive reinforcement is something the student wants. Social positive reinforcers include eye contact, tone of voice, touching, signals that mean "good job," proximity, smiling, verbal praise, materials/tokens (including food) as well as activities the student desires. For additional examples see **Appendix D: Differential Reinforcement Matrix**.

Type two is **negative reinforcement**. Negative reinforcement has two parts. The first is the withholding of a positive reinforcer when the inappropriate behavior is exhibited so as not to reinforce the unwanted behavior. In other words, if the student exhibits the unwanted behavior, the teacher does not positively reinforce the behavior in any way.

The second part of negative would be a consequence (cost to the student) following the inappropriate behavior. The cost (something not wanted by the student) that is recommended in a school setting is the giving up of some valued time (lunch, recess, before school, after school, etc.) during which the student is re-taught the appropriate behavior. The goal here is to replace the inappropriate behavior with the desired appropriate behavior. The teacher can then follow up with praise and encouragement. The ultimate goal is to replace the inappropriate behavior with a desirable behavior, or to extinguish (make extinct) the inappropriate behavior.

The third type of reinforcement is called **extinction**. This generally takes the form of "planned ignoring." As in negative reinforcement, the teacher does not reinforce the unwanted behavior but rather ignores the behavior intentionally so as not to unintentionally reinforce behavior that is unwanted. Planned ignoring/extinction has some definite merit (when students' behavior is not reinforced – it ceases), but it may not be the preferred approach in a classroom because of one important feature: uncontrollable reinforcers. While you can control your own reinforcement habits, you cannot necessarily control other forms of reinforcement such as those from other students, other adults, or even from the classroom environment. Because of this feature, using extinction when in a group setting may not prove to be effective.

Whenever a teacher desires to assist a student in changing behavior, it is imperative that any change be well thought out and connected to a thoughtful and reasonable **behavioral objective**. It is important that we make sure any attempt to change behavior is kept positive and business-like (i.e. it's about the behavior). We must know what the target behavior is (desired or appropriate behavior); what that target behavior looks like, sounds like and feels like; how we are going to achieve the target behavior (the plan or sequence of steps to learn, practice and implement the target behavior); the means with which we will evaluate our progress toward the behavioral objective (target behavior); and a sensible rationale as to why we need this behavior to change and what benefits for all will result from the change.

As we further consider Step #4 Reinforcement, a more detailed look at the reinforcement concept is required.

In the day-to-day application of reinforcement and reinforcers a seriously important consideration is warranted; often in our desire to move students in the direction of responsible behavior and performance, incentives (reinforcers) are offered. The thought here is that students (or youngsters or others) will respond positively if they are encouraged to do so by the upfront offering of something tangible or desirable. Some examples:

1. *If you come prepared to class then you will be given* ___________________.
2. *If you behave appropriately for the next* ____ *days, then you will be given* ___________________.
3. *If you achieve* ____________________ *report card grades then you will be given* ___________________.

In Daniel Pink's book <u>Drive</u> this approach is referred to as "if-then." In short, if you perform, accomplish, do ___________, etc. then you will be given ______________. Pink outlines some of the outcomes or effects of this approach as follows:

- ☐ They can extinguish intrinsic motivation
- ☐ They can diminish performance
- ☐ They can crush creativity
- ☐ They can crowd out good behavior
- ☐ They can encourage cheating, shortcuts, and unethical behavior
- ☐ They can become addictive
- ☐ They can foster short-term thinking

  (Pink 2009)

APL adds:

- ☐ Fosters entitlement
- ☐ Results in negotiations – If I do _______________, what do I get?
- ☐ Negatively impacts work ethic

APL suggests the following use of reinforcers as a positive, productive, and effective alternative to the "if-then" process. When reinforcers are offered to students on the front end of the desired outcome the students or the recipient is in control. The student decides whether the reinforcer is sufficient or whether he/she in fact even wishes to do what is asked. If, however, the reinforcers are put on the back end, then the teacher or adult is in control. In this instance the student does not expect it or see it coming, and as a result, the adult controls the effect. Doing the right or expected thing is its own reward. But, surprising the students or youngsters occasionally with something special reinforces the fact that the adult notices and appreciates the effort or behavior. We at APL often mention the fact that this act on the part of the adult acts as a stimulant to energize the student to continue his/her effort or behavior.

Some examples:

1. Teacher acknowledges that the class has consistently been coming prepared to class for the past _____ (weeks) (days), and as a result, today we will take a bit of time out to enjoy the following: ____________________________.
2. Teacher compliments the students for their exceptional behavior (specific examples here) over the past ____________ (days). As a result today we are going to _____________ for a short block of time.
3. Teacher provides a general overview of how the performance scores have improved over the past ___________ (weeks). The teacher further indicates that this is an obvious result of the sustained effort on the part of the class. As a result of this, today we will enjoy the following: ___________________________.

Step #5 Re-teach the Behavior

As you may know or have experienced, some individuals fail to deliver on the expected and taught behavior despite having gone through Steps #1 through #4. When confronted with this circumstance the student(s) in question need to have the behavior **re-taught** to them. This re-teaching will take place at a time that is valued by the individual (i.e. recess, lunch, study hall, after school, before school, etc.).

In the process of establishing the time for this "remedial" session, the student(s) need to know that you recognize that they are having difficulty with the desired behavior. As a result of this difficulty, you are going to assist them by re-teaching it so that they can be successful. In addition, the students need to clearly understand the fact that if they do not get it during the first re-teaching session that you will continue to re-teach the behavior, on the student's time, until they are successful. In other words, "I will continue to re-teach on your valued time each day for a short period until you get the behavior correct. However, I know that it will not be necessary because you are capable and, as a result, will get it the first time."

Once the process is complete to your satisfaction, periodically thank the students for the good job they are doing. This will underscore the importance and reinforce the desirable behavior. The frequency with which this is done will vary a bit depending upon the makeup of the specific class. Nonetheless, it needs to occur with regularity. On occasion, you may need to review the steps or content with the students. This is particularly true with younger, less motivated, or less capable learners. By revisiting Steps 3 and 4, you will find that the students will tend to deliver the desired behavior in a consistent manner. Periodic review is essential to positively affect both accuracy and long-term memory. Just as we systematically and periodically review content in the academic curriculum, we should systematically review content from the procedural and social curricula as well.

By stating those objectives, <u>you clearly identify for students their need to be accountable and responsible and that you will be persistent with your expectations that all students comply with the correct and consistent use of the expected behaviors</u>. As an aside, we call this re-teaching session a **seminar** in order to identify it as a learning opportunity and not a "punishment." We've also heard it referred to as a "camp" or a "clinic" or a "workshop." These terms assist in distinguishing the seminar from other school consequences such as detention, in-school suspension, etc. We do not want students to see the **seminar** as punishment. However, we do want students to view the seminar as one of the pieces of the process the teacher uses to hold students accountable for their classroom and school behavior. It is important to note that teachers should underscore this point (seminar is instructional not punitive) as you work through Steps #2 through #4. For example, as part of Step #2, you might state: "As a part of teaching this specific behavior, I know that you will be able to successfully deliver on coming to class prepared (or whatever behavior you're teaching). However, on the off chance that you cannot, I am prepared to help you by re-teaching at a time other than class time." **The re-teaching time should only be as long as it takes the student to show you the behavior**

correctly. Any time longer than that would appear as punishment to the student and could be lost as an instructional opportunity. What follows is an outline version and quick review of the **teaching a behavior process.**

Step #1 Brainstorm the Behaviors or Expectations and Determine and Teach the Content

1. Before students begin the school year, identify all your expectations and make a list of priorities (number them in order).
2. Identify all the parts of the behavior (task analysis). Make sure every part of the behavior is included.
3. Put all the parts in the correct sequence.
4. Try the behaviors alone, by yourself (rehearsal).
5. Some behaviors overlap so make expectations clear and clean-cut.
6. Make no assumptions when teaching behaviors. First, do not assume that your students know how to correctly demonstrate these behaviors; and second, do not treat them as though they know nothing.
7. During the first week of school, teach your top 2 or 3 expectation priorities for both instructional and behavioral expectations.
8. Get students to focus on the behaviors you will teach through an anticipatory set; tell the students that you are going to demonstrate a certain behavior (procedure).
9. Give students the relevant information that is part of the behavior. For example: "This is the process of lining-up at the door." You need to include the *what, when, how, where, who and why.*
10. Give consideration to the **three step maximum concept** as you teach the behavior so as not to overwhelm or overload the students all at once.
11. Be sure to **check for understanding** of the behavioral steps, rationale and expected outcomes before you move on to Step #2.

Step #2 Model the Behavior

1. Model the parts of each step one at a time. Demonstrate the steps with verbal annotations (narrate it as you show it). Examine the steps of the behavior with your students. Remember, modeling also affects retention.
2. Use the following Modeling Criteria:
    a. Model it 100% correctly.
    b. **Say** it as you **show** it (with each step).
3. Give consideration to the **three step maximum concept** as you model the behavior so as not to overwhelm or overload the students all at once.
4. Be sure to **check for understanding** of each part again before you move on to Step #3.

Step #3 Practice the Behavior

1. Have students practice the behavior. The teacher serves as a coach providing continual feedback on the accuracy of the practice for each student and for the group as a whole.
2. The practice session also provides the teacher with an opportunity to visually check for student understanding of the behavior.
3. Again, give consideration to the **three step maximum concept** as you practice the behavior so as not to overwhelm or overload the students.
4. Remember "perfect practice makes perfect" (Vince Lombardi). And, if it doesn't get used, you lose it. Practice is the hands-on piece reflecting the objectives and practice affects **competence which begets confidence**. In other words, "If I know what I'm doing, I'm more likely to do it."

Step #4 Reinforce the Behavior

1. Positive reinforcement is applied when students are doing the behavior correctly. This is the teacher action that increases the probability that the correct behavior will be done through praise and encouragement.

a. Praise and encouragement must be specific to the behavior, not the person; this will eliminate the perception of sarcasm (toward the student).
b. Praise and encouragement can be directed toward an entire group. Sometimes, however, it needs to be private to a single person.

Step #5 Re-teach the Behavior

1. Re-teaching is only for those students who don't do the behavior correctly once it has been taught.
2. It is also called a **seminar** (workshop, clinic, camp, re-teaching session).
3. Seminars must take place on the student's valued time, such as during recess, lunch, or study hall, before or after school, etc.
4. Seminars should only take as long as it takes to RE-TEACH Steps #2, #3 and #4 of the behavior (statistically that is 5 to 10 minutes).

Keep in mind that periodic and systematic review of the behavior is crucial in order to increase the consistency and efficiency of the behavior and to positively affect long-term memory. How often and how much review will be determined by the age, ability, maturity and success of the students. Keep the principle of **prime time** in mind when reviewing behaviors. Prime time is the first seven to ten and the last seven to ten minutes of class. These are the best times for reviewing. Remember also since **Mondays and Fridays** are prime time days of the week for learning and teaching, consider using Mondays and Fridays as your primary review times.

A sample **Lesson Plan for Teaching Behaviors** can be found in **Appendix C**.

There are several important criteria to use when applying the process of getting kids ready to be successful in your school and your classroom. We list them here for your consideration and use.

Additional Guidelines, Reminders & Recommendations

1. Be consistent with this system with all of your students.
2. Be dispassionate. This is business; it is not personal. Don't make it personal by bringing in unproductive emotions and attitudes. This is not a time to lecture the student; the intent of the seminar is to re-teach the behavior.

3. **Never use sarcasm or ridicule** during this or any teaching session or when you interact with students, parents or other professionals. When used, sarcasm and ridicule become weapons that injure the self-esteem of the person who becomes the target of the sarcasm or ridicule, and it creates animosity between you and the student(s).
4. **Be professional**. Approach the student privately and tell him/her that he/she will be attending a "seminar" with you and specify the time.
5. REMEMBER: **The *behavior* is unwanted, not the *student*.** Attack the behavior, not the student.
6. Once you've had a "seminar," tell the student you'll do the seminar over again until he/she gets the behavior correct. This statement works well: "If you have trouble getting it right again, don't worry, I'll help you in the next seminar."
7. Be consistent. Develop a reputation that you expect correct behavior and that you will always follow up on inconsistent or incorrect behavior with a **seminar**.
8. If students don't show for a "seminar," they've not only just broken a classroom rule, but they've broken a school policy by being insubordinate. At this point you should meet with the administrator to look at the written student policy for insubordination and follow the procedure. If there isn't one, administrators in the district with teacher assistance should write one.
9. It is a proven fact that in-school suspension (ISS), out-of-school suspension (OSS) and detention are not effective unless you **re-train** students to alter their behavior. Our recommendation is that the "Detention Center" be renamed to the **"Retraining Center."** The center has but one focus: to train all who are assigned to the Retraining Center on how to be a successful student (i.e. how to come to class on time, how to be prepared for class, how to interact appropriately with others, how to behave in the hallway, etc.). In other words, there should be a consistent "lesson plan" or process in place for the Retraining Center.

The ultimate goal in this entire process is to work cooperatively with students to ensure that classroom organization, efficiency and effectiveness are maintained consistently by giving the responsibility for those pieces of the classroom fabric over to the students.

Shaping

Shaping may be defined as reinforcement of successive approximations toward a new, desirable behavior. The intended instructional outcome is ***rate and degree.*** When we use the strategy of shaping, we systematically reinforce each step leading to the desired behavior. This process is called **successive approximations**. This is accomplished by creating a schedule of reinforcements. The schedule serves as a mental or written plan to guide the type and frequency of the reinforcers used to facilitate the increased use of the new desired behavior and the decreased use of the old, unwanted behavior. Shaping requires a thoughtful and strategic approach when reinforcing the target behavior. An example of shaping would be as follows: a student is frequently out of his seat and while so, is commonly disruptive to other students. The decision is made to assist the student with changing the out of seat/disruptive behavior (unwanted) to more appropriate in-seat/on task behavior (target behavior). In order to do this, the teacher and the student must identify the problem behavior, the target behavior, strategies for achieving the target behavior, and the reinforcer. Each time the teacher "catches" the student exhibiting the target behavior, a positive reinforcer is used. Each time the teacher witnesses the student exhibiting the old, unwanted behavior, the positive reinforcer is withheld, and the student is informed of the consequence (cost) for using the unwanted behavior. The teacher designs and implements a **schedule of reinforcements** for that particular purpose. A **schedule of reinforcements** is a planned system of reinforcements for both the target behavior and the unwanted behavior. The schedule could look something like this. During the first week, the teacher will reinforce every exhibition of the desired, target behavior and re-teach the student on the student's valued time for any exhibitions of the unwanted behavior. During week two, the teacher will reinforce every third exhibition of the target behavior, while continuing to use the same negative reinforcement schedule for each unwanted exhibition. During week three, the teacher may strive to reinforce target behaviors more randomly such as once in the morning and once in the afternoon while continuing to use the same negative reinforcement schedule for each unwanted exhibition. Eventually, the student will maintain the target behavior on his/her own with only occasional reinforcement. The teacher should continue to use the same negative reinforcement schedule for each unwanted exhibition until the unwanted behavior is extinct. If the reinforcement occurs in specific time increments (e.g. every 10 minutes), it is called **fixed-interval reinforcement**. Alternatively, if the reinforcer occurs in a more unpredictable pattern (i.e. the student does not know when the reinforcer will come), that type of reinforcement is called **variable-interval reinforcement**. If the reinforcement occurs after a specific number of exhibitions of the desired behavior (e.g. after every 2), it is called **fixed-ratio reinforcement**. We recommend a 2 to 1 ratio be used at the start of the process. Alternatively, if the reinforcer occurs in a more unpredictable pattern (i.e. the student does not know how many exhibitions are required before the reinforcer will come), that type of reinforcement is called **variable-ratio reinforcement**. Schedules of reinforcements are very important in maintaining the desired behavior. That being said, it is likewise important that teachers and parents eventually shift the responsibility of reinforcement to the student, thereby helping the student to become intrinsically motivated. An example of this shift of responsibility could sound like, "Joe, in regard to your behavior in class, what would you like to compliment yourself for this morning?"

Behavior Management and Teaming

Teaching has often been characterized as a lonely business. How strange an observation when you consider that it is a people-driven and focused effort. Teachers are interacting nonstop with students, parents, other staff and the community. In addition, each teacher is responsible for his or her own classroom world of a specific group of students, specific curriculum, within specified blocks of time. As a result APL has devoted a good deal of information in this book to those elements that result in more successful student behavior management. As part of our focus on student behavior, we would additionally recommend to all teachers that to assist each teacher in this effort, teaming is both recommended and essential. Teaming in this context is suggesting that the teaching staff in a section of a building, wing, corridor or hallway organize into a unit/team for the purpose of teaching agreed upon hallway, bathroom, classroom, etc. behaviors. The goal is to communicate consistent expected behaviors for all in that learning section of the building. In doing so the group can rely on the fact that response to behavior is not hit-or-miss, that students cannot play one adult against another, and that teachers in these areas can support one another. If retraining seminars or re-teaching is called for with an individual or group of students, then two, three or more can team to help one another in that process. Teachers often lament the fact that, given their schedules, they find it difficult to conduct re-teaching sessions on the students' valued time. Teaming for the purpose of following through with addressing unacceptable behavior can be more easily addressed by the team approach.

APL has received very positive feedback from teachers that have taken the time to organize themselves in this way.

Building Level Behaviors

We recommend that all staff members in a building (this includes custodians, secretaries, lunchroom personnel, bus drivers, para-educators, media specialists, art, music, physical education and computer teachers as well as administrators and classroom teachers) meet formally to discuss the types of building-wide behaviors students need to exhibit consistently to assist in ensuring efficiency, order and safety. Here are a few steps to follow when engaging in this process.

Steps for Determining Building Level Behaviors

1. Get together as a staff and identify behaviors for the school (Step #1). These behaviors should be identified by level of importance and subsequently taught in that order. Included in this step is the identifying of the essential parts and the sequential steps for each behavior. In addition, the group must identify the rationale for students using the behaviors, and then the group must write the behavioral objectives and the expected outcomes. These components become the **content** for the teaching of the behaviors.
2. In Steps #1 through #4, the entire staff is expected to teach students those behaviors in the identified order of importance. As a brief review, Step #1 includes **Teaching the Behavior**; Step #2 is **Modeling the Behavior**; Step #3 is **Practicing the Behavior**; Step #4 is **Reinforcing the Behavior**; and Step #5 is **Re-teaching the Behavior** when necessary. Keep in mind that even though teachers have the primary responsibility for teaching the behaviors, the monitoring of students is the responsibility of the entire staff. It would be

particularly helpful if some of the building behaviors were taught by staff members other than teachers. For example, if time and schedules allow, the lunchroom staff could be asked to teach the desired behaviors and procedures for use in the lunchroom. The prohibiting piece here might be that cafeteria staff (and other school staff) are busy with their regular responsibilities and do not have time in their schedule to teach behaviors. If that is the case, the teachers could assume the responsibility for teaching all the building level behaviors in their homeroom, but consider having the other personnel (i.e. cafeteria staff) present while the teachers are teaching cafeteria behavior. Either way it is important that the students equate the behavior with the place where the behavior should be exhibited and also with all the adults who are going to be monitoring those behaviors (the cafeteria staff monitors in the cafeteria, etc.).

3. In regard to Step #5, Re-teaching, it is the responsibility of all staff to monitor student behavior while in the building and on school grounds. It also could be the responsibility of any staff member (if agreeable with all building staff) to re-teach students who are not following the prescribed behaviors. Again, non-teaching staff have specific responsibilities that may prohibit them from undertaking the re-teaching piece; however, it does not absolve them from their responsibility to monitor students while on duty. If we use this premise, we will be communicating to all students that every staff member in the building is theoretically their teacher and vice-versa.
4. Remember, <u>what we ultimately want is a process designed to help students be successful by substituting self-control in place of teacher control</u>. By doing so, we increase the students' level of concern about personal responsibility for self-monitoring as well as helping them keep in mind the real and logical consequences of Step #5.

In summary, when **responding to inappropriate building level behaviors** you must do the following:

1. Act promptly when you observe inappropriate behavior.
2. Get the student's attention.
3. Identify the reason you are speaking with the student.

4. Determine the appropriate time and place for re-teaching. (It is most helpful if the re-teaching takes place where the appropriate behavior is needed.)
5. Re-teach the desired behavior, rationale and expected outcomes.
6. Model an example of the appropriate behavior.
7. Have the student practice the behavior while you coach and provide feedback.
8. Reinforce the student by encouraging him/her to succeed with this behavior.
9. Remind the student that if he/she has additional trouble with the behavior that you will re-teach him/her again as long and as frequently as necessary.
10. Thank the student and dismiss him/her.

This entire process should take only as long as it takes to re-teach the behavior, usually just a few minutes. Any longer and the student may consider the process as punitive rather than instructional.

One feature that we have seen used that resulted in very positive outcomes is one that called for the development of **retraining teams.** A retraining team is a small group of staff members (not just teachers) who specialize in the re-teaching of behaviors to students <u>who have broken the law</u>. One of the most effective retraining teams we've seen included members of the community who cared about kids and who agreed to give of their time toward the retraining process. These community members, when added to the retraining team, provided a believability that the other adults (teachers, administrators and school staff) could not provide with respect to instilling in the students that the entire community cares about them and cares about how they behave both inside and outside of school. This communicated a powerful message and one that the students were not quick to forget.

Remember, the best way to deal with students who habitually and chronically do not follow the rules is to re-teach them consistently and persistently. Most often, when students finally "get it" that you are not giving up, they will come around to understand and exhibit the desired behaviors. All too frequently, the teachers wear down before the students, and what we then communicate is that those particular behaviors are only to be followed by a select few students and the chronic offenders are not among that group. We then send a very harmful message that we will accept irresponsibility from some students, but not from others. Teachers quickly and sometimes permanently lose credibility and respect when that happens.

Section Two: The Beginning of Class

In Section Two we answer the key question of, "How will I manage the first 7 to 10 minutes of the class?" The strategies offered are those having a positive effect on getting classes started off on the "right foot" such as , , greeting students, using agendas, communicating the "what" and "how," bell ringers, and going over homework.

Setting the Stage

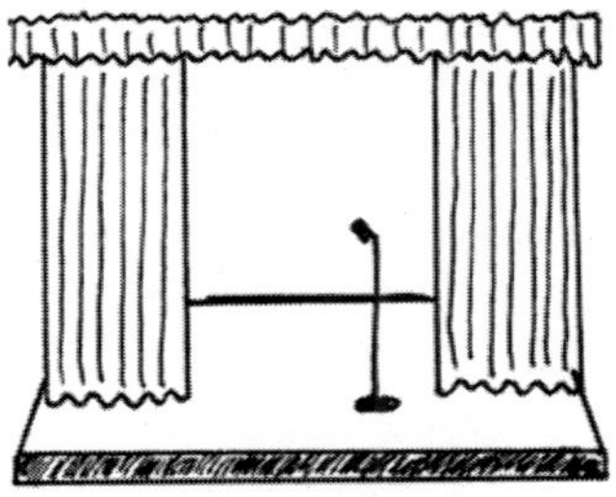

Setting the stage is essential in any lesson or instructional block. Therefore, starting class on time and in an organized fashion will, to a large degree, dictate the direction and focus of the remainder of the lesson. The following can serve as a set of recommendations to assist in setting the stage:

1. Posting an agenda, which would represent a breakdown of key items (skills, information, concepts) and activities, helps students mentally and physically organize for the tasks at hand. The teacher should then review the agenda with the students.
2. Posting the intended learning outcomes (instructional objectives) also helps students focus on the essential information that they will need to know at the conclusion of the lesson. Again, reviewing the objectives with the students helps them mentally organize for the lesson.
3. It is important that you involve students in a short reinforcement and review activity to "whet their mental appetite" for the content of the forthcoming lesson.

How we manage and organize the first 7 to 10 minutes of class has a significant impact on how organized, focused and efficient the class, for the most part, will become and remain during the lesson. Using bell ringers, sharing the agenda, communicating the lesson objective and going over homework are all key components of the first block of time we call **prime time 1**. There are several proven strategies that we recommend to assist you in facilitating your "setting of the stage."

Greeting Students

Taking the time and opportunity to greet each student individually and directly, particularly at the beginning of the day or class, produces several positive results. Teachers can begin to assess each student's attitude before beginning the teaching and learning processes. This brief interaction with each student gives the teacher a sense of who may be having some type of difficulty, problem or concern socially, emotionally, physically or intellectually. Greeting students and frequently interacting with students individually helps you create a warmer and friendlier classroom climate. As stated in Section One under feeling tone, our recommendation is to be at the door each morning, at the beginning of each class, or anytime all or most of your students are entering or returning to your classroom. Offering the students a handshake, pat on the back, high-five, or other symbol of friendship helps to warm up the climate significantly.

Using Agendas

Every time we teach a lesson, the three power words for teaching, **organization, consistency and specificity,** should be on our mind. We believe that human beings inherently desire structure. In structure lies security, predictability and ultimately the revelation of where we are going and why. Using agendas when teaching provides an opportunity to help both students and the teacher stay organized and be specific about the content and organization of a lesson. An **agenda** is a device used to inform learners of what activities will take place during the lesson and how much time will be devoted to each concept. Agendas help us achieve ***focus*** during the lesson and help us increase student ***retention*** of the content. Agendas provide additional support for students and teachers at the beginning of a lesson. The agenda communicates to the students the organizational format within which the teaching and learning will take place. Agendas can take a variety of forms. Here are three samples.

Our first example is the timed agenda. The **timed agenda** specifies the range of time within which a specific item, content or activity is going to occur.

A timed agenda will look something like this:

Timed Agenda:

8:20 – 8:24	Bell ringer
8:24 – 8:34	Go over homework
8:34 – 8:36	Record objectives
8:36 – 8:42	Review information on cell structures
8:42 – 8:57	Microscope identification activity
8:57 – 9:02	Closure
9:02 – 9:10	Getting homework started

The timed agenda takes some practice to get accustomed to using it. Don't be discouraged if you cannot adhere strictly to the time frames of the agenda. It is better to be thorough in the teaching and learning of content than it is to adhere to the agenda. That being said, teachers do not have unlimited time resources, and using a timed agenda can assist greatly in staying on track and accomplishing the lesson objectives.

The second example is a topical agenda. A **topical agenda** is a simple listing of the topics and activities in the order that they will be covered in a learning session.

Topical Agenda:

Bell ringer

Go over homework

Record objectives

Review information on cell structures

Microscope identification activity

Closure

Getting homework started

You will note that specific times are not included. Some teachers are more comfortable using the topical agenda rather than a timed agenda. As with any instructional strategy, the purpose is to help us be organized and accountable for the content of that lesson.

The third example is a combination agenda. A combination agenda has some of the characteristics of the timed and the topical agendas. The **combination agenda** is a sequential listing of the topics and activities to be dealt with in the lesson session with the number of minutes that it is estimated it will take to complete each item.

Combination Agenda:
Bell ringer – 4 minutes
Go over homework – 10 minutes
Record objectives – 2 minutes
Review information on cell structure – 6 minutes
Microscope activity – 15 minutes
Closure – 5 minutes
Getting homework started – 8 minutes

The teacher should briefly comment on the agenda by sharing it verbally with the students and thus drawing all students' attention to the format for the class. Agendas, like the sharing of objectives, lend a sense of organization, structure, purpose and seriousness to the learning session. Agendas are another key element in the initial focus segment, and they communicate the message that this is an important and valued process. Using an agenda models to students the power of organization and time management in an ongoing day-to-day fashion.

Communicating the "What" and "How"

There are tremendous benefits that result from the process of sharing your instructional outcomes (objectives) with your students. As part of the opening block of the lesson it is additionally important that the teacher effectively communicate the objectives for the learning session. Posting the objectives prominently, along with the agenda, further enhances the focus process for all the students. The communication of the objectives can be facilitated in a variety of ways. Here are four examples of ways to share the "**what**" and the "**how**" with students:

1. Post on the writing surface (chalkboard, whiteboard, or flip chart);
2. Project them using an overhead projector or a computer PowerPoint;
3. Post them on strips of paper on the classroom wall using masking tape;
4. Pass copies out to students.

Sharing objectives further reinforces organization, structure, purpose and seriousness of the learning experience. Objectives serve as targets and ongoing reference points throughout the teaching of the lesson as well as the focal point when conducting checking for understanding and closure activities. When we communicate the "**what**" and the "**how**" we are sharing our expectations, and in so doing, we are connecting to all four of the main outcomes of instruction: ***focus*** is enhanced, ***rate and degree of instruction*** increases, and ***retention*** and ***transfer*** are both improved. In and of itself, that would be reason enough to share our objectives with our students (Melton 1978; Veronin & Patry 2002; Schonfeld et.al. 1988). However, research has identified over 50 potential student benefits resulting from communicating the "**what**" and the "**how**." Among the most significant are the increase of test scores, the modeling of organization and time management, helping yourself and the students stay accountable for keeping all information relevant to the lesson objectives, and identifying for students specifically what the essential parts of that lesson are. Some of the other benefits include those listed in Table 2 below.

Table 2. Benefits of Sharing Instructional Objectives with Students

Time on task increases	Offers challenge to students & teachers
Reduce boredom	Better class management
Sets student goals	Eliminates student grouping by ability
Involves all learners	Equal expectations
Makes students responsible	Reduces stereotyping of learning
No copping out	Consistency
Sets up review	Models time management and organization
Facilitates closure	More student success
Motivates	Helps students acquire good life skills
Step-wise tasks	Students help others
Reduce student anxiety	Students can add own ideas to goals
Organizes mind set of student & teacher	Note taking skills are improved
Use for evaluation	Receptive and expressive feedback
Sets up student self-evaluation	Student ownership of learning
Stick to task motivation	Students & teachers control the learning

More than occasionally we meet teachers who object to this strategy. Many have said, "If I share the objectives with students they will know what will be on the test! I just can't do that!" We generally respond back with a question, "What is it about the essential content of your lesson or test (or course) that must remain a mystery to the students?" The obvious answer is, "nothing." How could any of us be accountable for information or skills that we did not know existed? The reasonable mind quickly sees the error in continuing to **not share** lesson objectives with students. It only makes sense that if we want students to accompany us on this educational journey that they have a right to know where we are headed and why.

Here are some final thoughts about sharing objectives. We know that sharing the "**what**" and the "**how**" is powerful in helping students achieve the outcomes. We also know that when teachers asked students to **record the objectives** in their notes prior to beginning the lesson that the lesson's outcomes are enhanced even more. The more frequently students interact with and think about the objectives of the lesson, the more we influence ***focus, rate and degree, retention*** and ***transfer***. In the recording of objectives process, we recommend that the objectives be numbered and sequenced by the teacher. The numbering allows for easy referencing (i.e. "Please locate objective #68 in your notebooks," or "The test next week will be over objectives 112, 113, 114, 116 and 117.")

Bell Ringers

A **bell ringer** is a class introductory strategy that asks the learners to recall information that was previously learned. Bell ringers contribute to the outcomes of both ***focus*** and ***retention.*** This strategy provides students with an opportunity to review previously learned material by assisting with the successful retention of information that was taught in the past, and needs to be remembered for the future. Bell ringers are one of, if not *the*, most powerful practice activities that exist. This activity is generally short in duration occupying from 5 to 15% of the overall class activity. Bell ringers contribute to ***focus*** by getting students immediately engaged in learning upon arriving in class. When students are immediately engaged in meaningful learning activities at the onset of class, better overall focus occurs for the duration of the learning session. There are three essential criteria connected to bell ringers.

Bell ringers:

- ☐ Are based on previous learning; (essentials only)
- ☐ Are a practice activity that facilitates the checking for understanding of a previous learning;
- ☐ Occur at the beginning of a class or learning objective.

There are specific instances in a classroom where additional time may be needed to adequately focus students and prepare them to move on to new content. The activities outlined below provide a structure for these extended focus activities:

- ☐ Extending the bell ringer activity on Mondays from a 3-5 minute activity to a 12-15 minute activity. This block of time is used to focus on as many essential learning processes and concepts as possible from the previous week's work.
- ☐ Following a vacation, it is recommended that one class period be spent looking back at key learning concepts from the pre-vacation time period (an extended bell ringer if you will).
- ☐ Another effective bell ringer strategy is the implementation of the **base group** exercise. Most teachers bemoan the fact that there seems to be no effective strategy for updating (instructing) students who have missed classes through absences by various causes. Creating classroom groups of 2 or 3 members (base groups) is an effective approach to address that concern and reinforce previous concepts, clear up any misunderstanding, and to clarify classroom and student expectations.

The following figure shows the **guidelines for the use of base groups.**

Figure 2. Guidelines for the Use of Base Groups

Step One: Teacher selects two to three students for each of the groups.

Step Two: Base group memberships remain intact over an extended period of time such as an entire marking period or semester.

Step Three: Base groups should meet every 7-10 days.

Step Four: Base group meetings should last for 15-20 minutes.

Step Five: During the base group meetings, the teacher assigns several items (based upon key learnings from the past 7-10 day period) that the group members will teach to each other in that 15-20 minute block of time as the teacher monitors by moving group-to-group.

Step Six: Each group has a spokesperson (a rotating role) who must respond to one question as posed by the teacher relating to the re-taught material. In other words, each group is responsible for re-teaching all of the essential learnings, but they are additionally responsible for reporting their results from one of the learnings back to the full class as a form of whole-class review. <u>The specific learning is not known until the teacher poses the question</u>.

Step Seven: If the spokesperson cannot respond, she/he needs to say "consult" at which point the group can quickly huddle to assist and support the spokesperson.

Some teachers prefer to use the base group strategy once every 5 days instead of 7-10 days. Those who choose to use it with more frequency felt that 7 to 10 days was too long and thus too much material or content needed to be reviewed in the allotted time. Using it once per week (for example every Friday) reduces the volume of material that needs to be reviewed. This strategy also works very well as a closure for the content of that week. The effective use of bell ringers, when implemented consistently, will create a more focused learning environment, promote better long-term retention, and improve student performance. It is another important part of your **retention system** along with checking for understanding and closure.

The following is a **very powerful and effective bell ringer activity.** Simply follow the instructions in order to facilitate a powerful version of the bell ringer strategy. This bell ringer is designed so that once it is prepared, you could use and re-use it many times.

Step One: Preparing the Cards

- ☐ Take 3x5 index cards (or any size you prefer);
- ☐ On each card **write essential items of content only**: a question, a process to describe, a definition/vocabulary, or a problem to work, etc. (example below);
- ☐ Then, number the cards in order to be able to reorder them in their proper sequence (you could actually put your entire curriculum on index cards);
- ☐ Limit each card to only one item (objective).

Step Two: Using the Cards

- ☐ At the beginning of class, hand a card to a team of two students as they enter the classroom (using teams of two keeps the students more accountable; you may also choose to use an in-basket and an out-basket to free you up from this (Aside: you have to teach kids how to work in groups).
- ☐ The students are directed to follow directions on the card and take five minutes to complete the given task or problem.
- ☐ At the end of the five minutes:
    - ☐ You call on five separate teams.
    - ☐ Have each team state the problem and their determined solution.
    - ☐ Have the class affirm or reject the selected solution.
        - *If affirmed, move on to the next team.*
        - *If rejected, the class must generate the answer before you move on to the next team.*
    - ☐ Call on the next team and repeat the process.
- ☐ The questions for your tests will come from these cards. This strategy will greatly assist in increasing your students' test scores.
- ☐ You may wish to include some additional cards to randomly allow students to have a break such as a:
    - ☐ Bathroom pass;
    - ☐ Kick back and take it easy pass; or

- ☐ Free cookie pass.
- ☐ This strategy allows you and your students to do recall, analysis, evaluation, and practice at the beginning of class or anytime you need a closure activity.

Again, it is our premise that what appears on a test at the end of a learning unit should not be a surprise to students who have been in class daily and participated actively in the learning sessions. Using bell ringers which are connected to your instructional objectives not only facilitates more organized reviews and retention activities, but produces more successful test results and becomes a powerfully positive motivational device as well. A bell ringer is a "chance tc look back before we look forward!"

Sample Bell Ringer Card

Rank these elements by atomic weight from lightest to heaviest:

Hydrogen
Helium
Oxygen
Nitrogen
Fluorine
Argon

Kindergarten Bell Ringer Example (based on previously learned material)

Students (working in pairs) are given a set of cards with color words printed on them. They are also given a set of cutout circles of different colors. Students are directed to take each colored circle and glue it onto the corresponding card.

First Grade Bell Ringer Example

In pairs, students are given multiple "coins" of different denominations (pennies, nickels, dimes). The teacher holds up a picture of an item with the price on it (i.e. a pencil costing 8¢). The students then must show 8¢ (using the "coins") on their desks.

Going Over Homework

As part of the beginning of class, homework will need to be given some consideration. If homework was assigned yesterday, then it needs to be gone over or used the following day. How much time to spend going over the previous day's homework will be a reflection of how much was assigned. We have a limited amount of time available in the first part of class. Therefore, we should not overload. In starting the homework in class we should do so utilizing homework partners (students can work on their homework with a partner). The same would apply when going over the homework. Working in pairs as they go over the homework will speed up this process and reinforce the correctness.

Section Three: The Middle of Class

In this section of the book we will detail the main features of what happens during class or the actual instructional delivery including the types of interactions we recommend between teachers and students. The strategies addressed here are designed to assist teachers in boosting student achievement during the actual teaching and learning processes. Those strategies include anticipatory set, active participation, wait-time, wait-time extended, interaction sequence, checking for understanding, clear directions and information, chaining, checking for understanding of directions, note taking, managing time to facilitate learning, the monitoring map, knowledge of results, modeling, interest and group work. We begin our discussion with anticipatory set.

Anticipatory Set

Anticipatory set is an instructional strategy proven effective in achieving ***focus*** and ***transfer.*** It is defined as a mental process where the learner is asked to search his/her past for information that he/she has about that which is to be taught. It is also referred to as "set induction." It is commonly an activity used to begin class, refocus after an interruption, or as a transitional activity when you move to a new objective. There are **three criteria to consider when using anticipatory set**. Those criteria are: 1) The anticipatory set must relate to the learner's past; 2) It must be relevant to the lesson's objective(s); and 3) It must involve the learner actively. Some examples of anticipatory sets are pictures or other visuals, humorous stories, asking students to imagine or think about something from their past experiences or a person they know, or asking students to draw, write, discuss or act out a thought or idea.

We have concluded that using a viable anticipatory set puts the teacher "on the road to controlling teaching." Anticipatory set helps you teach kids to be accountable for their focus, and it involves the learner by demonstrating that past knowledge, both personal and school, is important in the learning processes. It likewise provides the opportunity to activate memory as a type of advanced organizer for the new content to facilitate both learning and retention (Luiten et. al. 1980).

In creating an anticipatory set, the teacher needs to ask him/herself: *In what manner can I involve the students so that they are mentally moving toward the objectives of the lesson?* Effective keynote speakers ask themselves the same question. What can I do as I begin my speech to grab the audience? Often it is an attention grabbing story, a visual, or an experience that they use to connect with the audience. Therefore, the effective anticipatory set would relate to the learner's past, mentally or actively involve the learner and link the learner to the lesson's objectives. Much in the same way that a speaker at a large gathering would catch and hold the audience's attention, an anticipatory set catches and holds the students' attention in preparation for the sharing of new information and in order to connect it to past learning.

Anticipatory sets are not just for the beginning of class. They can be implemented at any point in the lesson where it is sensed that focus or refocus is necessary. Our **recommendations regarding when to use anticipatory set and for what purpose** are as follows. First, using it at the *beginning of class* will help gain the students' focus and will help students connect to their prior learning. Second, using it at the *beginning of each new objective* will compel the students to come with you as you make the transition into the new content. Third, using anticipatory set *following any class interruption* will allow you to accomplish all three purposes listed above. Since class interruptions are inevitable, using the strategy of anticipatory set provides you with the skills to start managing the classroom interruptions and to start minimizing their impact. A simple example here might be as follows, Teacher: "Prior to the P.A. announcement, I asked Samantha a question. What was that question?"

When using anticipatory sets in your teaching, consider the following **guidelines**. Use anticipatory sets:

- ☐ For the beginning of each new objective;
- ☐ Following interruptions;
- ☐ At the beginning of a new day;
- ☐ To break up lengthy objectives; and/or
- ☐ To help students focus and transfer information.

Remember the three criteria necessary for using anticipatory sets effectively. They must relate to the learner's past experience; they must be relevant to the lesson's objective(s);

and they must involve the learner. Anticipatory sets can and will make your teaching more interesting, more vivid and more learner-centered. Consider how you may begin to incorporate them into your teaching today.

Here are some **examples** of anticipatory set.

- ☐ Imagine that you're walking in a forest. What are some things you might see there?
- ☐ Remember the very first time you ate lunch in the school cafeteria? What are some of the things you remember about that experience?
- ☐ This morning when you arrived at school, what did you do first?
- ☐ Think about some of the ways that students might prepare for taking a test.
- ☐ Think about the scariest story you ever heard or read. What are some things that make stories sound scary?

Next, we'll examine strategies to help students more actively participate in the lesson.

Active Participation

Active participation is defined as the consistent engagement of the minds of all the learners in what is being taught. The intended instructional outcome is ***rate and degree*** of learning. Active participation assists teachers with efficient use of time and with student behavior. Let's define the main components of active participation: *consistent* means always, repeatedly and regularly; *engagement* refers to involving the students fully; *all the learners* means every single student regardless of the students' levels of achievement; *what is being taught* refers to the content objective for the lesson. Therefore, when we teach using active participation we always, repeatedly and regularly involve fully every single student with the content objective for the lesson. What we want is to have each and every student **"on-the-hook"** with our objective, and not "**off-the-hook"** with his/her own objective.

Imagine you are observing a classroom. There are generally three types of learners: the **high achievers**, the **low achievers** and the **in-betweeners**. When a teacher focuses solely on the high achievers, the rest of the class feels various things. For example, the low achievers may feel relief because they are not the group currently **on-the-hook**. The in-betweeners may feel left out or apathetic because they are being ignored. The high achievers will feel great and confident because they are the focus of the lesson. However, sometimes the high achievers will intentionally answer incorrectly in order to feel and show empathy for their other classmates. In this situation, the high achievers may defer their success, the in-betweeners may grow resentful of the teacher and the content, and the low achievers will continue to hide from true learning. The teacher may be fooled into thinking that he/she is bringing the entire class along on the journey, but actually, the majority of the students are not engaged to the level where they are able to succeed and meet the objectives of the lesson, the course, and those of the curriculum standards. "When the teacher is consistently interacting with the hand raisers or elite performers only, that's an indication that there is a serious problem in that classroom" (Schmoker 2011).

There are two types of active participation. They are **overt** and **covert** active participation. The best sequence for using them is covert to overt. Let's take a look at each type and how we may use each type to get kids "**hooked in**."

The first type of active participation is **covert. Covert activities** come first in the process of teaching and learning. When using **covert activities** we must adhere to the following criteria. First, it must apply to all students. Second, covert activities are not directly observable by the teacher. In other words, it is internal, not external. Third, covert activities involve providing students with think time through using the strategy of wait-time. Fourth, covert activities provide students with a mental rehearsal to get "hooked in" to the objective and in order to build their confidence with the content or skill. Some examples of covert activities are when students are asked to think, visualize, picture, imagine, look at, listen to, read, or to mentally pretend. Cognitive psychologists label this the "minds-on" component of learning. This is the time when students are building the mental schema for the content as they conceptualize the ideas and connect them to prior learning.

The second type of active participation is **overt**. **Overt activities** come after covert activities. When using **overt activities** we must adhere to the following criteria. First, overt activities do not always have to apply to all the students. In other words, you may ask only certain students to initially be involved in an overt activity. However, at some point it is critical that all students be given the opportunity to overtly demonstrate what they know by talking or writing about it, or demonstrating it. Second, the overt activity must be connected to the objective and let students overtly interact with the content or skill. This leads us to the third criteria for overt activities: the student interaction with the content or skill must provide us with observable data on each student's progress toward meeting the objective. You monitor student progress by frequently checking for understanding. It is important for us to remember to use **covert** active participation first in order to help students think before responding. One of the most powerful instructional strategies that combines both covert and overt active participation is called the **interaction sequence**. The interaction sequence provides for all of the above by involving all students in the instruction and learning process. We will take a closer look at this strategy in this section, but first, let's look at another important strategy that encourages active participation called **wait-time**.

Wait-Time

A critical element in encouraging active participation is giving students adequate time to focus on and think about the question in order to arrive at an answer. **Wait-time** may be defined as the amount of time you give learners to process (to focus on the question and to think about what you're asking them) before you call on a student to respond. We define **"adequate wait-time"** as **3 to 5 seconds.** Tobin & Capie (1982) found that students' attending and generalizing were enhanced when teachers paused approximately three seconds after asking questions before requesting a response. If you wait three to five seconds following the asking of a question before you accept a response, you allow for more processing time (student thinking time), and in turn you provide the students with a better opportunity to arrive at an answer because they have more time to accomplish the two pieces to the answer sequence that must be in place if students are to be successful. The first is time to focus on the question and the second is more time to think about their answer. Unfortunately, the average wait-time is less than 1 second. Rowe (1974) found that teachers usually react or ask another question within 0.9 seconds. Increase in pause time, as tested by Rowe, influenced pupil responses in many ways. Student responses were longer (average shift from 7 to 28 words) and there were a greater number of student responses which were unsolicited but appropriate (average shift from a mean of 3 to a mean of 37). An increase in wait-time led to fewer student failures to respond to a question. Children also appear to be more confident in their answers. Students listen to each other, there is an increased use of student inference statements backed up by evidence, and more student-initiated questions. As pause time increased, teachers showed greater response flexibility as indicated by fewer mismatches between student statements and teacher reactions.

Too frequently we see teachers use the following method. They ask a question and immediately call on the student whose hand was raised fastest. Regardless of that student's response (which may frequently be the right answer) the teacher immediately moves on to the next question and student. Several problems occur when using this method. First, students who didn't have the time or opportunity to arrive at their own answer are not being encouraged to move information from short- to long-term memory through the process of making a decision about an answer. In order for students to become metacognitive (to manage and analyze their own thinking), they need time to process and make decisions about the information they have. Second, when the teacher moves on too quickly, individual students who didn't arrive at the correct answer are left in the middle of two dilemmas: Why was my answer wrong, and why was the other answer right? Third, by using this ineffective strategy to monitor student learning, we also violate the guidelines of **knowledge of results** because students aren't given personal, immediate and specific feedback. The student and the teacher really have no idea who was wrong, and what went wrong and why. The teacher also does not accurately know who has the information correctly, who has incorrect information, who is missing pieces, and what pieces are missing. Finally, we fail to motivate students and create a reasonable **feeling tone** in the classroom when we use teaching strategies that are teacher-centered and non-effective. All in all it leaves huge gaps in the teaching and learning processes.

When using **checking for understanding** it is essential that we make use of **three easy guidelines** to make our checks for understanding more successful and organized. First, when checking for understanding, go back and use the lesson objectives for your check. The lesson objectives contain the "**what**" and the "**how**" that students should be able to know and do following the lesson procedure. So, phrase your questions around the "what" and "how" from each objective that you want to check. Second, use adequate **wait-time**, giving students the time to process and search their memories for the essential pieces needed to correctly answer the question. Before moving on to the third guideline, let's look more closely at **wait-time**.

There are two forms of wait-time: **wait-time #1** and **wait-time #2**. The first, **wait-time #1** looks like this:

- ☐ Ask all students the question.
- ☐ Pause by using the 3 to 5 second minimum. (Remember: The tougher the question, the longer the pause needs to be.)
- ☐ Call on someone.

The rationale for using **wait-time** is threefold. First, it actively encourages kids to focus on the question asked. This reason in itself is critical to student success. If a student didn't hear or isn't focusing on the question, a reasonable response will not be forthcoming. Second, the pause following the question gives the student time to think, searching his/her memory for the essential pieces needed for a correct answer. Third, using wait-time lowers the pressure on kids by diminishing anxiety of having to answer using the "quick draw" method. Fourth, this additional rehearsal of the information positively affects retention and strengthens the speed of the next recall of this information (Sousa 2006).

Wait-Time Extended

This second type of wait-time is directly connected to our third guideline for more effectively using **checking for understanding**, which is to <u>keep all students responsible for the answer</u>. We refer to this second type as **wait-time #2** or **wait-time extended**. It is "extended" because during the wait-time, you ask students to share their answers with a partner, thereby providing students with a "dress rehearsal" of their answer before they are asked to share it with the full class. Students are held responsible and made more successful through the use of **wait-time #2** by giving all students an equal opportunity to think about and formulate an answer because you have controlled hand raising, controlled the shouting out of answers by the few more competitive students, and by varying the type of student-responding strategies you use in the classroom.

Wait-time extended or **wait-time #2** (frequently called **think/pair-share**) consists of a 5- part sequence, as shown in the figure below.

Figure 3. Wait-Time Extended: Five-Part Sequence

Part One:

Ask the question of all of the students. It is highly productive when asking questions to put the questions out to all of the students as opposed to the common questioning strategy of prefacing a question with the name of one student the teacher has pre-chosen to respond. (Ex. "John, what is the sum of 39 plus 21?")

Part Two:

Teacher pauses to provide the students with a few seconds to process what has been asked (**wait-time**).

Part Three:

Put students **on-the-clock** (discussed later in this section) by giving them a specific amount of time for sharing. (e.g. "You have 30 seconds to share your answer with your partner.") The amount of time you allot will be based on the difficulty and complexity of the question.

Part Four:

Have the students, in pairs, share their thoughts regarding the question with one another (**wait-time extended**).

Part Five:

Select students to respond to the question or thought.

Keeping all students accountable and "on-the-hook" can readily be accomplished by using a more enhanced checking for understanding strategy that incorporates **wait-time #2**. We've developed a variation of **wait-time #2** that we believe will make you a more effective teacher and your students more successful learners. We call our strategy the **interaction sequence**.

Interaction Sequence

The traditional think/pair-share consists of the five-part sequence just described. The **interaction sequence** is a plan for managing student responses to teacher questioning in the classroom also by using **wait-time extended**. In the **interaction sequence**, we use all the parts listed above, but <u>we've added some additional steps</u>, as shown in Figure 4.

Figure 4. The Interaction Sequence

Step One:

- ☐ Ask the question of all of the students.
- ☐ Pause to provide the students time to process (**wait-time**).
- ☐ Put students on-the-clock.

Step Two: While students are discussing or sharing in pairs the teacher selects one or more pairs to interview or conference with regarding their thoughts. During this interview process, the teacher should check student answers, probe, or provide answers when information is missing.

Step Three: When the pairs are brought back on time, the teacher then calls on one or more pairs that were interviewed (with whom you conferenced). This is called **purposeful selection.**

Step Four: Next, the teacher additionally calls on a random student pair or two. These students were not part of the interview/conference procedure but did have an opportunity to share with a partner. This is called **random selection**. Random selection keeps all students engaged in the discussion because they do not know who the randomly selected students are beforehand.

Step Five: Finally, open the question up for additional responses by asking for "volunteers." This is called **volunteer selection**. Using volunteer selection allows you to acknowledge students who have the answer and want to readily share it.

Here are **3 guidelines** that facilitate the effective implementation of the interaction sequence:

1. For the interaction of all to be effective, the successful management of the "hand raising" process is essential. Simply put, it is recommended that students be informed that they need to refrain from raising their hands to respond to questions until the appropriate verbal signal by the teacher is given (i.e. "volunteers may now answer" or "the next question is for volunteers.")
2. Hand raising signals should be developed. In controlling the hand raising process, the teacher is also managing question asking by students. To accommodate question asking as well as question answering, it is recommended that the teacher create and teach **two hand raising signals**:

- ☐ If the student chooses to volunteer to answer a question, the signal can be hand up with palm facing the teacher.
- ☐ If a student has questions for which he/she would like a response, the signal can be hand up with fist closed.
- ☐ In either instance, the students can be taught that both signals are used without students verbally shouting or calling out.

3. In the <u>interview/conference segment</u>, if the students being interviewed do not have an answer, then the teacher can take that opportunity to "coach." Likewise, if the students being interviewed gave an incorrect response, the teacher can now remediate it in a safe and controlled manner rather than publicly in front of the entire class. An example of the interview/conference could sound like this:

    Teacher: *What is the sum of 24 plus 22?*

    Student: *44.*

    Teacher: *No. 44 would be correct if I asked for the sum of 22 plus 22. The sum of 24 plus 22 is 46. Students, say it with me please: The sum of 24 plus 22 is 46.*

    Then you move on to interview the next pair or return to the full class for the sharing of responses.

The **interaction sequence** is a very powerful strategy for ensuring the active engagement of all learners. It is quite effective in addressing questions regarding reluctant learners, the less confident, the defocused, and the less able as well as the focused, capable and higher performing students. We all have learners in our class who are somewhat reluctant to respond to questions. As a result we have difficulties ascertaining what they really know. If we wait until a quiz or test to find out what those students know, it may be too late to help them effectively. So, why do certain kids never raise their hands? Our experience has helped us identify four primary reasons: 1) they can't keep up with the stars (most capable students) in the class; 2) they never get called on even when they raise their hands because the teacher doesn't have confidence that they can answer accurately; 3) they are tired of being wrong; or 4) they can't handle the stresses caused by this competitive question/answer strategy. In order to move a student from the "reluctant" category to the "confident" category, we must build up his/her self-esteem by growing his/her confidence with respect to responding to class questions. We do this by "catching a student being right!" How do we accomplish this? We assist students in growing their confidence through the process of using wait-time extended and an interviewing process.

The **interaction sequence** has several obvious benefits. First, using the interaction sequence allows the teacher to deal with the problems frequently created when students use hand raising to signal that they have a response to share. When students compete to be the first to respond to any question, their primary goal may mistakenly be to get their hand raised first rather than to have an accurate response. In this situation, we often have lots of incorrect answers to go along with the raised hands. The interaction sequence places a higher priority on having an accurate response by reducing the competitive hand raising and through the use of **wait-time extended**.

Second, using the interaction sequence keeps students from blurting out answers. Frequently in classrooms without a question-answering strategy, one or two students will commonly yell out the answers to questions even before most of the students have had an opportunity to process the question, let alone think of an answer. In those cases, the majority of the students may just disengage from the discussion and let the more competitive and quicker students do all the answering of the questions. How, then, does the teacher know if every student has the correct information? Most generally a teacher moves on to the next question once a correct answer has been given by a student. It's possible that we may be leaving a substantial number of our students behind if we continue using very traditional yet ineffective question-answer practices.

Third, the interaction sequence provides an "equal opportunity" for all students to answer a question. If answering doesn't depend on speed, then students who process questions more methodically still have a chance to be the first to answer a question. (Remember: Success must come before motivation.) In other words, **responding to questions in class relies on accuracy, not on speed**.

Fourth, the interaction sequence counteracts the apathy of students. It does so by keeping every single student engaged in the process through the use of wait-time extended and the additional use of sharing answers with a partner, allowing students to "check" the efficacy of their answer before they undertake the risk of sharing it out loud in front of the entire class. This "dress rehearsal" of the student's answer is a key feature in making students successful and therefore increasing their intrinsic motivation and confidence. Keep in mind that when using random selection, you shouldn't always use the same people. Likewise, when using volunteer selection you should use volunteers from different groups. We call that "spreading the wealth around."

We often get asked about the hand raisers whose self-identity is closely linked to their ability to be "quick on the draw" with respect to the question-answer process. We recommend that you don't always put the volunteers at the bottom of the order because they may lose heart if they can't "show off" and/or they may become frustrated and act out inappropriately as a result. You avoid these problems by occasionally saying the following: "The next question is for volunteers." That way, students who like the competition of being the first to answer will still have that motivation built in; it will just be used with less frequency. We also recommend that you **use this strategy toward the end of the question/answer session** in order to keep all students engaged in the discussion process.

Ultimately, we offer the following additional benefits for using the interaction sequence in your lesson sessions.

Benefits of Using the Interaction Sequence

There are at least eight benefits of using the interaction sequence, as follows:

1. It gives kids a chance to talk which decreases boredom.
2. It reinforces student answers with another student (peer feedback).
3. It gives students a dress rehearsal in which to gain more confidence in their answers.
4. It allows students to "look good" in front of peers.
5. It develops positive relationships.
6. It provides a chance for the teacher to check for understanding while managing time effectively (by using on-the-clock).
7. It gives teachers an opportunity to interact with students individually and in pairs with frequency during every class session (during Step 2: Tell your partner/ conferencing and interviewing component).

8. It provides for multiple repetitions of the correct answer which is the most effective form of emphasis (Jersild 1928; Mayer 1983).

Much has been written about student self-esteem and self-confidence, all of which speaks to the question of student motivation. Making a student "look good" in front of his/her friends and classmates is an essential ingredient in promoting that healthy sense of self-esteem and self-confidence. It keeps students coming back, hoping for more, and extending themselves with the belief that they can succeed. We have not found any student active engagement process or strategy that rivals the **interaction sequence**.

Checking for Understanding (CFU)

Checking for understanding is a mental process wherein the learner is asked to summarize his or her perception of what has been learned. The primary intended instructional outcome is ***retention.*** Checking for student understanding of what has been taught helps students focus on the essential information, the "right stuff" if you will, from the lesson. Checking for understanding additionally contributes to the monitoring of the ***rate and degree*** of the student learning. Through the use of checking for understanding the teacher has the opportunity to assess the progress of individual student and overall group learning. Checking for understanding is critical to the process of **knowledge of results**. If we are to provide essential feedback to the learners about how well they are progressing in the achievement of the lesson objectives, we must use checking for understanding both **consistently** and **frequently**. It is easy to understand the consistent use of checking for understanding. It is an integral part of every teaching and learning episode. When we arrive at the end of the teaching to an objective, it is obvious that we need to check with the students to determine what they have learned and what they will remember about what they learned. We often see this process misused. For example, we frequently see and hear teachers check for student understanding in the following way. After finishing a lecture, a lab or seat work, teachers will commonly ask students, "do you understand what we've just done?" What usually follows is that students most commonly answer by either saying, "yes," or by nodding their heads. We must ask ourselves: *if I check for understanding using the method described above, just what is it that I really have learned about what students know about the topic we just finished?*

While most teachers just move on following that type of check for understanding, the actual answer to that question should be: "I have no actual idea what the students have really learned about this topic."

The frequency with which a teacher uses checking for understanding needs to be guided by not only when we've finished teaching to an objective, but also must be guided by the following two ideas. The first is **how much** students can remember before they are overloaded and begin to lose focus, start forgetting and/or begin to misconceive what is being taught. The second idea is **how long** a person can realistically manage to focus his/her attention before he/she loses interest, becomes overloaded, starts forgetting, or just moves over to his/her own agenda (daydream, think about later, the weekend, an upcoming job, a test in another class, etc.) We will examine the phenomenon of **how much** in the section on **clear directions and information**.

Another phenomenon about memory is that it is also impacted by the time of the day the learning occurs. In a conventional school schedule (school starts at 8:00 a.m. and dismisses at 3:30 p.m. for example), students will be able to learn and remember more in the morning sessions than they will in afternoon sessions. This phenomenon is influenced by biological events called circadian rhythms (Sousa 2006). Students may be easily able to accomplish three or four objectives each in morning classes, but only two or three each in their afternoon classes. In fact, students experience a protracted period of time in the afternoons where learning and focus is more difficult (Sousa 2006). Let's examine the phenomenon of **how long** in a bit more detail here.

The phenomenon of **how long** is impacted by what we know about human memory and attention. Ebbinghaus' 19th century research on memory discovered the following:

- ☐ **After 20 minutes, up to 45%** of what you've taught is gone without practice and checking for understanding.
- ☐ **After 60 minutes, up to 55%** of what you've taught is gone without practice and checking for understanding.
- ☐ **After 24 hours, up to 65-75%** of what you've taught is gone without practice and checking for understanding.

For appropriate reasons, this phenomenon is called the **forgetting curve**.

Memory is additionally impacted by the total length of time that a person can maintain focus or attention to the primary learning activity or stimulus. Russell (1979) concluded that for preadolescents the average attention span is 5 to 10 minutes, and for adolescents it is 10 to 20 minutes. **For the majority of adult students, twenty minutes is about the maximum length** of time they can maintain optimum focus. Beyond the twenty minutes, information begins to be lost and/or incorrectly understood, learned and remembered due to mental fatigue. **For the majority of adolescents, ten minutes is about the maximum length** of time they can maintain optimum focus. In order for us to prevent the problems earlier identified with how long a student can maintain focus, we recommend using the **10-2 rule in high school** when checking for student understanding of the lesson content and ultimately the lesson objectives. This rule states that for every ten minutes of instruction, you stop and take at least two minutes to check for student understanding of what has transpired during the previous ten minutes of the lesson. By using this strategy (rule) you will never need to re-teach more than the previous ten minutes if students have not achieved the essence of the objective. We frequently see teachers who may teach an entire class period before asking students to summarize what they perceived was the content of the previous 40 to 50 minutes (or in block scheduling this could be up to 90 minutes). It is amazing what answers students will give, or not be able to give, because the time between the initial delivery or interaction with the content and the point when the students were asked to share what they learned about content could be up to 40 or more minutes. This violates the human attention span maximum and it disadvantages students by asking them to remember it **all** before they have a chance to rehearse it again for memory. This is not only unquestionably a poor strategy, but it often places students in the position of building misconceptions about content and in situations where, due to memory incompatibility, they fail to remember any essential information relative to the objective. We believe that by following the **10-2 rule in high school** you will be setting up your students for success, providing them with memory compatible methods for remembering information by building schema and fostering student hope that they not only can learn, but they can more deeply and easily understand the material and remember the essentials for far longer. While this ratio works well in high school and adult learner settings, we do recommend smaller ratios for younger learners. It is best to take a look at the students in front of you and estimate the length of time that they can focus. Let that estimate become the **rule**. Remember, for a significant percentage of your students this will be their first exposure to this new content. Therefore, they will need more processing and rehearsal time in order to learn and remember the new content. For middle school settings (grades 6-8) we recommend that you adjust the ratio down by following a **7- or 8-2 rule when checking for understanding**. For the intermediate grades (3-5) we recommend that you further adjust down by following a **4- or 5-1 rule when checking for understanding**. For primary grades, we recommend that you further adjust down by following a **2- or 3-1 rule when checking for understanding**. Using these ratios will tremendously assist your students with greater memory success and better understanding of the material. They will also help you monitor learning and remembering more effectively and keep your more able students from the boredom they most assuredly must endure if you must re-teach frequently because you did not use appropriate checking for understanding strategies.

Guidelines for Using Checking for Understanding

The **checking for understanding** process is easy if we follow a few basic guidelines. First, ask the question of **all** the students. We do this by not using anyone's name, we only ask the question. Second, use wait-time (3 to 5 second rule) to provide all the learners with an opportunity to formulate an answer. Third, select a student or a group of students to provide a response.

The benefits to using these guidelines are as follows: first, by asking the question of **all** the students rather than using the more common method (i.e. "Jon, what formula is used to find the circumference of a circle?"), we engage all the learners in **covert active participation**. If we ask the question using Jon's name first, we engage many fewer students; generally, we may engage Jon and those other students who are genuinely interested, but in most cases, we engage only Jon. It is equally important that we avoid using the other common strategy of saying something like, "Who can tell me what formula is used to find the circumference of a circle?" Asking questions in this manner just seems to beg for a smart aleck student to respond with this answer, "No one!" So, ask the question of all the students, not just Jon and certainly, not just "who."

Second, by using **wait-time** we are providing important processing time for the learners. Not all students have hair-trigger responding skills. Those who don't have hair-trigger response skills appreciate the opportunity to be able to potentially be the first one to answer a question without needing to arrive at the answer immediately. Third, when you decide who answers (instead of one or more students blurting it out before all have had some processing time) you decide who responds, thus giving you control over the participation of every single student in the class, thereby guaranteeing that no one gets left out. Remember: our primary goal here is to know which students have an accurate response and which students do not. We accomplish that by "*catching students being right*" (having the correct response) through using these simple guidelines for checking for understanding.

Clear Directions and Information

Clear directions and information is a strategy that addresses the question of how much information students can manage and the degree to which it is received accurately. The intended instructional outcomes are ***focus*** and ***rate and degree***. Clear directions and information like checking for understanding is impacted by what we know about human memory. In other words, how much information can a person handle before he/she reaches overload and starts to break down. Most kids can handle 3 items of information before they reach the point of overload. According to Smith (1977), adults, in theory, are able to handle 5 to 9 items (+/- 1) of information before they reach the point of overload. However, in application it actually translates to an average of 4 items for adults and adolescents. For preschoolers the average is 2 items, and for preadolescents the average is 3 items (Miller 1956 in Sousa 2006). This translates into an instructional strategy that we call the **three step maximum concept**.

While it is possible to remember larger groups of items (larger than 3 to 5), we remember more successfully if those several items are broken into smaller groupings or sets of two or three. To illustrate this phenomenon, think about the number of digits in a telephone number (either 7 or 10 with the area code) and the number of digits in a Social Security Number (9). What do you notice about the way those digits are communicated? They are not communicated in an unbroken string of 7, 9 or 10 digits, but they are broken up into smaller sets of 2, 3 or 4 digits. Hence, we are better able to remember phone numbers or our social security numbers because the numbers are presented to us in a more **memory compatible fashion** of 3 groups. For this reason, teachers need to think carefully about and plan for these human memory needs within our lesson structure by using teaching and learning strategies that are **memory compatible**. When designing a lesson, we need to keep in mind that for maximum memory capacity and compatibility, we must organize the lesson objectives in groups of two or three for younger learners and groups of three or four for more mature learners.

Memory is also impacted by the time of the day the learning occurs. In a conventional school schedule (school starts at 8:00 a.m. and dismisses at 3:30 p.m. for example), students will be able to learn and remember more in the morning sessions than they will in afternoon sessions (Sousa 2006). Students may be able easily to accomplish three or four objectives each in morning classes, but only two or three each in their afternoon classes.

Memory is additionally impacted by the total length of time that a person can maintain focus or attention to the primary learning activity or stimulus. For the majority of preadolescents **five to seven minutes is about the maximum length,** and for secondary students **ten to twelve minutes is about the maximum length** of time they can maintain optimum focus. Beyond twenty minutes, 45% of the information begins to be lost and/or incorrectly understood, learned and remembered (Ebbinghaus 1885). In order to prevent this type of memory breakdown, an instructional strategy called **chaining** can be used effectively to purposefully and positively affect accurate learning and remembering. Let's look at an example of a lesson which has four objectives and examine how the idea of memory compatibility using **chaining** would translate into a learning session.

Chaining

Chaining may be defined as a process designed to positively and accurately affect learning and remembering by systematically linking the teaching to the lesson objectives with **frequent and multiple checking for understanding**. For example, in a lesson where a teacher needs to teach to and students need to master four learning objectives, a teacher using the strategy of chaining would follow a specific sequence of activities during the lesson. Here is an example of the use of chaining to teach four lesson objectives.

Table 3. Chaining Sequence

Phase One	Teach the 1st learning objective	Check for understanding of the 1st learning objective
Phase Two	Teach the 2nd learning objective	Check for understanding of the 2nd and 1st learning objectives
Phase Three	Teach the 3rd learning objective	Check for understanding of the 3rd, 2nd and 1st learning objectives
Phase Four	Teach the 4th learning objective	Check for understanding of the 4th, 3rd, 2nd and 1st learning objectives
Phase Five	Prime Time 2	Run a closure on all 4 objectives

This type of process provides for multiple repetitions of each of the learning objectives (Mayer 1983), but also takes advantages of the concept of **primacy and recency**. If people remember better and more of what they see and hear first and last, the **chaining** strategy plays right into the hand of that human characteristic of primacy and recency. Overall retention is enhanced which affects next day memory, improves test/quiz scores, and has even been documented to increase attendance for older students due to increased rates of success in classes which use the concept of **chaining**.

Checking for Understanding of Directions

One final piece of advice under this category of clear directions and information deals with the idea of **checking for understanding of directions**. It is imperative that we habituate the use of checking for understanding of directions for several important reasons. First, when we don't check for understanding of the directions we give, we create two types of students in our classrooms. Type one we will call **lifters**. They are the students who always hear, understand and retain the directions for a task or assignment. We call them **lifters** because they do the work; they do it well; and they complete it on time. The lifters always pull their own weight in a classroom.

The second type of students we create is called the **leaners**. The **leaners** are those students who depend on the **lifters** to hear and understand the directions. The lifters therefore become the **designated listeners** for the leaners in our classroom. The **leaners** lean on others to know what to do, how to do it and when it should be done. If we do not check for understanding of our directions, we will be sentenced to repeating directions with increasing levels of frequency. It is our observation that the average teacher repeats the directions multiple times before all the students begin the task or assignment. If your directions conservatively take one minute to complete, you could conceivably waste up to six additional minutes just repeating the directions over and over again for the leaners in your classroom. Even if you are able to avoid repeating the directions personally, the lifters (designated listeners) will have to spend their precious work time explaining the directions to the leaners who were not held accountable for their own listening because the teacher had not helped them become responsible. In other words, we, the teachers, have trained our students to be non-listeners by our undesirable habit of repeating directions often and louder. To counteract that practice, we recommend the strategy of **checking for understanding of directions**, as shown in Figure 5.

Figure 5. Check for Understanding of Directions

Step One: Say the directions once, or **have the students read** the directions if they are printed on the assignment or task.

Step Two: Check for understanding. Ask students to pair-share the directions.

Step Three: Put them on-the-clock. Give students the time allotted for the CFU of directions and then the teacher interviews/conferences during the student sharing.

Step Four: Bring them back on time. Call on students in the following sequence: 1) Interviewed pairs; 2) Randomly selected students; 3) Volunteers.

Step Five: Give students the amount of time they will have to complete the assignment or task last (see below for rationale).

Step Six: Do not let them begin the job until the directions are understood.

It is our recommendation that you always check for understanding of the directions for any task or assignment, including the directions that may be written on an assignment or a test or quiz. In reference to **Step Five: Give the Time Last**, we recommend that step for one very important reason: **kids are very time-oriented**. As such, if you give them the time first, they will more than likely fixate on the time and may forget the directions of the task. Therefore, we recommend that you do not give kids the time first because in doing so, it de-focuses them from the task and how the task is to be accomplished. When dealing with more mature learners, it makes no difference whether you give the time first or the task first. **Adults are very task-oriented** and hearing the time first generally will not de-focus them from the specifics of the task.

Note Taking

As in the case of checking for understanding (CFU), APL has developed and refined a variety of instructional skills and strategies that are taught in the workshop sessions. This book is designed to support the workshop experience and therefore refresh and review as needed.

As part of our ongoing research in refining the workshop content, we frequently encountered pieces that focused on note taking. It became increasingly apparent that this skill was one that contributed mightily to student success. The ability to take in essential items of information and translate to the written word is essential in support of student performing (Marzano 2001).

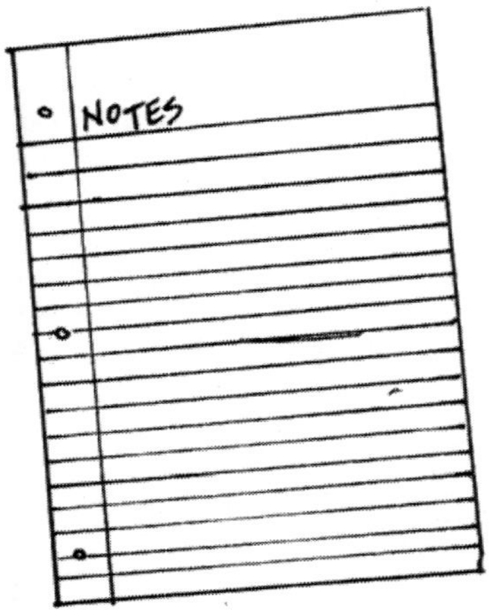

When discussing note taking and note taking strategies with teachers, it was clear that most stated that they learned to take notes through self-teaching. It is a skill that, over time, they refined. It was a trial and error process that for those who consistently pursued it paid off in the form of improved classroom performance.

It is with this in mind that we include this section on notes and note taking. We will suggest here that this skill is one that needs to be taught and practiced. It is a tool that elevates students and teachers alike when taught as a process. This note taking effort should begin early on in the school experience. We are now recommending that grade three is a productive starting point. Third graders are, for the most part, developmentally at a point where they can understand and manage information recording; this, of course, with organized teacher guidance and support. What follows is a description of and rationale for productive, focused and manageable note taking.

Supporting the note taking sequence and format that follows is the literature that suggests that **verbatim note taking** (students recording notes as the teacher is teaching) is the **least** effective. While attempting to record information, students are not synthesizing. Recording takes up too much of the working memory and therefore one cannot analyze incoming information (Marzano 2001). "Thinking is effortful; it takes concentration. You can't think about something else while you're working on a problem," is another way of looking at verbatim note taking (Willingham 2009). This suggests a radical departure from what has become accepted practice in student note taking. Our prior research on best practices provided APL a note taking strategy that would facilitate learner focus on the objectives for that lesson and result in an accurate and complete set of notes for all. We have emphasized that as part of daily instruction teachers should consistently check both directions and content. On the content side we suggested that the rule of 10-2 should apply (5-1 at the elementary level). Translated, it means that, for every 10 minutes of instruction, there should follow approximately 2 minutes of checking (review, closure) prior to pursuing another 10-minute instructional increment. It is during these 2 minutes of review that the teacher and students could collaboratively create the notes on the previous 10 minutes or 5 minutes of instruction. This would ensure that all students had complete, organized and accurate written information taught in that lesson. As a matter of classroom balance, guided notes should be offered for those students who require learner support (less able, identified, resource, learning support, etc.). Guided notes are skeletal versions of the notes all students will have, with blanks, which with some assistance, can be filled in with the key elements of the day's lessons. All students then have a complete set of accurate notes.

As part of the note taking sequence and format that follows, it is basic and essential that objectives for each lesson be posted. Daniel Willingham (2009) clearly states that when you plan a lesson, you start with the information you want the students to know by the end. This is the beginning of the effective process of quality note taking. Posting objectives should take a specific format and should be neat and legible, posted in a specific classroom location and in complete sentences. Students should then be taught that at the beginning of class, in addition to the bell ringer, they should copy the lesson objectives in their notes. Our practical recommendation for this process, of posting and recording, is to number the objectives by course or subject sequentially for the year. (You may find that you have hundreds of objectives for that year.) Additionally, we encourage that a second number be attached, and circled, at the end of each objective as follows:

Sample objective #1:

[29] You will be able to:

Write one interrogative and one declarative sentence.

(10)

In this instance the teacher has determined that 10 lines would be necessary to record the relevant information in each student's notes.

Sample objective #2:

[68] You will be able to:

Describe the difference between invection and convection.

(12)

In this instance the teacher has determined that 12 lines would be necessary to record the relevant information.

We have included here one elementary objective [29] and one secondary objective [68]. The number of objectives serves several very useful purposes as follows:

- □ **Referencing:** the teacher can direct students to locate objective #68 in their notes to review previously taught information.
- □ **Studying for tests:** the teacher can specifically identify, for students, the objectives and accompanying information that they need to review for an upcoming test.
- □ **Absences:** students can easily access accurate notes for when they were absent.
- □ **Skill development:** the teacher is communicating and modeling it consistently. In acquiring this skill students can apply it in future classes.

Equally important to the organization of notes is the format or structure within which the notes will be taken. Literature (Marzano 2001) suggests that there is no best note taking method or format. However, he goes on to suggest that there is one widely recommended method. This method is commonly known as the **Cornell Method.** The Cornell approach is a simple structure that is easily managed by the students and the teachers. What follows here is both a diagram and description of this note taking approach with some accompanying guidelines and recommendations.

Figure 6. Cornell Method

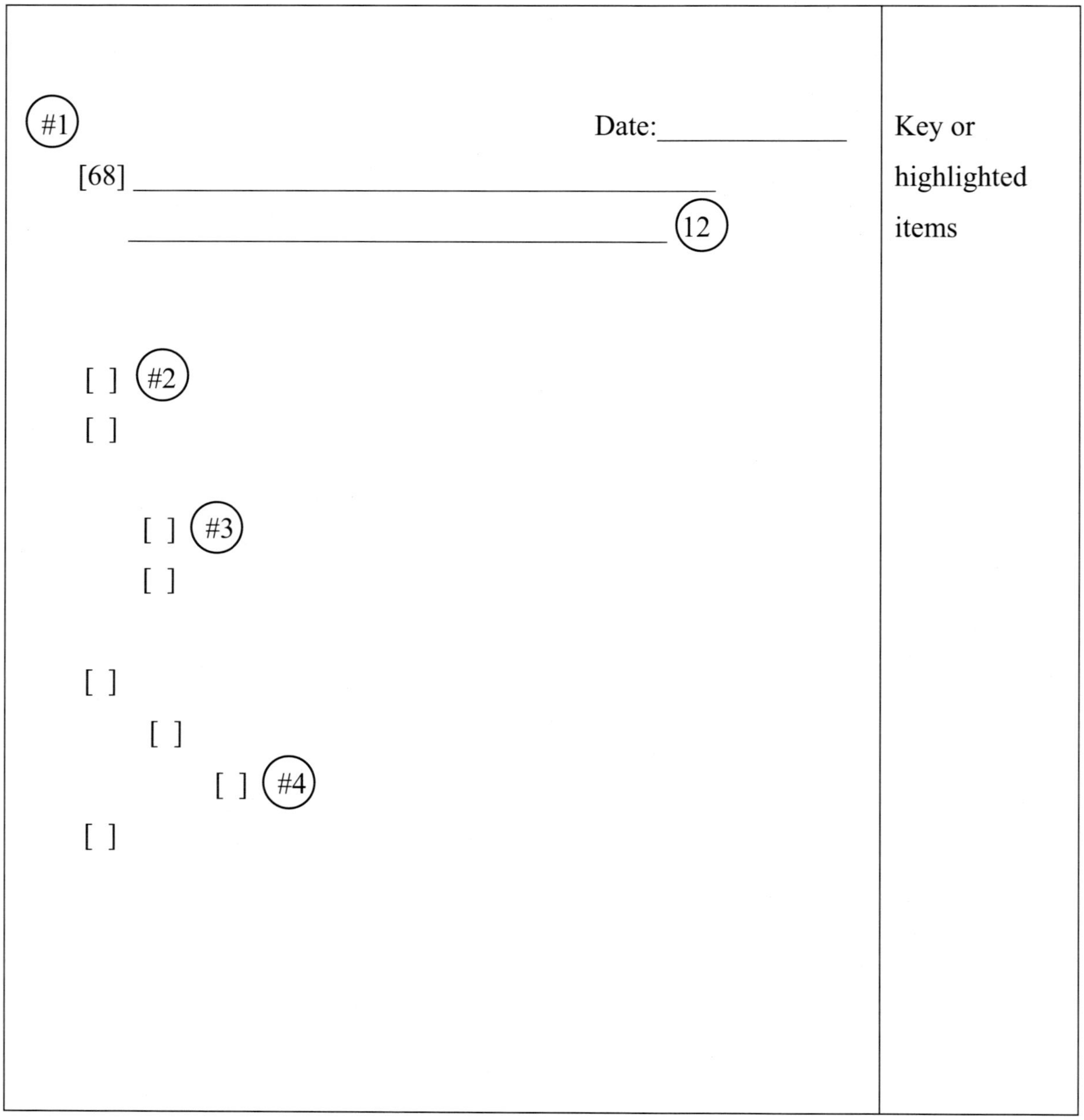

As you can see this note taking process is based on indentation only. The only portion of the notes numbered is the item at the far left margin. That is the objective for that lesson [68]. Students record this objective in their notes with the accompanying circled number (12) which indicates how many lines they should count off before recording the next objective. As the teacher proceeds to teach objective [68] the students are engaged and interacting with the teacher (listening, answering teacher questions, sharing with a partner, etc.); there is no note taking by the students at this point. The total focus is on the teacher and the content being delivered. After about 5-10 minutes of teaching, the teacher stops, and with interaction with the class, they collaboratively create the notes from that 5-10 minute teaching segment (rule of 10-2 / 5-1). This process continues through the successful completion of the identified objectives for that lesson. As indicated the teacher and the students collaboratively identify what should be included in the notes from that teaching segment. As in the diagram, main ideas or points would be indented and are represented by (#2) in the diagram. Subheadings of supportive information would be indented under these main ideas or points and are represented by (#3) in the diagram. If additional related and supportive information is required, then you just need to indent further as illustrated by (#4).

Early on in the school year the teacher takes the lead in this process with input from the students. As students become increasingly skilled in the process they can assume a greater role in what should be included for notes under the specified objective for that lesson. Given the above you have:

- □ A high degree of student engagement throughout the lesson.
- □ **All** students leave class with a complete set of accurate notes.
- □ Studying for tests becomes very focused and efficient.
- □ Organization and note taking skills are being developed, reinforced and refined daily throughout the year.

Again, as previously noted, there may be a handful of students who require a guided note taking experience.

As you look back to the diagram of the **Cornell Method** take note of the vertical column along the right margin. This area is for key or highlighted items that give the note taker a quick and uncluttered look at essentials from that page of notes.

Sample items that could be included here are:

- ☐ Key points
- ☐ Key terms
- ☐ Sample test items

Our goal here has been to elevate all students' information recording and note taking skills. In doing so, we elevate all students.

Managing Time to Facilitate Learning

We have suggested throughout, that time and time management is an equally important consideration when coordinating the instructional delivery process. Therefore, we include here **managing time to facilitate learning.**

Managing time for learning may be defined as strategies designed to facilitate the effective management of instructional time while assisting students in becoming better time managers. The intended instructional outcome is both ***focus*** and ***rate and degree of learning***. It is fair to say that disorganized people do not know how to manage time. To avoid being disorganized, students need to be taught to be aware of time both inside and outside of class. Fisher, Berliner et.al (1978) discovered that in the average achieving elementary classroom, daydreaming, socializing and misbehaving occupied about 8 minutes of each hour, but in high achieving classrooms that time was reduced to only 4 minutes per hour. In a study of junior high students, Evertson (1980) found that low-achieving students were engaged in academic activities only 40% of the time and that high-achieving students averaged about 85% engagement. Powell and Eash discovered a positive correlation between achievement and the reduction of the number of disruptions in a study of 184 high school classes. In the high achieving classes 25% of the available on task time was wasted by interruptions, while in low achieving classes this figure rose to 49%. These research findings strongly support the use of **high quality time management strategies** that support **quality time-on-task** by most fully engaging learners from the start of class (bell ringers), keep students focused on the tasks during class (agendas, instructional objectives, and above all, the interaction sequence), make optimum use of time management throughout the entire lesson (on-the-clock), guard against boredom and loss of focus (10-2 rule for checking for understanding), and keep students engaged until class is over (closure and getting homework started). The following **time management strategies and guidelines** were created to assist you in the task of managing time in your classroom.

Successful time management requires a teacher to purposefully account for not only how time is used, but also, who is responsible for the allocation and monitoring of time during a learning session. Time is significant because it is a fixed commodity. It has been given much attention in the educational community and much emphasis has been placed on the Time-on-Task phenomenon and its impact on learning. Therefore, it is important that in the interest of successfully managing time we examine some guidelines to assist in managing teaching and learning time effectively.

Time Management Strategies and Guidelines

It's troublesome to attempt to conduct a conversation about time management without initiating that conversation with a serious look at instructional organization. Instructional organization is a key first step for the teacher and students toward classroom success. As we look at the act of teaching, first and foremost, **begin and end your classes on time**. If we want our students to respect time, we must model respect for time. Time lost can never be reclaimed. When we fail to start on time we insult those who arrive on time ready to work. Do not let the stragglers control when you start class. Start class on time. Some examples of things which get in the way of successful time management are intercom interruptions, assemblies, field trips, equipment failure, fire drill, lunch count, attendance taking, school pictures, mowing the lawn outside your classroom, surveys conducted during class, substitute teachers, etc. We presuppose that we have 180 days times 6 hours per day, BUT actually, we have only about 45 to 50% of that time available for instruction (Powel & Eash 1974). It is our estimate that for every minute after three minutes you fail to get class started, it takes twice that amount of time to focus the class. Here is an example: if it takes you four minutes after the bell to begin class, it will take 8 minutes from then to focus the class (the original 4 minutes + [4 minutes x 2] = 12 minutes total). Over a week's time, we could easily waste the equivalent of an entire class period by failing to start class on time. When we fail to **end class on time**, we insult the students (who have other things to do and places to go) and we insult the teacher(s) of the next class(es) those students will be attending. Letting students out late jeopardizes their ability to arrive at the next class on time and prepared to work. If we hold that expectation for our classes, we should respect our students and colleagues and make sure we are not the cause of students arriving late and unprepared.

Second, since interruptions are inevitable, **after an interruption, run a check for understanding** to refocus the learners and yourself.

Third, consider **using a timing device** such as a timer, stopwatch, computer, sand timer, clock or watch. The use of any type of timing device will make us more aware of time and help us monitor the use of time. This helps us communicate to students that time is valuable, it is finite and should not be wasted. This also provides interest for students (if you keep time accurately). Have available as many time measurement devices of various kinds as possible (egg timer, game timer, stopwatch, cooking timers, etc.). Match the device to the activity. In doing so you communicate that time is important here, and it helps to break the routine.

Fourth, if the **clock in your classroom does not work**, get it fixed, unplug it, or cover it up. The clocks in school must be synchronized or they are of no support to instruction and the daily schedule.

The following paragraphs are written in response to questions we are most commonly asked about time management issues and problems.

Question: What if you put the students on the clock, you're walking around monitoring students working, and you see the students aren't going to finish the task in the given time because you underestimated the amount of time needed. What do you do?

Answer: Immediately get the attention of the students and tell them you have underestimated the amount of time needed for the task, and that you are adding/extending the time (then give an exact number of minutes).

Question: Why not just let them keep working until they complete the task?

Answer: It is important that you don't turn the time management over to the students, but that you keep the students on-the-clock. If you turn the time management over to the students, the work quality will go down. You must intervene in order to keep the students from hurrying to just get the work done without regard to quality. In the event that you don't intervene, many avoidable errors will occur, and the resulting work will be sloppy.

Question: What should students do who finish early?

Answer: Create and teach a menu of choices of things students who finish early can choose to do with your approval. Make sure you check their work to see if the finished product is acceptable before letting them choose another activity. We recommend:

1. *Listing the menu items, and you choosing one, two or three for them to pick from for that day.*
2. *Some example menu items are:*
    - ☐ *To review materials (you may wish to provide the list for review)*
    - ☐ *To engage in silent reading*
    - ☐ *To get a start on homework from a previous class*
    - ☐ *To work on an ongoing project*
    - ☐ *To start tomorrow's reading*
    - ☐ *To engage in an art or other enrichment activity, such as learning centers.*

Remember: This is a behavior management strategy to keep students on task, so you will need to teach students this strategy of choosing from the menu items and the parts of each job on the menu.

Question: What should I do with students who hurry and do a poor and sloppy job?

Answer: Give students who rush only part of the assignment at a time. One recommended strategy is to ask that student to:

- ☐ *Do the first two problems only; and*
- ☐ *Raise his/her hand when finished with those two; and*

- ☐ *I will then come around and check the work before he/she may continue on with additional problems.*

This strategy helps you gain quality output from a student who commonly hurries and typically does not engage in quality work output.

Question: What should I do if all my students finish early?

Answer: If all students finish ahead of time, DO NOT give them more of the same work. If you give them more of the same, it seems like punishment and the next time they may well slow way down to avoid receiving more work. If all your students finish early, review the assignment or activity with the time remaining, transition to a new topic, or give all students a choice from the Menu Items.

Again, it is a matter of respect for the students in our classes that we make the best use of time by starting on time, ending on time and using strategies like **on-the-clock** for time management.

Using On-the-Clock for Time Management

On-the-clock is a strategy designed to help teachers manage time and managed tasks. This strategy consists of **three basic components**. First, describe the task, job or assignment that students are to accomplish. Second, give students a specific and reasonable amount of time in which to complete the task. Use the formula on page 144 to determine how much time to give the capable student to complete the work. Third, hold students accountable to the time allotted. When the time is up, the work on that task is finished.

The results of using **on-the-clock** are significant in meeting the needs of both time and task management in the following ways. First, **on-the-clock** meets the criteria of **consistency** (one of the three power words for teaching addressed in the Introduction) with respect to time management and helps students to make more accurate predictions about the instruction, the tasks and the teacher. Second, **on-the-clock** meets another of the three power words for teaching, **specificity**. When we are more specific about the *what, how, why and when*, it means more success for both students and teachers.

Here are some of the benefits of using **on-the-clock**:

- ☐ Trains students to listen, to focus and pay attention to directions and information given by the teacher;
- ☐ Trains students to be on-task and on the teacher's agenda for the learning session, not their own;
- ☐ Both the students and the teacher get more done during a class session because less time is lost and/or wasted;
- ☐ Students gain confidence in their ability to complete tasks competently in reasonable length of time;
- ☐ Teachers are more respected by students, colleagues, and supervisors because of their competent time and task management skills.

How, you may ask, are teachers to monitor time usage and student on-task behaviors? There are two critical features of this process. The first is to use a timing device that frees the teacher up to assist students who need help. There is no need to "watch the clock" if one uses a timing device. The second critical feature is to use physical proximity to monitor student on-task behaviors. We call this teacher behavior **management by walking around** or **MBWA** for short. We use the following phrase, "On your feet – not on your seat" to help us remember that proximity 1) increases the student's level of concern; 2) puts you in a position to readily know what is going on; 3) allows you to quickly assist students who need help; and 4) allows you to ascertain if the students will complete the task in the time you have allotted. This brings us to the point of addressing the question, "what should I do if the task is not completed in the allotted time?" If you see that students will not complete the task in the allotted time, but are close to completion, you may extend the time for everyone in order to complete the task. If it is obvious that you seriously underestimated the actual time needed and that you will definitely run out of time, you may stop the activity in the time allotted and either continue it at a later time or let what has been completed suffice. Remember, if you want to truly reap the benefits of using **on-the-clock** as listed above, you must always be **consistent** and **specific** in your use of **on-the-clock**.

Monitoring Map: Using the Hit-Run/Push-Pull Strategy

The interaction sequence is an ongoing process that students come to know and understand. Along with the interaction sequence is the ongoing monitoring that the teacher uses for purposes of assessing, supporting, encouraging and feeding back. Again, this too needs to be planned and implemented in a sequential format. Where the **interaction sequence facilitates** discussion, thinking, processing communication skills, critical thinking, problem solving and overall involvement, the **monitoring process facilitates** effort, independent work, group work, completion of tasks, and successful pursuit of activities. As was the case with the interaction sequence, a plan or format of monitoring should be developed and pursued in a consistent manner. To accomplish a more consistent approach to monitoring, the **monitoring map** approach should be implemented. Monitoring can often become random or hit-or-miss as the teacher moves around the room. It is **clear** that random monitoring is not effective and can be very inefficient. Therefore, it is recommended that monitoring should follow a plan that has several key components as follows:

- ☐ In the monitoring map approach the teacher should **first** go to those <u>students who have consistently shown that they do not complete in-class tasks but are capable of doing so</u>. These are the <u>procrastinators</u>. When approaching these students (**hit**) the teacher should clearly specify what should be accomplished within a specific time frame (**push**). For example, "I'm going to be back in three minutes. See if you can have this completed by the time I return." The teacher then moves on to help other students (**run**). This procedure is repeated in timed increments through the completion of the activity and is repeated for all activities where the class is working on independent tasks (seat work). Initially, the teacher is applying the **hit-run/push** approach as described above. If three to five attempts to encourage the student to begin do not work, or if the student is consistently completing the portion you've requested, then the teacher should shift to the **hit-run/pull** approach. In the **hit-run/pull** approach the teacher gives the student the decision-making power over what can be done in that amount of time (**pull**). It sounds like this: "I'm going to be back in three minutes. What is it that you can have completed by the time I return?" In this latter instance the teacher is working toward a commitment on the part of the student (**pull**). If the student responds to the question, "What do you think you can have completed?" with, "I don't know," or a "shrug," the teacher should immediately shift back to the **hit-run-push** strategy. The full procedure is referred to as **hit-run/push-pull**. Once the student is completing the work, the teacher should continue to purposefully but not intrusively monitor progress.

- ☐ As the teacher moves along in the monitoring process (applying the monitoring map concept) the student or set of students that the teacher will engage **next** are those that we will loosely describe as less able. These students, although in a regular classroom setting, are usually assigned a Resource/Special Education teacher as part of their support and instructional system. When approaching these students, the teacher will spend a bit more time than with the first group. It's with these students that the teacher adjusts the task to match the needs and abilities of the students. It is recommended, therefore, that the approach taken by the teacher be one of task adjustment, not time adjustment. In other words, **reduce the task; do not add on more time**. Over time the teacher will increase the task expectation in increments with the goal in mind of getting these students to produce more and better work applying the concept of **successive approximations**. Time adjustments (extensions) for the "less able" are very appropriate under specific conditions (e.g. testing, skill building, etc.). However, on a day-to-day basis and in regular settings, it is a process that is difficult to manage from the teacher side, and over time can result in the outcome of "learned helplessness" whereby the student won't do the work unless the adult constantly stands over him/her.
- ☐ The third tier of students that the teacher will go to as part of this monitoring map approach, will be those members of the class who can be relied upon to consistently get at the tasks and work them successfully to completion. These are the capable students. However, they must be consciously built into the route that the teacher takes as part of the monitoring map planning process. If not, the monitoring again becomes random and therefore not focused, productive, and efficient for all, and the most capable students are left out, which reduces teacher-

student interactions along with relationship building and maintenance. Additionally, some capable students have been known to begin doing less or begin doing poorly in order to gain more attention from the teacher. This is an avoidable outcome if we keep the capable students in the "monitoring loop."

The **monitoring map** looks like this:

- ☐ Give everyone a job to do (seatwork, worksheet, start homework, lab, etc).
- ☐ Check for understanding of the job you have assigned.
- ☐ Give a specific amount of time to complete the job (you will have 10 minutes to complete this job).
- ☐ Check for understanding of the time allotment you've given.
- ☐ Then begin using the **monitoring map** by first going to your procrastinator(s) (**hit**): [group one] and use this sequence **hit-run/push**:
  1. Example: Please put your name and the date on your paper (**push**). I'll be back in two minutes to check your progress. Then walk away (**run**) to help another student [in group one]. Go to the less able students next, and the capable students last in the monitoring process.
  2. Go back in two minutes to check on the progress of the first student. Do this in turn for each student from group one. You must become a "broken record" by saying the same thing again and again if the student has not completed the task.
  3. If the student has not completed the task, repeat the first directions again, repeat the time frame again, tell him/her you'll be back in the time frame indicated, and move on to help the next student (**hit-run/push**). You may extend the time for completion of the task as necessary. ("I'll be back again in two minutes.")
  4. If the students have completed the task, direct them to move on to the next part. In other words, after the students have completed step one, direct them to move on and complete step two, giving them the time allotted for step two (continue using **hit-run/push**).
  5. This process works best if you break the task down into its tiniest parts. This is called **successive approximations.** Break the task down into its micro

parts and reveal only those parts the student needs immediately in order to begin or continue working.

6. Once students are consistently responding to the **push** approach, move on to using the **pull** approach by giving students the decision-making power over how much they can get accomplished before your next return.
7. If you're dealing with a student who may be less capable, **do not change the time but rather change the amount of the task**. Modify the task, not the time. The reason for this suggestion is to stay consistent with time allotments for the sake of the entire group and for yourself. If you alter the time schedule for some of the students and not the others you create a time monitoring nightmare. The same rationale holds true if you personalize different submission deadlines for each student. You also create a bookkeeping nightmare.
8. Remember the formula you may use to determine how much time to give the capable student to complete work? For grades K-6 it will commonly take the student 4 to 5 times the number of minutes it takes you to complete the task. For grades 6-12 it will commonly take student 3 to 4 times the number of minutes it takes you to complete the task. When grade 6 is in an elementary setting, use the 4 to 5 times formula. When grade 6 is in a middle level departmentalized setting, use the 3 to 4 times rule. This presupposes that you **do the work first to ascertain these time allotments**. If you aren't willing to do the work yourself, should you really be assigning it to your students?
9. Repetition is the key. Do not give up. Be specific. Be consistent. Be polite. The objective is that the student(s) must understand that you will keep coming back until you are satisfied that the first part (and each subsequent part) of the task is successfully completed as directed.

When we use the **monitoring map** we are helping students gain a very important life skill: helping them learn how to **break the cycle of procrastination** that many of them face when it comes to initiating work by showing them how to break larger tasks into smaller more manageable segments. Using this strategy consistently and correctly will make a difference in your classroom by teaching students how to begin the work and how to get the work completed.

Now let's take a look at a strategy called **knowledge of results**. This strategy is designed to help teachers give students helpful feedback that identifies what students know and the degree to which they know it.

Knowledge of Results

Knowledge of results is defined as the immediate and specific feedback to the learner. The intended instructional outcome is ***focus***. All humans, learners most of all, need feedback as to the progress and disposition of their work. As part of the day-to-day teaching and learning process teachers must automatically and systematically build in feedback as part of those processes. In instructional delivery we refer to that feedback process as providing **knowledge of results.** Without feedback, it may be impossible to know if we are moving toward successful completion of a task, or if we are actually moving away from the goal. There are two types of feedback (knowledge of results) teachers provide to learners. Those types are verbal (oral or written), and non-verbal feedback. Before we examine each of the two types of **knowledge of results**, we want to explain that, when using any of the types of feedback, there are **two important criteria** that must be considered if the feedback strategy is to more effectively benefit students. The **first important criterion** is that the feedback must be **immediate** or as immediate as possible for the following reasons. First, the feedback must be immediate so the students will be able to minimize confusion and make the appropriate link or connection to the accuracy of their task or response. Second, to reinforce the student's effort and degree of correctness so the students will know that if it's being done wrong, it must be corrected now. The degree of correctness is important in increasing the desired degree of accuracy for retention, and in promoting continued effort on the part of the learner. Third, we use feedback in order to provide the students with confidence in their responses or actions. Fourth, we use feedback in order to reinforce the student for the correct behavior. And the final reason is so that the student won't forget. Feedback communicates to the student that we are modeling what we expect, which is the power of being timely, specific and organized.

The **second important criterion** is that the feedback must be **specific** to have any value. We want to specifically reinforce that which the student has done well so as to increase the likelihood that it will be repeated in the future. Also, we want to specifically highlight items which need to be corrected or improved so as to prevent repetitive mistakes. Consequently, specific feedback allows us to avoid confusing the student if we were to leave the feedback open to interpretation by virtue of its vagueness. For example, if we use ambivalent statements such as, "good job," or, "your work is too vague," students are confused by the lack of specifically knowing what is good and why, and what is vague and why. A student's answer may not be all wrong, and students need to know which parts may be correct or incorrect if they are to adjust their answers to increase their degree of correctness. Finally, the student may not be able to believe you if you are not specific as to the degree of correctness.

Now, let's take a look at the **two types of knowledge of results**. Type one, **verbal/oral feedback** allows us to highlight the part of a student answer that is particularly noteworthy using phrases such as, "Great answer. The part of your answer that I think is great is . . ." or to identify incorrectness, "No, that is not correct. You were incorrect in saying …" Note the care with which these examples go beyond the usual "good answer" or "sorry, that's not correct." In order for feedback to be effective, it must meet the criteria of being **specific** as discussed above. Despite our best efforts during the teaching and learning process, incorrect student responses will still occur. When confronted with wrong answers from students, it is recommended that you indicate to the student that the answer is incorrect and that you will help him/her to come up with the correct information. It is further recommended that when dealing with incorrectness in the verbal form, that you not shift the responsibility to another student in your pursuit of coming up with the desired response. What commonly happens in classrooms following the receipt of an incorrect answer in order to minimize "the damage" is that teachers tend to immediately move to one of the most capable students whose response is usually correct. Doing this can result in student #1 feeling demeaned in comparison to student #2 who has given the correct answer, thus setting up a *student-to-student; have-to-have not* comparison. Teachers should avoid using this pattern because it could well prevent students who have been incorrect from being willing to answer in the future. We believe that it is the teacher's responsibility to "fix" wrong answers. Let us demonstrate what we recommend that you do when dealing with incorrectness by the following example. Let's say we've just asked students to answer the following question: "What is the sum of 12 plus 15?" After using the appropriate amount of wait-time, you call on student #1 who answers: "29." Instead of saying only, "You're wrong" you should respond to the student as follows, "No, 29 is the sum of 14 plus 15. The sum of 12 plus 15 is 27. Now, what is the sum of 12 plus 15? Yes, 27 is the correct answer. Class, what is the sum of 12 plus 15? [Choral response: "27."] Yes, the answer is 27." Using this method preserves student dignity and accomplishes your need to ensure that students have the correct information. Additionally we recommend the use of an instructional strategy called the **interaction sequence**.

Also included in type one is **verbal/written feedback**. It is often easier to be more specific in terms of identified errors and items that are correct when the feedback comes in written form. As with verbal/oral feedback, the <u>criteria of immediate and specific</u> again come into play. With written work or projects the prompt returning of the work in as timely a fashion as possible is critically important.

Here are some **guidelines to consider with respect to written feedback**:

- ☐ For the day-to-day work, it is recommended that you return items within three to five working days.
- ☐ For more detailed work (long-term projects, research papers, book reports, major tests, etc.) it is recommended that a calendar date be identified and shared with the students as to when they can reasonably expect their work to be handed back. This strategy assists the students and the teacher in maintaining focus in the work and feedback processes. It further communicates that the teacher is serious and organized.
- ☐ In recording written feedback on the various pieces of student work, the criteria of specific is again, significant. In doing so, it is recommended that the teacher address two feedback categories entitled **glow comments** and **grow comments**. **Glow comments** are written comments which are designed to specifically highlight items on the student work for which the student needs to be complimented. At least one item should be identified on each piece of student

work. All humans need to feel that at least something in their work deserves merit and thus positive feedback in a complimentary manner.

Grow comments is a category of feedback that addresses items that the teacher determines need correcting, improving, or remediating. It is tempting to just randomly check items as incorrect or to casually communicate that something is deficient by using single words or briefly worded phrases (i.e. poor, too vague, not well thought out, missed the point, etc.). Again, specificity is critical here. If the students are to know and understand where and how they need to improve, the feedback must be specific in terms of **grow comments**. We also advise that you control the number of **grow** items to one or two that you wish a student to focus on improving. The **grow** process has to appear to be doable on the part of the student. It is easy for the student to feel overwhelmed and therefore futile and hopeless. Teachers should want to focus on developing more complete, competent, successful and confident students, particularly those students who have a history of poor or mediocre performance. Teachers need to have patience and pursue the growth of student quality performance in increments, not quantum leaps!

Type two feedback is **non-verbal feedback**. Non-verbal feedback includes two specific forms: **signals** (a very powerful communication tool) and **body language**. In order for non-verbals to be effective they must agree with your verbal responses; in other words, they must communicate the same message, but on a non-verbal level.

Teachers who use signal systems have a wide variety of non-verbal signals that are built into the teacher-to-student communication process. Signals tend to be less defocusing and disruptive to the teaching and learning process. Signals support a good organizational model and contribute positively to an efficiently run classroom. Some teachers are enjoying a good deal of success along this line by incorporating signals into the classroom that are borrowed from American Sign Language.

With respect to body language, we refer to the teacher's use of the whole body in the communication process. Eye contact, proximity, stance, movement, facial expression, tone of voice, and other non-verbal expressions such as sighing, laughing, shaking or nodding the head, winking, and looking surprised, angry, pleased, frustrated, or unhappy may be considered as components of this category and should all be measured thoughtfully. Students are sensitive to non-verbal communication. They watch for and assess the adults (and other students) total communication through the careful process of observation. We must ask ourselves this question: "Are we communicating the intended messages of caring, interest, support, dissatisfaction, concern or worry appropriately?" Observe other adult faculty and their non-verbals at a distance. What is your sense of what the person is communicating? How do you think students would feel or react to what you are seeing?

Some interesting facts about non-verbal communication include that adolescents are very perceptive to non-verbals, and that up to 60% of what a person interprets as the true meaning of what has been said comes from the non-verbals that accompany it.

We want to offer these **cautions on knowledge of results**. First, when using **verbal** feedback, teachers must never use **sarcasm**. Sarcasm is not a viable form of verbal feedback because it hurts people. Second, **ridicule** is a companion to sarcasm and neither has a place in the classroom because <u>they are verbal weapons and they victimize students</u>. Finally, as a reminder when using written feedback, observe the following **recommendations**:

1. Give papers back as soon as possible but always within five working days.
2. When dealing with long-term assignments such as projects, tell students specifically which day they will get the assignment back.
3. Clarify the symbol systems you use (e.g. +/- or check marks, etc.) for feedback purposes so that students do not misinterpret your remarks.
4. Anytime you write comments on paper make sure you provide the following:
    a. One to **glow**: stating specifically what the student did well, and
    b. One to **grow**: stating specifically what needs improvement.
5. Remember, it is recommended not to have students exchange papers for correcting. Too many bad things can happen when students exchange papers to grade, such as a student feeling pressured to cheat or even refusing to complete an assignment, quiz or test if the student believes that the results of her/his work will be made public. <u>Since grades on projects are the private property of the student, communicating one student's grade to or discussing one student's work with</u>

another student is unethical and raises the issue of the breeching of confidentiality.

As an aside we want to explain that using the strategy of peer-editing is not the same because that is completed before any grading is done. However, when choosing to use peer-editing, the teacher should remove students' names from their work so that honest feedback is provided, and students' fears of having their work identified and exposed is removed. If you choose to incorporate peer-editing into your students' class work, be sure you teach the behavior "peer edit" which includes what you want the editors to look for as they edit another student's work and what types of comments are acceptable when providing peer feedback.

6. Many teachers hand back tests and go over them for instructional purposes (to help students to learn). If you choose to use this strategy, consider not placing a grade on the paper because that may stifle any positive outcomes that could have resulted from the use of the test as a learning activity. In other words, the student sees the grade and views the test as over, not as an additional opportunity to correct inaccuracies and add to his/her knowledge.

Modeling

Modeling is the demonstration of a process or the examination of a product. The intended instructional outcome is ***retention***. Most educators believe deeply in the power of modeling as an important teaching strategy. The great Greek teacher Aristotle said, "We simply need to put the students in the presence of adults who know the difference between right and wrong, who will articulate it to them, who will remind them of the human experience with that difference and who will live that difference in their own lives." In other words, we should, "walk the talk."

There are **two criteria for modeling.** First, you must model the behavior with 100% accuracy. If we want students to remember something accurately, we must show it to them accurately in order to help students to remember it correctly. Second, you should Say it as you Show it. This in turn helps the students to be more successful in remembering the process through the use of both visual and auditory learning modalities. We believe that it is the teacher's responsibility to model the behavior for his/her students. This reminds us to offer **one caution about modeling**. It is important that you do not use students to model a behavior unless you have rehearsed them thoroughly, and they can do the modeling with 100% accuracy.

There are also **two types of modeling**. The first is called the **product approach** or the whole-part-whole approach. In this type we let students see it all, then we take it apart and finally we reconstruct it for them. We move from the **general** (the whole) to the **specific** (the parts) and back to the **general**.

The second type of modeling is called the **process approach** or the part-whole-part approach. In this type we let students see the parts, we put it together for them, and finally we take it apart again. We move from the **specific** (the parts) to the **general** (the whole) back to the **specific**. The following table offers a listing of benefits of using the modeling process with students.

Table 4. Benefits of Modeling Processes

Process	Benefits
1. Organizing schedules and deadlines	1. Get things done on time, have materials needed, feel successful, allows students to participate fully.
2. Managing homework time and strategies	2. Completed homework successfully
3. Steps of writing a term paper	3. Term paper completed
4. Adjusting a microscope	4. Clearly seeing the specimen
5. Conflict management	5. Orderly, safe environment
6. Lining up in the hallway	6. Orderly, safe environment

We close this portion on modeling by quoting another famous Greek philosopher, Plato, who stated that, "Modeling is **not** the best way to teach – it is the **only** way to teach." Another powerful strategy in teaching is the creating of interest in the content and activities in our classroom. Let's take a closer look at this idea.

Interest

Interest refers to the activities that the teacher creates that are novel or vivid and provide greater interest within the teaching and learning context. Interest is another instructional strategy that enhances the outcome of ***focus***. Interest may be achieved in a number of ways such as using guest speakers, taking a field trip to a museum or job site, bringing in "real world" materials for students to examine and study, or simply showing a video. There are some simple rules that teachers should follow when working to achieve higher levels of interest.

Movies and Videos

If you spend more time showing videos than actually teaching, that is a misuse of videos. A ***few simple cautions*** can help guide the use of videos in class. First, the movie or video must be relevant to an objective within the curriculum. Second, **you must view it in its entirety** before showing it to students. If you can't view it, don't show it. Third, teach the behavior for viewing a movie. Consider what behaviors are important for students to exhibit if we are to get the most out of watching this video. While remaining quiet, staying awake, taking notes may seem like the common sense thing to do, do not assume that your students have the same expectations that you have with respect to video viewing behavior. Remember, any specific behavior you want, you must teach. We recommend giving students a specific job to do while viewing the video such as taking notes by using a note-taking framework with specific questions that follow the sequence of that video. Another effective video viewing strategy is to remember the following ideas that result from memory research. Students at the elementary level can handle 5 to 7 minutes of a video before they shut down. Students at the secondary level can handle up 10 to 12 minutes of a video. In order to avoid losing student focus during a video, you should stop after that duration (5 to 7 minutes for elementary and 10 to 12 minutes for secondary) and have the students do something using what they have seen/learned. Asking students to share the information that they have written in their video note-taking framework for specific questions is one proven strategy to keep students engaged for the full duration of the video. If you are working with adults, it is helpful to know that most adults can handle 20 minutes maximum of video viewing before losing focus. It's not the same as watching a movie for entertainment. Additionally, it is important that you do a **closure** activity at the end of the video to assist students in focusing on important information presented in the video. Using these strategies is not only indicative of good teaching, but they ensure ***focus and retention***.

Field Trips

Field trips are an excellent way to extend learning, and to move the learning into "real world" contexts. Field trips are generally motivating for students and can definitely contribute to learning interest and focus. If you are planning to use field trips to achieve any of the above mentioned goals, keep several important ideas in mind. First, the activities and content examined during the field trip must be relevant to an objective in the curriculum. Field trips can certainly be entertaining, but if entertainment is the only outcome, the teacher must rethink the undertaking of the field trip with respect to the use of financial, time and other resources that are both limited and precious. Second, you must teach the behavior needed for the field trip to be successful. This will have a major impact on the success of the event. Make a list of behaviors students should know and be able to do while on the field trip. Keep in mind that the students, chaperones, bus drivers, and you are representing your school, school district and community. Teach, model and practice the specific behaviors needed to ensure success. Specify verbally and in writing to students and parents your expectations and requirements for making this trip successful. One poorly-arranged, disorganized and badly-implemented field trip could result in the elimination of field trips for you and possibly your entire school. It could even end your teaching career. So here are some additional suggestions. If at all possible, take the trip yourself before you take students there. That will give you a better idea of what to expect and will help you avoid the "unknowns" that can sabotage even the best-organized trip. When the students are at the field site, give them a data collection activity so that they are engaged in a meaningful examination and interaction while on-site. When you get back, run a closure activity on the field trip by asking students to explain why, where, how, and what was accomplished during our outing. Also, secure adequate numbers of adult chaperones to assist in monitoring and aiding you and students when necessary during the trip. Our recommendation is that you have one adult chaperone for every five students. Your chaperones need to attend chaperone training before the trip. Elements included in this training should include the duties and the responsibilities of chaperoning students. It should be made clear to chaperones that no smoking or drinking is allowed on school trips. That includes the chaperones. Chaperones will need to be informed about how to dress appropriately for the event, what is appropriate language and behavior, and what to do in the event of an emergency. The advent of cellular phones now makes field trips a bit easier to supervise on site. However, keep in mind that certain places such as museums, concert halls, and hospitals do not allow for the use of cellular phones while on their premises.

It will also be necessary for you to obtain permission forms signed by parents or guardians for each of the students taking the trip. On that permission form should be a medical release form allowing you to get medical assistance for a student who may become ill or injured during the trip. This is of particular importance if you are taking an extended trip (overnight or beyond) or if you are taking students out of the immediate vicinity. Chaperones need to be "on duty" around the clock for overnight trips; that means staying in the hotel hallways throughout the night.

One final thought about trips involves dealing with bus drivers. It is important that all participants on the trip treat the bus driver(s) with courtesy and respect. You will have to remind students and chaperones of the need to regard the feelings and obey the directions of the drivers. Remember, your safety is foremost in the mind of the drivers, but they also have other responsibilities such as the care and maintenance of the bus equipment. They may have specific rules for you and your students and chaperones to follow. If that is the case, obtain a copy of those rules beforehand, provide copies of the rules for all those participating on the trip and speak directly to your students and chaperones about those expectations. There are two other courtesies that you should consider extending to the drivers. First, before you leave on the trip, ask them if they would like to attend the field trip activity with you. If so, make sure you have purchased or have the means to purchase admission for the drivers. Second, after you return home **send thank you notes** from the class and the teacher to the chaperones, the bus drivers, and the people at the field trip site.

Guest Speakers

Guest speakers can bring a vividness or reality to the classroom that you cannot bring. A guest offers several benefits for you and your students. The guest speaker should have expertise in areas where you do not. In that event, the guest can speak with greater authority, yet all the while be reinforcing the information you have already provided your students. The guest speaker can share personal and professional insights that will be of benefit to the students and to you. A guest speaker can inspire and motivate students to embark on more elaborate examinations of that topic or profession. With those benefits in mind, you must additionally take the following items into account. First, make sure the guest speaker's information is relevant to an objective in the curriculum. Second, teach the behavior your students need to properly interact with a guest speaker. Third, sit down with the guest before the appearance to discuss the following important areas:

- ☐ What is the speaker's understanding of why she/he has been invited?
- ☐ What does he/she specifically plan to say?
- ☐ What materials, if any, does she/he plan to use?
- ☐ Finally, work out any discrepancies in content, delivery method, philosophy, connection to your objectives beforehand.

Teachers should never leave students alone with a guest. Teachers need to be present at all times with their students: it's the law. Never be discourteous to the guest. You and your students are making connections to the public. It is important that even if we disagree with something the guest says or does, we must remain courteous. Keep in mind that every community has undesirable people with an agenda other than ours, or the schools. That is precisely why we must confer with our guests in person beforehand to ascertain any questionable ideas or topics that could be infused in the guest's comments or materials. Remember, just like you the teacher, the guest has a captive audience. We cannot let the guest prey on the students' young minds. If a guest says or does inappropriate things, stop the activity immediately and remove the guest from the setting.

Group Work

Rarely can a discussion take place regarding instruction, instructional strategies or instructional delivery without cooperative learning surfacing as part of that conversation. Over recent years cooperative or collaborative learning has been widely promoted as facilitating effective classroom instruction, organization and management. All of which, it is felt, lead to improved student performance and therefore student success.

When reviewing the four desirable or highly sought after 21st century skills, the ability to collaborate (work effectively and productively with others) stands out prominently as one of the four as follows:

- Professionalism and work ethic
- The ability to collaborate
- Problem solving and critical thinking
- Communication skills, both written and verbal

As you consider these four skills it becomes apparent that there is a very close relationship between these skills as they interface one with another. As students improve their collaborative skills they simultaneously work more effectively and productively. They also are able to work things through to resolve problems or think through critical issues as communication skills are improved or polished.

Students are particularly motivated by learning opportunities that may also include opportunities to be sociable with their classmates. Hyatt and Gottlieb (1987) studied the phenomenon of why people fail. They uncovered nine reasons for human failure. At the top of their list was *poor interpersonal skills*.

Louisell and Descamps (2001) in *Developing a Teaching Style* have determined several important benefits for students and teachers resulting from group work. First, it helps educators meet the needs for students' **active participation in learning**. Second, it gives students an opportunity to **solve problems** while **learning how to work cooperatively with each other in a team** with adequate **positive interdependence**. Third, group work provides an opportunity to foster **individual accountability** to the group and to oneself.

SECTION THREE

Fourth, it provides an opportunity for the **acquisition of interpersonal skills** through coaching and practice. Fifth, cooperative interaction and support lead to **higher achievement** and more **effective problem solving**. Last, cooperation affects positively many different personal, instructional, and interpersonal outcomes simultaneously (Louisell & Descamps 2001).

Additional outcomes (via Johnson and Johnson, Kagan and Slavin) are:

- ☐ Positive face-to-face interaction
- ☐ Group processing skills (the ability to reflect on how group members interact as they work together)

APL Associates has added:

- ☐ The successful completion of the class or project objectives (APL Associates 1986)

The effectiveness of cooperative or collaborative learning or grouping for instruction, as APL Associates has come to refer to this strategy, is well documented. Effective implementation of a cooperative process requires that we address some key areas as follows:

- ☐ Group size considerations
- ☐ Criteria to consider as we assign students to groups
- ☐ A strategy for matching students
- ☐ Troubleshooting and resolving problems as students work in their groups
- ☐ Prerequisites to the successful functioning of groups

As we work through each of these topics there exists the underlying notion that we are training (teaching) students how to successfully navigate the working together process. One of the key teacher considerations along this line is the size of the groups that you plan to create. There are several factors that play into this decision as follows:

- ☐ Age – the younger the learner, the smaller the group
- ☐ Ability – the less able the learner, the smaller the group
- ☐ Task – what size group will best facilitate the successful completion of the activity

Example:

- ☐ Science labs might work best with three in a group
- ☐ Daily instruction and interaction might work best with pairs (wait-time extended)
- ☐ Group projects might work best with four
- ☐ Review sessions (base group activity) call for groups of three

It's common for teachers to think that most grouping for instruction activities should be organized around a group size of four. However, it is appropriate to have varying size groups working on a specific activity. In other words, group size need not be divisible by a specific number (all groups of equal size – 2's, 3's, 4's, etc.). An over-the-top example might be that in a class of 28 students, you could find the following arrangement:

☐ Two groups of 4	= 8
☐ Four groups of 3	= 12
☐ Three groups of 2	= 6
☐ Two students working independently	= 2
TOTAL	28

As you analyze this unusual grouping arrangement it might be explained as follows:

- ☐ You have eight students who can work effectively in groups of four.
- ☐ You have twelve students who can manage working in groups of three. However, they are not at the point where they could be productive with a fourth person being added.
- ☐ You have six students in groups of two. These groups might include your less able students who at the moment cannot function in either a group of four or a group of three (example: inclusionary students).
- ☐ Finally you might have two students who appear to be working independently. In this instance, the teacher has identified these two as students who will work with the teacher. In identifying these the teacher is partnering with students who:
    - ☐ Have serious behavior issues
    - ☐ Refuse to work with others
    - ☐ Are unusual to the point that it would be troublesome for others to work with them, etc.

It's important to note here that this is a temporary arrangement only. These students will be made aware that the goal for them is to be able to work with at least one other student within a specified time.

This unusual grouping of students format is outlined here to communicate that as a teacher you have a variety of options when it comes to establishing group size.

If the grouping of students for the purpose of pursuing instructional objectives is a strategy that you choose to implement, then in addition to group size, successful matching up of students must also be considered. It's here that specific criteria should be applied as a way of establishing your groups. When discussing this with teachers they easily identify three criteria as follows:

- ☐ Ability
- ☐ Personality
- ☐ Gender

As we assess ability as a specific criterion it is important to note that a high-low match of two students would not be in the best interest of either. Therefore we have outlined here a step-by-step process by which you can efficiently match up students using their ability. To begin, we ask that you construct a master list of your class. The number one student at the top of the master list would be that student that you sense is the most able. The last student on the master list would be the student that you sense is the least able.

1. Jacob	________________	most able
13. Stephanie	______________	midline
26. Amanda	_______________	least able

In our illustration we have Jacob as most able and Amanda as the least able with Stephanie as midline (number 13). This sheet serves as a visual guide as you begin the matching up process. Step two in this effort calls for the use of 4x6 index cards. Using these 4x6 index cards, create a card for each student, with his/her name at the top of each card.

Jacob ________________
1.
2.
3.
4.

Under the name on the top of the card, list the names of four students who you think this student can work with productively. Again, use your master list as a reference and a guide. Continue this process until you have a card for each student. At this point, the matching up process, using ability only, can begin. In this instance as you look at Jacob's list of four possibilities you can check those four students' cards to determine if Jacob's name is on one or more of their cards as well. If so, you can now put those two cards together. You have a match.

Example:

Jacob ________________	Stephanie ________________
1. Eric	1. John
2. Stephanie	2. Tim
3. Gretchen	3. Jean
4. David	**4. Jacob**

Continue the card match sequence until you have all students matched up with a classmate. At this point you have created pair sets. If the activity that you plan calls for large groups, you can continue to pursue the same sequence.

As you review your criteria you have a comfortable feeling that, as it regards ability, you're well positioned. The next task is to look at your groupings to determine whether the personalities fit the ability matches. Some personality considerations along this line can be:

- □ Dominant – submissive types
- □ Task – non-task types
- □ Passive – aggressive types

Your day-to-day observations plus input from other staff can help here (previous teachers, guidance, etc.).

The third criterion for grouping considerations is gender. There is no hard and fast rule for matching same gender or mixed gender groups. Your decisions will be influenced in part by the personality and ability criteria, and secondly affective domain outcomes (for example, students can work productively with other same sex or opposite sex students).

On paper we now have your class organized in a grouping format. To further prepare your students, it is very important to teach them how to interact successfully (interaction sequence; teaching behaviors). It is not practical or fair to assume that even though you have done an excellent job of matching students to form the groups that the groups can function effectively. They now need to be taught how groups should function (again, teaching behaviors). They need to be provided all of the essential information on how successful groups function, they need to have it modeled for them, and they need to be provided the opportunity to practice (mini-practice sessions). As you work through these teaching/practice sessions some essential prerequisites need also to be taught, as follows:

- ☐ Brainstorming
- ☐ Status Report
- ☐ Summarizing

These prerequisites facilitate a smoother functioning of each of the groups and result in their being more focused and productive. The skill of brainstorming has too often been overlooked as a skill essential to the successful functioning of groups at almost any level. You need only to think back to groups that you were a member of to visualize how individuals tended to interact (committees, various meeting groups, classroom group experiences, etc.). The skills that we brought to these sessions were learned (or not) through a hit-or-miss or trial-and-error process. Working together toward a common end is a difficult process at best. Therefore, it is critical that the skill and process of brainstorming be introduced and taught early on.

The brainstorming process has several guidelines that must be taught and practiced as follows:

- ☐ All members contribute. *Specify a minimum of 1-3 contributions/member.*
- ☐ No interrupting (turn taking).
- ☐ Stick to the topic.
- ☐ All input is accepted.
- ☐ Identify a recorder.
- ☐ Specify the time (timed event).
- ☐ No criticism of an individual or individual's ideas or contributions.
- ☐ Identify a spokesperson.

It is interesting to note that the successful management of the brainstorming guidelines results, very effectively, in the realization of the collaborative learning outcomes outlined previously (positive interdependence, positive interpersonal skills, individual accountability, group processing skills, etc.).

One of the concerns often mentioned by teachers when considering the grouping strategy is the possibility of student defocus and socializing. Teacher monitoring of groups will assist greatly in keeping students on task. As part of that monitoring process we encourage teachers to employ **status report** as a specific strategy. This strategy is designed to assist students in staying on task while providing a sense of how the class as a whole is functioning. Most group activities are timed events. The students have been instructed that they have a specified block of time in which to work. Periodically during these group work sessions (every 5-10 minutes – teacher discretion) the teacher announces a status report to all. At that point each group, through a spokesperson, will briefly report on how much they have accomplished to that point and what, if any, problems they are encountering. After all groups have reported, the teacher will set the groups back to work. This process serves to keep students on task and productive and also serves to illustrate what the various groups have accomplished to that point. It also allows the teacher to troubleshoot and resolve problems that specific groups are encountering as described by the group spokesperson.

As you read through this content on grouping you can rightly conclude that it is a complex process that requires some serious thought and organization. We have taken you through a step-by-step process that will significantly increase the likelihood that those grouping outcomes that we spoke of earlier will be realized for all.

What remains is the third prerequisite that tends to bind the process as a final accountability measure. Many instructional skills strategies refer to this as closure. A student or group summarizes the efforts of the group; this summary activity is key (Marzano 2001). It should address two ends:

- □ A summarization of the group's efforts and therefore the outcome or product.
- □ A summarization or look back at the process and interaction (group processing).

One item to consider in the summarization of the group's efforts or product is what the group has accomplished, which speaks for itself as a group summarization. In addition, each member of the group should produce an individual summary as well. To facilitate the creation of the individual summary statements, we recommend fill-in-the-blank or open-ended summarization as a productive first step for students pulling their thoughts together. Some sample fill-in possibilities are:

- ☐ We produced ________________________________
- ☐ We accomplished ______________________________
- ☐ We solved ___________________________________
- ☐ We created __________________________________
- ☐ We answered _________________________________
- ☐ We developed ________________________________
- ☐ We built ____________________________________
- ☐ We shared ___________________________________
- ☐ We practiced _________________________________
- ☐ Etc. Etc.

As students develop a comfort level in creating their short statements they then can work on being more descriptive by adding additional information. The expanded portion of the short summary statement would include, "by doing <u>blank</u>." The student, for example, now can say, "We created <u>fill-in-the-blank</u> by doing <u>blank</u>." Here they add a description of the kinds of things that their group did to achieve their group outcome.

The second summary consideration should focus on individual student feedback on how their group tended to function and interact as they worked together. This is done by having each member confidentially share his/her thoughts. A short form could be used to provide this thoughtful feedback. The group process is set in motion to work toward a common end. In addition, it is also essential for each group member to reflect on how this all happened. (Did each member contribute? Was there appropriate face-to-face interaction? Were there behaviors evident that facilitated or got in the way? Etc.) This can be achieved by having each student complete the following:

Figure 7. Individual Student Feedback on Group Work

GROUP TASK:

____

Did your group successfully complete its assigned task?

- ☐ Yes
- ☐ No

If yes, identify two things that contributed to this success:

____

____

If no, identify one major barrier that kept your group from being successful:

____

____

Based on this feedback the teacher can lead a general discussion on the factors that lead to the success in some groups and the factors that caused some groups to struggle. The process of group work should, over time, result in students becoming more comfortable and skilled.

You now have a complete, well-organized "grouping for instruction" plan, which is designed to address that highly sought after 21st century skill of successful collaboration. Setting the students on the path to being able to work effectively with others requires thoughtful effort on your part.

Section Four: The End of Class

Section Four provides a look at strategies that heighten effectiveness at the end of a class and tie in directly with the strategies discussed in Sections Two and Three. The strategies examined in Section Four are closure, practice, homework, work orders, reflecting on the day and planning for tomorrow. The question of how we should both manage and organize the last 7 to 10 minutes of class is the **prime time 2** block of time in the serial positioning sequence we call **recency**. Bringing specific content to a logical and organized conclusion is critical. The instructional skill of closure does that for us. However, as you read further on closure you will note that **closure** can be utilized at the end of any block of instruction.

Wright and Nuthall (1970) found that review of material at the end of a lesson is positively related to achievement. Good and Grouws (1979) examined the effects of review on 4th grade math students. The review strategies used by the teachers of the experimental group proved highly effective in advancing student achievement. Those key variables include a review at the beginning of a new lesson along with weekly and monthly reviews to sustain daily learning. The teachers who used these strategies with the experimental group were significantly more successful in inducing student achievement than the teachers of the control group.

Rosenshine (1982) reported that when review is programmed into learning materials, teachers are more likely to use it, resulting in student achievement increases. These findings are further supported by the work of Good and Grouws (1979) and Emmer, et. al (1982). Weekly and monthly reviews were found to be one of the effective instructional functions identified in these studies. Medley (1977) found in his review of research on teaching that structuring reviews at both the beginning and end of a lesson were positively correlated with achievement in both kindergarteners and first grade students in arithmetic. This was true for both low and high SES students.

Ausubel and Youssef's (1965) study of retention confirmed the findings from earlier studies by Spitzer (1939) and Reynolds and Glazer (1964) that spaced review increases retention more than mere repetition. In a very important study on the effects of early and delayed reviews, Gay (1973) found that students who received both an early and a late review achieved a higher mean score on delayed retention tests than did students who received only early reviews and students who received only late reviews. The late review only group retained 20% more information than the early review only group, but the group receiving both early and late reviews retained 20% more than the late review only group and 40% more than the early review only group. This study revealed that both early and late review strategies produce the most significant differences in student achievement. Prime time 1 review is best achieved through the systematic use of bell ringers on a daily basis. Prime time 2 review is best achieved in two ways. The first is **closure**, and the second is **homework**.

Closure

Prime time 2 is the final segment or end of an instructional period (the last 7 to 10 minutes) and should be divided into two blocks of time. The **first block** is devoted to summary activities which we call **closure**. The **second block** is the portion of the lesson that allows students an opportunity to begin the homework for that lesson. Let's begin by discussing the first block more fully.

Closure is a mental process where the learner is asked to summarize his or her perception of what has been taught and learned. Closure is the summative form of **checking for understanding**. Closure helps students achieve the instructional outcome of **retention**. Closure is a combination of reinforcement, monitoring, feedback, active engagement and focus activities. Essential to the effectiveness of closure are **clearly stated** and **shared instructional objectives**. Also essential to an effective closure is the **engagement of the learner** in the process. The students need to summarize what they perceive they have learned or are now able to do and how it relates to the instructional objectives. Closure activities can take a variety of forms including: written, verbal, application activities, responses to questions, working with other students in small information sharing groups, problem solving activities, quizzes, etc.

There are two important criteria for closure. Let's look at each in detail. First, in order for closure to be effective, **the students must do the summarizing**. Four key benefits result from this student summary:

- ☐ Students rehearse the material and strengthen their encoding (moving concepts from working memory into long-term memory)
- ☐ Students learn the process of self-assessment (what do I know, how well do I know it, and what do I still need to learn?)
- ☐ If the students learned it well, then they should be able to teach it to others accurately
- ☐ The teacher has an opportunity to check the students' perception of what was learned to check for accuracy and rate and degree.

The second important criterion for closure is that it must be **relevant to the lesson objectives**, in other words **closure** must be directly matched, linked, and connected to each of the objectives for that lesson. What students do during the closure activity should assess how much and how well they have achieved the lesson objectives.

Closure can be conducted at almost any point in the class. Closure can also be conducted following a larger block of time such as a day, week, or several weeks. General guidelines for closure suggest that the most appropriate times to consider using closure would be at the end of each instructional objective, at the end of class, at the end of a day of instruction, prior to or after a planned interruption, and at the end of a unit of study. Stated another way, **you should use closure**:

1. When you shift objectives within the lesson;
2. At the end of the lesson or day;
3. At the end of a unit or other times when a broad review by students is desired;
4. Prior to or after any classroom interruption.

Closure contributes to learning in two very important ways. Its primary focus is to reinforce essential content, concepts and skills by providing for another repetition of that content, concepts and skills. Secondly, closure serves as one of the processes implemented as a part of an ongoing system of repetitions designed and implemented by teachers. By intentionally building and implementing systems that reinforce essential learning, the teacher significantly increases the likelihood that all students are able to perform successfully by being able to recall and apply the essential information or skills from the lesson (Gay 1973). Through the systematic repeating of the content we are increasing and influencing the retention of what was taught and learned.

Here are several important **reminders** with respect to using **closure** at the end of any learning session. First, on average, students will remember what you teach for 20 seconds to 20 minutes. Ebbinghaus' **forgetting curve** research discovered that without practice and systematic checks for understanding, the following is true:

- □ after 20 minutes, 45% of what you taught is gone;
- □ after 60 minutes, up to 55% of what you've taught is gone; and
- □ after 24 hours, up to 65-75% of what you've taught is gone.

There are several effective and easy preventions that can be used to counteract memory losses. The first is to use **check for understanding** frequently, consistently and at the appropriate times (following the **5-1** or **10-2 rule** and always immediately at the end of an objective or activity). Second, use **wait-time** and **wait-time extended** to allow for deeper processing of content. Third, run a **closure** at the conclusion of any major activity, end of an objective, a lesson, the end of class, the end of a school day, week, or instructional unit. Fourth, use **bell ringers** at the beginning of class to assist students' retention by giving them a job to do as soon as they enter the classroom. The bell ringer involves recall of material learned yesterday or earlier. **Remember: it is a chance to look back before we look forward**.

Remember the following premises:

- □ Check for understanding is the reason for retention
- □ Bell ringers are the reason for retention
- □ Closure is the reason for retention

Closure is closely connected to and should be used in conjunction with two other primary instructional strategies that were discussed earlier in this book. Those strategies are **knowledge of results** and **practice.** Through the **closure** processes, students gain important **feedback** (immediate and specific) on their progress and another opportunity for **guided practice** of the content, concepts and skills. Let's remember that **closure** is a mental process where the learner is asked to summarize his or her perception of what has been taught and learned. It is the summative form of **checking for understanding** that helps students achieve the instructional objectives and the outcome of **retention**.

Closely related to checking for student understanding is the concept of practice. Let's take a closer look at this idea.

Practice

When considering the several criteria used to measure professionals, two stand out when applying the criteria to educators. Being an expert is one that often heads the list. In the case of teaching being an expert means that you are an expert in the content or grade level subject matter and that you are an expert in how teaching works (instructional skills and strategies).

As mentioned in earlier sections, instructional delivery is one of the primary focuses of this book. Knowing and consistently applying the instructional strategies that we have outlined thus far will contribute mightily to student and teacher success. Equally key, however, is having a firm grasp of the content and skills (being an expert in the curriculum).

Recently there has been increasing attention being paid to those elements of the curriculum that we would characterize as essential. Essential is described here as those elements of the subject area content that must be mastered in order for students to experience success.

A concept that is receiving increasing attention in education circles in this regard is the Pareto Principle, developed by Vilfredo Pareto in 1906. This principle in its simplest form is known as the 80-20 concept. In its day-to-day application this translates to mean that 80% of what we tend to accomplish is generated from 20% of our energy and activities. The application of this principle has existed primarily in the private sector (business, corporate, manufacturing, etc.). Most recently the Pareto Principle has begun to be applied in education circles as well. In the world of teaching and learning, the application of this concept centers on the identification of the 20% of any curriculum (subject matter) that we would determine is absolutely essential to the success of all students. This is not to say that the 80% of the remainder of the curriculum is not important. The goal is to deliver (teach) all of the identified curriculum but in doing so provide heavy emphasis to those concepts and skills that would fall into the 20% category. Ensuring that the 20% is in place for all will result in students performing much more successfully in that subject or grade level. It has been suggested in widening circles that students are not performing at desired levels because the basics of the essentials are not in place. Therefore, it has been further suggested that because the basics (essential learnings) are not mastered, the students are not able to function as successfully in areas of application, critical analysis, or problem solving. We are not suggesting here that we should reassess "what" and "how" much we teach and therefore cut back. A good deal of very high quality work has been done by teachers, coordinators and others in both developing and aligning curriculum. Our thinking has to focus on those essentials (20%) in the various curricular areas that we deem to be essential. In this regard, practice is essential.

Practice, after all, is an instructional skill. When appropriately applied, practice contributes in very significant ways to student success. **Practice** is a strategy that is defined as: the consistent engagement of the learner in a repeated activity designed to correctly produce the desired outcome or product. The key words in this definition are: *consistent*, *repeated activity (repetition)*, and *correctly*.

There are two essential points here. Point #1: The degree to which a student can be successful is in direct proportion to the student's willingness to invest in "sustained practice." Point #2: Student success is also a function of the number of repetitions that the student has experienced with those essential skills of areas of content. The essential question becomes, "how do we build the sustained practice (repetitions) regarding the essentials (20%) while continuing to move forward in pursuit of the curriculum?" The interesting fact is that higher performing students (sometimes referred to as elite performers) have developed and implemented their own practice systems and pursue them consistently as part of how they function from day-to-day (systems for reviewing and studying for tests, note taking procedures, completing homework, coming to class on time, working on projects in a timely manner, coming to class prepared, organizing their time and procedures, seeking help, etc.). Too many students do not have these same defined and well developed procedures in place that contributes to their overall success. In other words, they do not have the well defined systems that build the repetitions or reinforce the defined learning outcomes.

Before we outline specific strategies that facilitate ongoing practice and repetitions for all, we need to further develop the case for sustained and meaningful practice. The forgetting curve developed by Hermann Ebbinghaus in 1885 helps build that case. Figure 8 shows what the curve looks like in most literature.

Figure 8. The Forgetting Curve *(Ebbinghaus, 1885)*

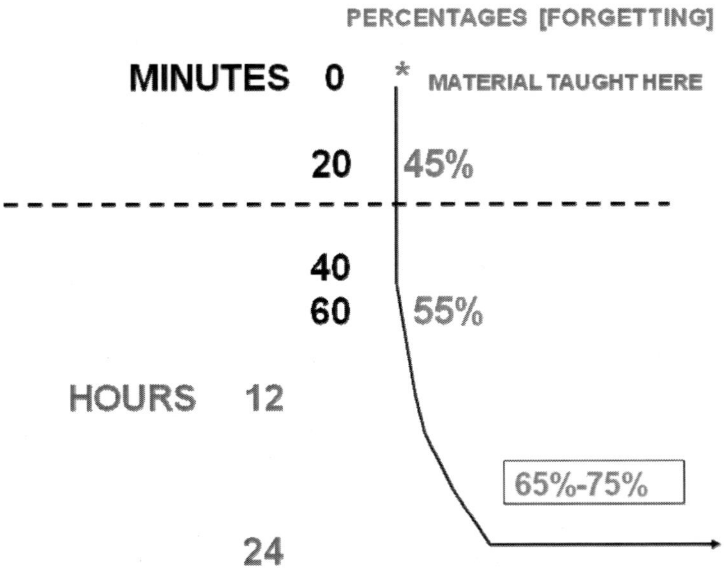

Some critics dispute the widespread application of this. However, there is general agreement that students do lose a significant amount of what has been taught over a rather short span of time. Experienced teachers lament the fact that students are not retaining the content. They often attribute that to lack of effort, not studying, distractions, lack of motivation, etc. However, we also now know that those teachers who have systematic and consistent strategies of repetition as part of their day-to-day teaching are experiencing very impressive and improved student performance results for all.

To reinforce this notion we also refer you to a concept known of as **learning line**. The learning line is shown in Figure 9.

Figure 9. The Learning Line

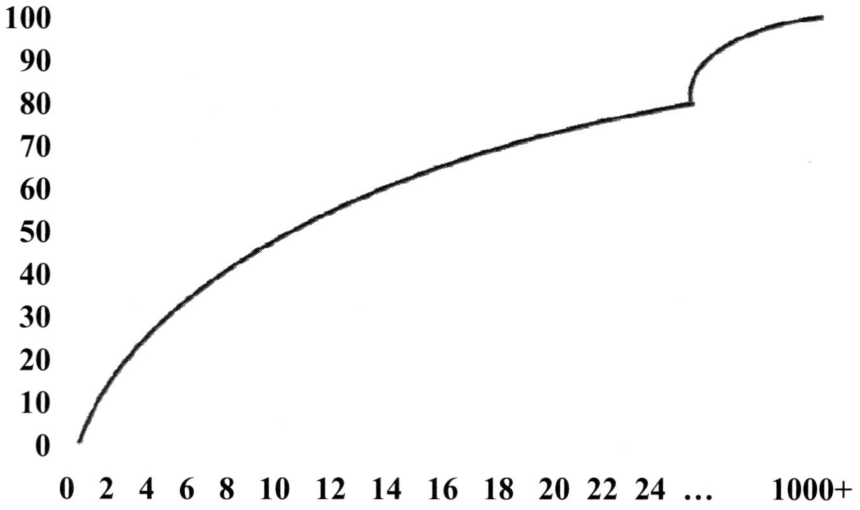

NOTE:

- ☐ *Vertical scale represents improvement in learning (100 represents % of mastery).*
- ☐ *Horizontal axis represents the number of practice sessions.*
- ☐ *Students have to practice 25-30 times to reach 80% competency.*
- ☐ *It's only after a great deal of practice that students can perform a skill or retrieve knowledge with speed and accuracy.*

Anderson, J.R., 1995 and Newell & Rosenbloom, 1981

When suggesting that repetitions are a key variable in the retention of essential content, we are also suggesting that teachers need to construct and implement systems that provide ongoing and meaningful repetitions to all students. What follows are specific strategies that when consistently implemented result in significantly improved student performance.

The first of these is the ongoing and consistent use of a **bell ringer**. A description or definition of a bell ringer is a task that students pursue at the beginning of a lesson or class. This task focuses on previously taught essential skills or content (the 20% that we referred to previously). The bell ringer focus can be from that which was taught over the past few days, weeks or even months. The most commonly used bell ringer format is to post a task for all to work on (flipchart, whiteboard, smart board, etc.). All students are expected to work on this common activity immediately upon arriving to class. In so doing we are again reinforcing key concepts or skills for the first 3-5 minutes of class. All students are engaged in a meaningful task while the teacher can immediately attend to some very necessary housekeeping chores (handing out, collecting, taking attendance, addressing a student question or concern, etc.). A quick check of the bell ringer will follow prior to pursuing the lesson objectives. In this instance all students are working on the same bell ringer task. It is recommended that one bell ringer be assigned for all when the content is that with which all students seem to struggle. For the day-to-day application of bell ringers, APL recommends that teachers utilize the 3x5 index card bell ringer approach. This bell ringer strategy, when used with consistency, has been found to have a very positive impact on student performance scores for all. This simple but very effective strategy relies on itemizing essential content on 3x5 index cards as follows:

- ☐ A key question to answer
- ☐ Vocabulary / terminology
- ☐ A process to describe
- ☐ Labeling
- ☐ Fill-in-the-blank
- ☐ Sample test question
- ☐ Multiple choice
- ☐ Etc.

These cards can be created as part of your ongoing planning and organization process before or following instruction. As you create your cards it is suggested that you number them in sequence for the entire year (example #1 through #300 plus). The numbering facilitates organization and follows the order with which the curriculum was delivered. As you distribute the cards at the beginning of class it is easy for you to collect and therefore put them back into the same order of the curriculum sequence. Teachers are finding that if the cards are color coded by unit or subject area, it tends to further facilitate the effective organization and application of this strategy. When distributing the bell ringer cards at the beginning of a class it is recommended that students should work in pairs.

Doing so results in:

- ☐ Immediate, active engagement of all students
- ☐ The consistent completion of the task
- ☐ A very high instance of correctness
- ☐ Significant repetitions

The teacher can then check with four or five pairs before pursuing the lesson objectives. Teachers have become very creative as they develop and implement this bell ringer activity. Some teachers computerize their essential bell ringer target questions and then print them off as labels, lists or study guides. We are aware of at least two teachers who printed label cards for each of their students (labor intensive but very effective). When preparing for a test the teacher could indicate that the upcoming test will focus, in part, on index cards 53-87. A number of teachers have indicated that the bell ringer cards were very useful and effective when preparing for a substitute. It can become the central activity for the substitute teacher. In this instance it becomes a very productive and effective strategy as students are reviewing previously taught essential content (again in pairs), thus making for a productive, focused and practical substitute experience.

As we expand on the application of bell ringers and the need for meaningful repetitions we turn our attention to Mondays. This first day of the week has been found to be unique from other days of the week in a variety of ways as follows:

- ☐ There has been a minimum of 48 hours away from the content of the previous week (consider the forgetting curve and how much is lost after 24 hours).
- ☐ Sleep patterns have changed.
- ☐ Routines and patterns of life have changed.
- ☐ Life's up-and-downs and the accompanying baggage from the weekend tend to come through the doors on Monday.
- ☐ Reestablishing social connections becomes a primary focus for many students.

As a result, Monday bell ringers need to be structured differently. The **Monday bell ringer** structure should vary from the other days of the week in two basic ways, as follows:

- ☐ The activity should be longer on Mondays (approximately 10-15 minutes).
- ☐ The activity on Monday should focus exclusively on essential content taught from the previous week.

The students have had a minimum of 48 hours away from the content of last week. Recreating some essential learning from the previous week sets a solid base and focus for the content that we have in mind to be taught this week. Again, the rule-of-thumb applies here: **always go backward before you go forward**. Both the consistent application of **daily bell ringers** and **Monday bell ringers** does exactly that in a powerful way.
An ongoing concern for teachers is how to catch students up on the content (instruction) missed due to absences. Most of the traditional recommendations seem ineffective or unmanageable (keeping students after school, copying a classmate's notes, staying in at recess, etc.). In most cases strategies to address the concern are hit-or-miss at best. To address this dilemma APL developed a process commonly referred to as **base groups**. The base group activity that we developed is designed to reinforce previously taught content, catch students up who were absent, and build repetitions for all students. The base group structure has several recommended components as follows:

- ☐ Divide your class into groups of 3. (In lower grades it is recommended that the groupings be pairs.)
- ☐ The base groups should meet every 7-10 days.
- ☐ These small group sessions should last from 12-15 minutes.
- ☐ In these sessions the students will review (teach to each other) teacher-selected essential items of content taught in the previous 7-10 days. (Each group has the same items.)
- ☐ Following this review each group will have a spokesperson who will respond to one teacher question based upon the reviewed content.

If the spokesperson cannot answer the teacher question, he/she can respond by asking to either *consult or confer*. *Consult or confer* is the student's way of gaining permission to huddle with his/her group mates so that they can help with the teacher question, and then the spokesperson can give the correct response.

Teachers implemented this process with great success. In doing so, however, they recommended adjustment. Instead of conducting this activity every 7-10 days, teachers chose to conduct the base groups every 5 days. They gave the following reasons for the adjustment:

- □ The 7-10 day format was too long a block of time.
- □ The 7-10 day format covered too much content to be able to conduct an effective review. The teachers, therefore, recommended that it be conducted every 5 days. They also recommended that it should be implemented each Friday and thus serve as a closure for the week.

It was an essential goal for APL to develop strategies that would address the need for repetitions so as to reinforce the intended objectives. As stated previously higher performing students build their own systems of repetition which contribute significantly to their success (note taking, studying strategies, consistently prepared for class, following through with homework and longer term projects, etc.).

It is our experience that a significant percentage of students do not develop or pursue these practices. The reasons are many and varied. Recognizing this dilemma APL not only created the above three strategies (index card bell ringers, Monday bell ringers and base groups), but also highly recommended that an instructional week center on these strategies, as follows:

Monday	Tuesday	Wednesday	Thursday	Friday
Monday bell ringer activity	Regular index card bell ringer	Regular index card bell ringer	Regular index card bell ringer	Base groups

This consistency of reinforcement throughout the week and thus the year strengthens each student's grasp of the objectives. It further results in a smoother pursuit and flow of the curriculum and improved performance scores for all, particularly those who tend to struggle.

When asked about the importance of practice as a classroom activity or strategy, teachers unanimously agreed that it is essential for student success. In support of that belief they stated that practice:

- Is a checking for understanding activity
- Builds confidence
- Builds repetitions
- Significantly improves overall student performance

The foregoing statements are based on the assumption that the practice activity is focused, safe, at the appropriate level of difficulty, directly linked to the intended objectives, not perceived as a waste of time, and does not overload and thus take an inordinate amount of time to complete. This applies to both guided practice (in class) and homework (out of class). The out of class practice (homework) is of particular concern in that it is subject to overload and can be perceived as a waste of time when students are asked to pursue less-than-quality assignments.

Homework

There has been much written in recent years about the negative impact of homework overloading. In the instance of overload the damage can be extensive and long lasting (Cooper 2001). Therefore, the well worn guideline of *quality, not quantity* makes clear sense. To accommodate this recommendation, time guidelines have been promoted by many based upon Harris Cooper's (2001) extensive work centering on homework as an instructional strategy. The often quoted time guidelines look as follows (Table 5):

- ☐ 10-20 minutes per night in grade one, and 10 minutes multiplied by grade level for grades 2 through 12, per night:

Table 5. Time Guidelines for Homework

Grade Level	Minutes
2	20 minutes
3	30 minutes
4	40 minutes
5	50 minutes
6	60 minutes
7	70 minutes
8	80 minutes
9	90 minutes
10	100 minutes
11	110 minutes
12	120 minutes

It has been found that students can manage the homework, within these time guidelines, if teachers consider dividing their grade level figure by the number of possible subject area assignments possible on a given night (Example: Grade 8 x 10 minutes = 80 minutes, divided by 5 subjects = 16 minutes per subject per night). At the secondary level where departmentalization is the standard model, managing the quantity and time can easily get out of hand. Individual subject area teachers can lose sight of how much total homework they are assigning as they pursue instruction and the delivery of the curriculum. The homework assignments and quantity and time guidelines that we have been considering here represent the day-to-day assignments. These time and quality guidelines do not account for:

- ☐ Upcoming major tests (all subjects);
- ☐ Long-term assignments or projects; and
- ☐ Other school related activities in which students are engaged.

When considering all of the above it is easy for us to imagine how serious overload can evolve. Managing homework over an entire staff can, at first glance, be troublesome or appear unmanageable. We at APL have found that the fundamental first step in managing homework is the development of a district-wide homework policy. A policy developed and endorsed by a district is not a set of guidelines or recommendations, but rather the rule or policy that has been formally adopted by the district. Once adopted each teacher is bound by the policy. Short of having a specific district policy, individual buildings or individual teachers should at least be able to clearly state their homework beliefs, procedures and policies. To do less is hit-or-miss, disorganized and will negatively impact all students.

After reviewing a variety of homework policies, APL has identified some common elements as follows:

- **Time:** Each of the reviewed policies had the element of time as a common thread. As a general rule the time constraints are specifically outlined by grade level. Using the maximum time guidelines developed by Harris Cooper, we can easily manage homework loads. (Example: As outlined previously, 9th graders should not be assigned more than 18-20 minutes worth of homework per night per subject. Or, in other words, the grade level x 10 = 90 total minutes maximum per night for all subjects. The average 9th grade student might carry five subjects where homework could be assigned per day. Dividing the 90 total minutes, as Cooper recommends, by the five subjects, results in the 18-20 minutes per subject per day total.)
- **Quality:** Teachers should only assign homework that is based upon previously taught content and skills. Homework, by definition, is a practice activity. This practice activity adds additional reinforcement or repetitions to what teachers have identified as the essentials. Bell ringers, Monday bell ringers, base groups and now homework build these consistently ongoing and necessary repetitions. However, homework has to be managed carefully to be effective, particularly the homework assigning structure. As APL researched the homework strategy it became evident that the traditional homework assigning process did not result in the desired effect and became problematic as students pursued their assignments. When considering the previously shared forgetting curve, it becomes clear why many students struggle with their assignments. They forget a significant amount of the content taught over a 24-hour period.

One-Two-One Homework Assigning Process

We at APL designed a homework assigning structure that would effectively strengthen the previously taught essential content and result in more students successfully completing their daily assignments. We refer to this structure as the **1-2-1 homework assigning process**. This process reinforces the notion that homework should strengthen the student's grasp of the essential content being taught. This homework assigning sequence is described as follows:

- ☐ The first numeric **one** in the **1-2-1 sequence** simply indicates that the students should only be assigned a very limited amount of homework based upon that which was taught that day. (Again, the forgetting curve tells us that the student will forget a significant amount of what was taught that day and therefore is doomed to struggle with the assignment.)
- ☐ The number **two** in the **1-2-1 sequence** indicates that the bulk of the homework assignment for that day would focus on content that has been taught over the past 7-10 days. At this stage in the process students should feel a bit more comfortable and confident, thus increasing their chances for success.
- ☐ The final number **one** in the **1-2-1 sequence** indicates that the students should get a bit more homework on content taught over the past several weeks.

This then becomes a limit-more-limit homework assigning concept which is very nontraditional in homework assigning circles. Again, the teacher has to keep a sharp eye on the amount of time that it will take to do any assignment.

As you read through this section on practice and homework we have outlined specific guidelines and recommendations as follows:

- ☐ Limit the quantity. Homework should facilitate and strengthen the intended learning – not create frustration, negative attitudes and incorrectness.
- ☐ Manage the time. Have a sense of how long it will take the average student to complete the assignment.
- ☐ The quality of the homework should be such that it does not result in being viewed as busy work.

What follows now are some additional homework guidelines for your consideration:

- ☐ Assign the homework at the end of class so as to manage student focus. (Some students tend to work on the new homework during class or are defocused on the lesson as a result of their being concerned or upset about the new homework assignment.)
- ☐ Homework should never be assigned as discipline. We often hear teachers recounting their own negative experiences along this line. (Teachers threatening students to add to the homework assignment as a method of dealing with unruly or unacceptable behavior, writing something 50-100 times, copying segments of the dictionary, etc.)
- ☐ Students should know how the teacher plans to use the homework the next day. Going over all of the homework is both desirable and recommended. Teachers often lament the fact that they do not have time to go over all of the assigned homework. Therefore we make two recommendations:
    - ☐ **Assign less.** There is no literature that suggests that assigning large quantities of homework is productive. In reviewing Harris Cooper's work in this regard he stated that, "assigning large quantities of homework results in students becoming bored with it and tended to depress the student performance scores."
    - ☐ **Be creative and efficient in how you go over the homework.** For example: organizing the class into groups of 3-4 and assigning each group a segment, question, or problem that they have to be prepared to share with the class. Assign to the task a reasonable amount of time to complete. Have each group share with the whole class their answer or solution.
- ☐ Most students wish to know whether the homework is going to count. (In their terms, is it going to be graded?) The common recommendation is to not grade the homework. Remember, homework is not a test. Completing homework does three basic and important things: the first is to provide feedback to the teacher and to the student (checking for understanding); second, to build additional repetitions; and the third is that it can be a significant confidence builder.

Teachers have reported to APL that the grading of homework can seriously complicate the averaging process to determine report card grades.

It is generally felt that, rather than grading, it should be given a value. The logic here is that students are investing their personal time in addition to the regular work day. (Students have already put in a full work day.) To accommodate this student desire to know whether it is going to count, we at APL recommend a value added approach. A simple and uncluttered sample of value added could consider the following:

- Most value added homework systems are based on symbols (check marks, stickers, rubber stamps, etc.).
- Using or placing one of the above on a student's paper is an indication that he/she has completed the assignment. It is not an indication that the homework was correct or incorrect, but rather that it was done to completion.
- At the end of the grading period (often 8-10 weeks) the teacher can count the number of checks or symbols that each student has accumulated against the number of assignments given. The teacher can then assign a value to the homework assignments done during that marking period.

When conducting a survey of students around the question of, "what is it that teachers can do to increase the probability that students will attempt to complete the homework?" students unanimously identified the two previous items:

- How will it be used?
- Is it going to count?

In addition to the two student questions, APL added recommendations and strategies that also contribute to more consistent homework completion by all. In considering serial positioning it was pointed out that the end of class was an essential block of instructional time and had to be carefully and thoughtfully managed. Conducting a closure, of course, would be an essential element of the thoughtful managing of the end of class. The conducting of a closure would then be followed by 2-3 minutes where students would actively begin to work on the assigned homework. The teacher needs to be very specific here:

- ☐ Specific on the amount of time that the students have to work on the assignment.
- ☐ Specific on what must be completed in that 2-3 minute session. (By the end of the allotted time, each student must have at least "X" amount of homework done.) Failure of the teacher to state specifically the minimum that must be completed results in too many students choosing to not take it seriously.

In addition we at APL have found that pairing up students to pursue this homework session (homework partners) contributed significantly to:

- ☐ Students following the teacher directive.
- ☐ Students completing at least the minimum required in the 2-3 minutes prior to the end of class.
- ☐ The overall quality and correctness.
- ☐ Students tending to add to the assignment on their own time and as a result more students with completed homework.

As we discuss the question of homework, it is important to note that not all students can get the homework finished. (They did however get it started in class.) The circumstances and attitudes that contribute to non-completion are many and varied. In most instances the trained eye can easily identify who these students might be. They do not exist in overwhelming numbers, but they do nevertheless exist. Please consider:

- ☐ Knowing who these students are; and
- ☐ Developing an individual plan whereby the students can get the assignments completed. The plans typically outline a process whereby these students can complete the assignments before they leave the building.

Homework can be a very productive instructional strategy. In summary, if we consider doing the following, homework can be a very positive contributor to overall student success, help develop and foster a positive attitude and contribute significantly to a healthier work ethic:

- ☐ Limit the quantity. (Don't overload.)
- ☐ Know and be reasonable about the amount of time that it will take to complete the assignments.
- ☐ Utilize the one-two-one homework assigning process.
- ☐ Provide time to get homework started in class. (2-3 minutes)
- ☐ Assign homework partners when starting homework in class.
- ☐ Go over **all** homework.
- ☐ Create a homework valuing system.
- ☐ The above guidelines apply to both the elementary and secondary school levels. However, at the elementary level it is also highly recommended that in addition to starting a small portion of the homework at the end of each lesson, that a bit of time (5-10 minutes) be set aside at the end of the day to get out the homework assigned during the day and add a bit to it before dismissal. Too many elementary youngsters, it was found, were unclear as to what their homework was for that night and did not have all the necessary materials to pursue it.

Work Orders

As we reflect on our school experiences we can visualize those instances where we were assigned a longer term project or paper. In most instances the teacher was reasonably specific about the expectations and details (when it's due, format, elements that need to be included, appearance, structure, rubric by which it will be assessed, etc.). As part of that process the students were reminded from time to time that they needed to be producing and that specific elements needed to be completed by a specific date.

Of major concern to most teachers is whether or not students are actively engaged in working on their projects in order to submit a quality product by the appointed date.

What follows is a strategy designed by APL to minimize the above concern by having students work on the activity in a timely manner.

The strategy is called **work order**. Like work orders in the real world, this work order process specifies what must be completed by a specific date and by whom. Its effectiveness lies in the fact that, rather than having teachers establish interim dates by which specific elements of the project be completed, the students establish both the elements and the time frame for completion of these elements.

The format can be rather simple in its design and has in it the flexibility for the teacher to add appropriate design elements (See Figure 10).

Students complete a segment of their work order in class and project or predict what will be completed on the project by a specified date which appears in the left column of the work order. As part of this process students are instructed to bring their work order and completed elements to class each day.

A few minutes can be spent having students share what they stated they would have completed by a specific date and some information to validate that fact. This can (and should) be done randomly throughout the completion of the project.

As the students work vertically down the work order form, a new date (3-4 days from then) is established with a description of what each will have completed by this new date. This process is repeated in 3- to 4-day increments until the project reaches completion. At that point the finished project should be ready to hand in (due date).

As part of the completed project the work order(s) need to be attached for submission to the teacher. The attached work orders should be part of the rubric by which the overall project is evaluated and/or graded. (Example: a completed work order, attached to the completed project, will account for ____% of the grade for that project.)

This strategy or process has been shown to be very effective in getting students to work on their longer term projects in a timely fashion. The resulting effect has been the production of higher quality products and the development of a set of life skills (goal setting, action plan creation, time management, organization, a strategy for attacking large tasks, etc.).

Figure 10. Work Order

Topic: **Project Label or Name**	
Dates: The dates by which a specific element is to be completed	**A description by the student of how much and/or what will be completed by the accompanying date**

Reflecting on Today

At the end of most teaching days, teachers may often find themselves tired enough to consider skipping the task of reflecting on that day's progress. When we don't reflect on the nature of what happened that day and why, we neglect a significant growth opportunity. Professionals in all walks of life are given to professional reflection in order to grow their skills and attitudes about how to become more efficient and therefore more effective. While comprehensive reflection cannot occur every day, some daily reflection is necessary if we want to maintain or move toward Super Star Teacher status. In the interest of growing your professional skills, consider how the following questions may assist you in that process.

1. What went well today in terms of overall organization? Why?
2. What organizational strategies do I need to continue to use? Why?
3. What did not go well today in terms of overall organization? Why?
4. What organizational strategies therefore do I need to implement? Why?
5. What went well today in terms of procedural organization? Why?
6. What procedural strategies do I need to continue to use? Why?
7. What did not go well today in terms of procedural organization? Why?
8. What changes should I consider making in my procedural organization? Why?
9. What went well today in terms of instruction? Why?
10. What instructional strategies do I need to continue to use? Why?
11. What did not go well today in terms of instruction? Why?
12. What instructional strategies do I need to consider fixing and/or adding to my repertoire to be a more effective teacher? Why?
13. Were my lesson plans satisfactory? How and why?
14. Was I able to achieve the instructional objectives set for today? Why or why not?
15. How did the learning activities I chose to use go? Were the students well-engaged? Did they seem to be motivated? What adjustments do I need to make before I use these activities again?
16. What strategies did I use today that helped my students make connections between their learning and real life? Why were those strategies effective?
17. What strategies do I need to consider using to be more effective in helping my students make connections? How will those strategies help?
18. What strategies did I use today to help my students grow their level of responsibility? Why were those strategies effective?
19. What strategies do I need to consider using to be more effective in helping my students grow their level of responsibility? How will those strategies help?
20. What went well today in terms of building more positive relationships with my students? Why?

21. What relationship building strategies do I need to continue to use? Why?
22. What relationship building strategies do I need to consider adding to my repertoire to be a more effective teacher? Why?
23. How am I a better person and professional for what I experienced today with my students? Why?

Obviously, while this is not a comprehensive list, it does provide substantial opportunity and a quality place to start with respect to taking time to reflect on the nature of what we do each day to enhance the lives of the children with whom we work and to enhance the quality of our professional and personal lives.

Planning for Tomorrow

In your overall organization model for your classroom, daily lesson plans are the cornerstone. When teachers return to work the next day without lesson plans waiting for them, several serious problems can result. Even a cursory examination reveals how significant the problems are when no lesson plans are in place.

Some of those problems of trying to teach without lesson plans are listed here:

1. A serious lack of organization;
2. A serious lack of understanding of the scope of the job of teaching;
3. A serious lack of understanding of the responsibilities of the job of teaching;
4. A serious wasting of the students' time;
5. A serious loss of instruction and wasting students' time when substitutes must try to function without adequate (or any) lesson plans;
6. A serious wasting of taxpayers' money;
7. A serious void in the making of connections between our lessons, the district's curriculum and the state and national standards;
8. A serious disadvantaging of the students in terms of their achievement on classroom and district level assessments and standardized tests; and/or
9. A behavior that borders on professional malpractice.

While the final item on the list may seem a bit harsh, how would you like to visit your doctor, lawyer, dentist, investment counselor or other professional only to find out that he/she did not have any plan in mind to deal with you during your time together (time that you are paying for his/her services, we might add)? It seems preposterous to even consider paying someone for a service he/she does not deliver with exceptional competence. Yet, too frequently, we encounter teachers who neglect to plan adequately in formal ways in order to be **organized, specific and consistent** (remember the **three power words for teaching** from the Introduction). Our recommendation is to follow the same type of professional behaviors expected from the other professions in our lives, and not only will we be more competent and confident in what we do, but we will also more probably be treated with the type of respect the teaching profession should have. In order to be respected as professionals, we need to show our respect for our students, their parents, and our community by demonstrating our competence in the ways we organize, manage and deliver instruction.

Section Five: Parents and Teachers

In this part of the book we present strategies for parents to use that are effective in helping their children be successful in school. Those strategies include making school a priority for your child and you, parent-teacher conferencing, assisting children with homework, managing home behaviors, and dealing with bullying.

Making and Keeping School A Priority

The primary focus of this book has been to support teachers through the development of instructional skills and strategies. By implementing these strategies teachers significantly increase the performance scores of the students they serve. To think that these worthwhile outcomes are achieved in isolation from the other environments that students experience is to deny the influence and power of these other forces.

An equally important focus for teachers is to involve parents in the teaching, learning and overall school experience. Involving parents better serves students and contributes mightily to their immediate and future success. What follows are strategies, processes and plans that are directed at linking parents, students and educators together toward a common goal. Those strategies include assisting children with homework, managing behaviors at home, and parent-teacher conferencing. The goal is to more efficiently and productively forge a quality educational experience that will be the ticket for the future for every child.

The fundamental home/school bond is developed and nurtured out of the relationship between teacher and parent. Much has been written about the critical nature of this relationship. To create and foster this relationship requires that the school and the teaching staff pursue a specific course of action that results in closer ties and a positive sense about the home and school relationship. This obviously means a positive, continuous and regular process of communicating with the parents of your students.

The first step in that process is for the organization and the teachers to clearly communicate to parents who they are, what their procedures and expectations are, and that the staff is available to support and serve. This provides a broad view of what the organization and the classroom is set up to accomplish in support of their youngsters. It should be stated clearly that they can expect ongoing communication regarding their children's progress and should feel comfortable contacting the school when concerns or questions arise. All of this information should be framed in terms that communicate that parents and students are valued. We cannot be successful overall if lines of communication are not well established and if parents do not feel comfortable with the process. This section has been designed to focus on that home-school connection in support of student success and parent and school communication. A well-designed and focused conference format contributes in significant ways to a positive parent and school connection.

Schools can be very intimidating to many adults. This feeling of intimidation can arise out of what those adults remember about their own personal school experiences as well as from how they are greeted and treated when they come to the school. Treating them with courtesy and consideration when they do come to the school is a key consideration in developing that feeling of being welcomed.

When the occasions arise that call for parents to come to the school for the purpose of chatting about their youngster, whether initiated by the parent or the school, there are conferencing processes which will lead to very productive and positive results. These processes should be implemented in instances where the school and the teacher are providing a student status report to a parent.

What follows is information on parent-teacher conferencing, including some general principles regarding conferencing and a description of an APL Teacher-Parent Conference.

Parent Conference Process

Part One: Introduction

In the **introduction** portion of the conference the teacher or administrator should focus on three key elements: **hi-line; feel fine;** and **outline.**

- ☐ The first element, **hi-line**, represents the welcoming of the parent to the school and to the meeting. (Example: "Thank you for taking the time to come in. I/We know you have a demanding schedule. I/We have been looking forward to meeting and working with you.") No comments should be made at this point regarding their youngster. This is strictly for the parent and initially making the parent feel welcomed.

- ☐ The second element, **feel fine**, focuses on making the parent comfortable as well as welcomed. The seating arrangement is a critical consideration in achieving this sense of comfort. There should be comfortable seating in fairly close proximity for all the participants, with no desks or major obstacles separating any of the meeting participants. In other words, the teachers or administrators should not position themselves behind their desks for these meetings. Some additional thought should be given here to providing refreshments. Offering a soft drink or a glass of water, snacks, fruit, etc. are all possibilities. This communicates that the parent is of value, and this is a professional, high level, and valued experience.
- ☐ The third element, **outline**, is the agenda that will be shared with the parent. As part of this agenda sharing you will follow the **"3R" approach** of **recall, reinforcement** and **review**. The outline may sound like this: "First you (referring to the parent) will have an opportunity to tell me anything about (son or daughter's name) that you believe is important for me to know. Then I am going to compliment _________ for doing the following (______________________), and finally we will take a look together at a concern and outline a plan that we have implemented to address the concern."

Part Two: Recall

The first of the "**3 Rs**" is the **recall** section. It is designed with the parent/guardian in mind. In this portion of the conference, the parent speaks first. This section of the conference provides the springboard for the parents to share information about their son or daughter that might not otherwise surface in the conference. We must communicate the fact that we are willing to listen and value the parents' point of view which demonstrates school support for the student and the student's family. During this part of the process, teachers and administrators must refrain from commenting and offering opinions and allow the parents to speak and, in essence, "get some things off their minds." Often parents bring to conferences agenda items which they sense that they may not get an opportunity to adequately express. Not being provided this opportunity may result in significant parent frustration and defocus that could result in a less than successful parent conference. This problem can easily be averted by giving parents an uninterrupted opportunity to answer some questions and make some statements about and on behalf of their child. By listening to and weighing the parent comments, the teacher or administrator obtains additional information in support of or in conflict with whatever conclusions the teachers and administrators hold regarding that student.

Part Three: Reinforcement

The third part of the conferencing process features the second of the "**3 Rs**" which is **reinforcement**. Following the **recall** segment of the parent conference, the teacher can shift the conference focus to the **reinforcement** portion. **Reinforcement** refers to the identification and sharing of skills, behaviors, circumstances, characteristics, and abilities that the student possesses or exhibits for which they need to be positively complimented. The thought here is to point out to the parents positive things about their child that we wish to make apparent to both the parents and the child. The goal is to communicate that the student has some very positive things going for him/her, and to strengthen by reinforcement those behaviors through this identification and sharing process. Sharing positives also keeps the conference positive and headed to the ultimate objective of identifying and creating an action plan to assist the students in the areas which need improvement. To share these positives is particularly crucial to provide a balance of positives (**glow comments**) with the areas of concern (**grow comments**) that the teacher has identified and of which the parent must be made aware during the **review** portion of the conference.

To this point in the conference, the parents have been made to feel comfortable (hi-line, feel fine, outline) by the teacher or the administrator, have been actively listened to (recall) and now have had the opportunity to receive some specific positive feedback about their child (reinforcement). Too many conferences are set up and conducted with the sole purpose in mind of outlining deficiencies, problems, or concerns, often with 2-3 or more staff in attendance. How overwhelming and emotionally distressing that can be for parents, particularly when all the information they hear from several sources is negative.

In sharing with the parents the items that we wish to compliment the student for doing, the teacher should encourage the parent to share this information with his/her son or daughter at the first opportunity. It is wise to present that list of **glow comments** in writing to the parent. Kids are very interested in knowing what was discussed at these sessions. To facilitate this, the teacher can provide the parents(s) with a printed list of these compliments or the parents can take notes or jot down their thoughts for future reference.

Part Four: Review

The fourth part of the conferencing process features the third of the "Rs" which is the **review** portion of the conference. The conference may have been necessitated because the teacher or administrator has identified some academic weaknesses, deficiencies, or behavior concerns that need to be addressed. At this point it should be stressed that the concerns regarding the student were arrived at thoughtfully and carefully and are rooted in the school's desire to do what is best for the student. What we are **reviewing** here is not only the identification of the concern but the **outline of a plan** that we have developed to address the issue or concern. The identification of the concern is both obvious and easy. The more difficult task is how to successfully address the identified concern through a plan of action or a behavioral contract.

Let us digress here for the purpose of offering a **caution** about the conferencing process. It is often unfortunate that parent conferences deteriorate into a problem sharing or complaint session only. It is in these sessions that the conversation focuses exclusively on the child's problems or the problems that the child is creating. It is in these types of meetings that frustration and, at times, emotions can run high if the primary focus is solely on problem identification and problem clarification and no discussion of remediation ensues. As a result of these types of meetings the parents or guardians are left generally with the message that they now know what's wrong with the child and that they (the parents or guardians) should immediately go home and do something to fix the child's problems so as to eliminate or minimize the problems at school in the future. Let's examine an appropriate analogy here.

In the medical field we use an appointment with the appropriate personnel often for the purpose of addressing a specific health-related concern. Our goal in doing so is to clarify and pinpoint what seems to be the nature of the health problem and to arrive at a course of action to treat that concern. In other words, we would like our health care professional to outline a plan to treat our identified ailment. How distressing it would be for us to spend time with our doctor only to find out that all that they did was share that, "yes, you do have an identified medical or health concern. Now, you must go home and plan to treat the ailment so that you can become a healthy and thus happy and productive human being." As silly and ridiculous as this might sound, this is often the message that we (teachers and administrators) are sending to the parents as a result of a visit to the school and as a result of a parent conference: "Okay, parent, we've outlined the concerns and/or detailed the problem, now do something about it. We expect results and improvement." We need to outline our concerns for the parent as part of the "review" section of the conference. However, the crucial piece at this stage of the conference has to be the sharing of the plan that we have designed to improve, remediate, or fix whatever we previously shared as the concern or deficiency.

In this **review** section of the parent session we should be prepared to detail the plan that we have in mind to help the student. We want to have the parent exit this conference clearly understanding the procedures and steps that we plan to implement to cause improvement (a plan of action). It should be specified, focused, positive and consistent. In some situations it may be the "behavior teaching" approach outlined in earlier sections of this book. In other instances it may be providing instructional support through a tutorial. It further might be specific changes in a class schedule. It could be a system of accountability between home and school where parents need to see and sign-off on an assignment(s) or assignment book or homework or projects. There could be regularly scheduled in-school meetings for the student with a mentor or counselor. There could be a specific intervention strategy that is to be employed when things get out of hand or there are uncontrolled student outbursts. In some more extreme cases, the need to design and implement a specific "shaping plan" (**behavior contract**) to improve performance or behavior through an incremental approach while carefully utilizing reinforcers is appropriate. The parent, nonetheless, deserves the right to know and understand the plan. As an extension of the plan it should also be communicated that the key school personnel will be in regular contact with the parent to provide an ongoing progress report. It's through this regular communication that updates and modifications to the plan can be shared with the parents.

Often as part of the conferencing, parents will look to teachers for suggestions as to what they might do to assist and support their child's instructional efforts and school experience. How can I help my son or daughter with schoolwork/homework? Is there something that we could do to help him/her prepare for tests? Again, they are looking to us as experts for answers to these very important questions, and we must be ready with the answers, or in the immediate absence of answers, to take the time to find appropriate answers for the parents.

Part Five: Closing

The final part of the conferencing process is the **closing**. In this part, we want to do three very important tasks in order to insure the success of the plan that we've created with the parent. First, we want to answer any and all questions the parent has about the steps of the action plan, the plan timeline, the evaluation criteria, who is responsible for what steps in the plan, and the ongoing communication process between the parent and teacher or administrator. Second, we want to run a **closure** on the conference. Each party will have a brief opportunity to think about the essence of the conference and then briefly, in turn, state those thoughts to the others in attendance. Lastly, we want to thank the parents for their time and efforts in helping you manage their child's educational and social/behavioral progress. If appropriate, the setting up of a subsequent meeting could be decided at this time.

All in all, the parent-teacher conference is about the plans you make to facilitate that student's progress and success in school and life. It is important to note here that some problems are of a serious enough nature that additional professional help may be necessary. We encourage you not to hesitate if that is the case and to help the parents find the necessary professional help. Lending your support to the parents can be a major encouragement to them and of tremendous assistance in taking the first step toward seeking additional help for their child.

Let's shift our focus now and take a look at some strategies that can help parents assist their child in being successful.

Assisting Children with Homework

Parents are constantly looking for advice when it comes to assisting their children with homework or other schoolwork related items. Teachers are frequently asked to provide parents with ideas respective of these parental needs. It is important to note that today there are many resources available to parents when it comes to seeking and providing their children with assistance for school. Easy access to professional learning centers and online tutors now puts parents in a more proactive state of mind when it comes to their children's success in school. We want to add to these resources by offering some ideas of our own that parents can consider using as strategies and suggestions for providing assistance and structure in order to help kids be successful in school. These strategies include: providing the students with a calendar of weekly tasks and activities, emphasizing and teaching the concept of neatness, working on time management skills and supervising homework, and providing a specific time and place for homework. Let's look at each of these strategies individually beginning with a calendar of weekly tasks and activities.

Calendar of Weekly Tasks and Activities

Helping your child create a calendar of weekly tasks or activities that covers the days of the week from Sunday to Saturday (see Figure 11) can go a long way in teaching important life skills to youngsters such as how to manage work time, how to meet deadlines, how to keep track of work progress, how to keep track of activities and obligations, and how to manage leisure time. The calendar, which should be filled out or completed in advance by the student, could look something like what we've included in **Figure 11**. Across the top of the calendar are the days of the week for a 7-day stretch.

Down the left-hand column should be the time slots, starting with the time slot that represents school dismissal time. The ending time should be the time slot that represents the time that would be the typical bedtime for that youngster. Creating vertical columns of the days and horizontal columns of one-hour time blocks will create a calendar grid as you see in Figure 11.

The parents can then have their youngster fill in the blocks of time for the corresponding day by entering activities for each day of the week. Having a child fill out the calendar for the week helps the child create the mental framework for the week by forecasting and focusing on what events and activities are occurring during that time frame. The next step is to prominently post the calendar so it communicates to all members of the household what's in store for the week. If homework has been slotted for a specific time block, it is easier for the parents to hold their child to that homework time block. In the hectic world of parents and kids this process of calendar management tends to get kids focused and to cause them to be more organized and productive. While some young people are more adept or are "quicker studies" with respect to this organizational piece, we must remember that none of us is born organized. Organization is a learned skill. So, make no assumptions about whether or not your child is "mentally" organizing his/her days and weeks. It is very important that we teach our children a process and the skills to manage their own schedules. Parents should take the lead on this one. In addition, since we learn best with modeling and practice, it would be extremely beneficial if the parents likewise create their own personal weekly calendars so that the children see how adults manage time and events in their busy lives as well.

Figure 11: Calendar of Weekly Tasks and Activities

Jenna's Calendar of Weekly Tasks or Activities for Week of ____________________________

Day Time	Monday	Tuesday	Wednesday	Thursday	Friday	Saturday	Sunday
2:30	School dismissal	School dismissal	School dismissal	School dismissal	School dismissal	Homework	
3:00	Soccer		Soccer	Soccer Game	Friend's House	Homework	
4:00	Soccer		Soccer	Soccer Game	Friend's House		
5:00				Soccer Game			
6:00	Dinner	Dinner	Dinner	Dinner	Dinner	Dinner	**Dinner**
7:00	Homework	Homework	Church Youth Group	Homework		TV time	**Family Night**
8:00	Computer Project		Church Youth Group	Computer Project		TV time	**Family Night**
9:00	TV time	TV time	TV time	TV time	TV time	TV time	**Family Night**
10:00	**Bedtime**	**Bedtime**	**Bedtime**	**Bedtime**	**Bedtime**	**Bedtime**	**Bedtime**

Neatness

Emphasizing that neatness makes a difference is an important parental responsibility. The appearance of any product when given a first glance by the teacher can certainly provide an edge if that product is neat and attractive. Ask your child to describe in his/her own words what the teacher expects with respect to neatness and attractiveness. The following questions may assist you in having that conversation.

1. What does a "neat" paper look like?
2. If you were the teacher, would you describe this paper (the child's paper) as "neat"?
3. What parts of this paper are neat? Why would they be considered neat?
4. What parts of this paper are not neat? Why would those parts be considered not neat?
5. For those parts which are not neat, what could you do to make them neater?
6. How can I help you get started on that process?

As with the other strategies for assisting kids, the strategy for neatness will take both specificity (what does neatness look like?) and consistency (has neatness become, and is it continuing to be, a permanent feature in the work of my child?). You as a parent will need to be constantly monitoring your child's work for this important characteristic.

There is a very significant lesson to be learned from this process, and that lesson is: "You only have one chance to make a first impression."

Time Management and Homework Supervision

It is vitally important in the early going (particularly with younger students) that parents take a more active role in the management of homework time and effort. When assisting children with homework, it is advisable to have them work on school work in short manageable blocks of time with short breaks in between. Getting started on homework can be a struggle for kids particularly when the task at hand (homework, project, etc.) seems overwhelming in terms of task size or perceived time required for completion. The use of a digital timer (cooking timer) can be very helpful here. Identify your child's focus limit by asking the child how long she/he thinks they can actively do quality work before needing a break. Be reasonable here and remember the focus limitations of preadolescents and adolescents. For elementary students 10 to 15 minutes might be a reasonable focus limit. For secondary students 20 to 30 minutes might be more appropriate. However, you know your child, so do your best not to over- or underestimate his/her needs and abilities. Set the timer for the length of time you have identified. Encourage the youngster to work as hard as he or she can on the activity until the timer goes off and then he/she will be able to take a short break (example: 5 minutes) and get away from the work briefly (have a snack, walk around, do exercises, read for fun, etc.). Reset the timer following the break and have the child work for another block of time. Repeat the process as needed. It is extremely difficult for any of us to sit and focus nonstop on an activity for prolonged blocks of time and remain productive while producing a quality product. To meet those basic needs, it is most advisable to break the work down into manageable "chunks" and to undertake the work one "chunk" at a time. In the beginning the parent should assist in the time management strategies with the eventual goal of turning time management over to the child when the child is ready to assume that responsibility. Parents should monitor discreetly the working process from a short distance (like the next room) and not right next to the child. The child needs to acquire the confidence to do the work on his/her own. However, when help is needed, parents should provide assistance by answering questions, providing encouragement and remaining in the vicinity to assure the child that help is available if needed. Your primary role is to encourage the child -- not do the work for the child. You want your children to feel good about themselves and about their ability to competently complete the work. The Amish have a wonderful proverb by which they live: *"A positive self-worth comes from feeling capable."* One of your important tasks as a parent is to orchestrate opportunities for your child to learn to how to be capable.

Providing a Time and Place for Homework

As part of the ongoing school experience, students are going to be consistently bringing home various assignments to work on, both long-term and short-term. Setting the stage for where the schoolwork needs to be done is a critical part of that ongoing process. It is recommended that the choice of location be well established (same place most of the time). This location should be as free from distractions as is possible. Some examples of distractions are television, radio, CD player, video games, noisy and high-traffic areas in the home, etc. To facilitate the successful completion of the schoolwork, the materials that might be required should be in that schoolwork location. The following is a basic list of **common materials/equipment** to which students frequently need access during their homework time.

Common Homework Materials/Equipment List

- ☐ pens and pencils
- ☐ paper
- ☐ tape
- ☐ stapler
- ☐ construction paper
- ☐ paper clips
- ☐ magic markers
- ☐ crayons
- ☐ three-hole punch
- ☐ string
- ☐ scissors
- ☐ hi-liters
- ☐ dictionary
- ☐ glue, glue stick
- ☐ rulers
- ☐ eraser
- ☐ calculator
- ☐ computer

When pursuing schoolwork a major inhibitor (and sometimes excuse) to the successful completion of the assignment is the lack or unavailability of the necessary materials. Providing these items removes the hurdle or the excuse. If a specific location is not realistic at a home site (desk, room, etc.), the materials could be stored in a container and brought to the spot where the student will be working on the assignments. Some examples might be the living room, grandma's house, bedroom, den, etc. Something as simple as a cardboard box or a plastic container will do nicely. These helpful hints and strategies further reinforce the notion to the students that you are here to assist them in being successful.

The next section is an important one with respect to dealing with behaviors at home. For us, we have lived by the axiom, **"If you want it – teach it!"** That applies not only to classroom behaviors, but to home behaviors as well.

Managing Behaviors at Home

The process of teaching behaviors for classroom and school use discussed in Section One can also be applied at home. For example, you might teach your children how to do the dishes, make their beds, clean their rooms, or how to behave at the supermarket. In each instance, the process remains the same. It is important that you make no assumptions when teaching procedures or behaviors. You should not assume that the child knows how to correctly exhibit the effective and efficient behaviors necessary to be successful in the situation or at a certain task. We call this process, "**If you want it - teach it!**" The intended instructional outcome is ***focus***. We further define these ideas as a process designed to help kids be successful by substituting self-control in place of parent control. Let's review the steps to teaching a behavior.

Step #1 Brainstorm the Behaviors or Expectations and Determine and Teach the Content

To initiate the behavior teaching process, you will need to brainstorm a list of specific behaviors or expectations that you wish to see exhibited on the part of your children that are essential to the successful operation of your home. In addition to the examples of home behaviors listed above, others might include how to keep your room organized, how to take out the trash, how to mow the lawn, how to take care of a pet, how to come home on time, and a myriad of other essential behaviors which, when used, make home a more orderly, predictable, safe and efficient place to be.

Once you have brainstormed the appropriate or expected behaviors, you will then need to decide which of these should be taught first and an approximate timeline by which others will also be taught and implemented. As you make this decision, keep the **three step maximum concept** in mind and consider teaching no more than two or three behaviors the first week, and then add one or two more per week until your list of essential behaviors have all been taught. Remember, when children are very little (under 6 years of age), behaviors must be taught non-stop for months.

After identifying the desired behavior to be taught (i.e. doing the dishes) you will need to list all the items of information you can identify that your children need to know about this behavior. Most importantly, this list will include each of the steps in this behavior that are necessary for success. This list will be the content of the lesson for teaching that identified behavior or expectation. Your brainstormed list will then need to be reordered to reflect the order or sequence (**successive approximations**) in which a behavior is to be taught. You will then need to identify your **expected outcomes** that result from the correct and consistent use of the behavior.

After completing the first parts of Step #1, you will need to teach your procedure to your child or children. During the teaching session, first share the learning objective for the session. It might sound like this: "Children, today you are going to learn how to wash, dry and put away the dishes." Next, share the rationale as to why this behavior is important. The rationale might sound like this: "The reason we are undertaking this lesson is so that we all share the workload required to keep our home running smoothly." Then, share your pre-determined sequence of the steps of the behavior and other relevant information with your children as part of what you are teaching them. This is where your **modeling** (Step #2) of the behavior (saying it while showing it) comes into play. Children will remember more of this behavior if they can both see and hear it. It is also crucial during this teaching session that you adhere to the **5-1 Rule** or **10-2 Rule** and frequently **check for understanding** of one part before moving on to the next part. Next, we recommend that you also share your expected outcomes from using this behavior. In other words, what will be the resulting effects in our home when we all use this behavior correctly and consistently? Finally, following this information sharing, we recommend that you run a **closure** of the content and correct sequence for this behavior to ensure accuracy before moving on to modeling the behavior (Step #2).

Step #2 Model the Behavior

As you pursue the steps in teaching the identified behavior, each behavior will need to be modeled so that each child will have a clear picture of what is expected (i.e. how the behavior looks and sounds). The model must be 100% accurate. Parents should do the modeling themselves first.

Depending upon the age of the child or children, you may find it necessary to model the various elements of the behavior that you are teaching in blocks of two or three items (remember the **three step maximum concept**). This will be determined for the most part by the ability and, in some instances, the ages of the children. Remember, you want them to be successful in reproducing the behavior, so do not give them more than they can handle in any one modeling session. Again, following the modeling, we recommend that you run a **closure** of the content and correct sequence for this behavior to ensure accuracy before moving on to the child's practice session (Step #3).

Step #3 Practice the Behavior

This is the key element in the teaching a behavior process if you desire the behavior to be consistently exhibited. This practice session will immediately follow your modeling of the behavior. You will want your children to **practice** the task while you monitor and provide feedback (coaching) for their actions. The children, as a group or individually, can practice a single element, a group of elements, or the whole process or behavior. You should monitor their progress and make appropriate adjustments. Throughout the practice sessions, children must receive specific and immediate **knowledge of results** (feedback) in a positive atmosphere. It is important for the children to **hear, see** and **feel** what the job entails if you really want it done correctly and remembered with certainty. Children should continue to practice until you see them able to do the behavior with reasonable accuracy given that this may be their first exposure, and with consideration of their ages and the complexity of the task. Again, how much practice is a parent decision based on ability, complexity of the task, considering attention spans, the ages and the maturity levels of the children. **Remember:** short bursts of practice will result in significant **quantities** of practice overall, and it will increase **quality** when the increments are small and time durations short.

Step #4 Reinforce the Behavior

If the children have struggled in the practice session to produce the behavior as you described and modeled, you need to indicate that the behavior is not quite what you want. Provide specific points (feedback) as to where the behavior broke down and then ask your children to watch and listen as you teach and model it again, emphasizing that you know that they can do it this time. Following the correct performance of the behavior by the children, the parent needs to reinforce the behavior using verbal and/or non-verbal reinforcers such as, "Nice job demonstrating that you can wash, dry and put the dishes away properly." Or, "You're a class act, and as a result you make our jobs easier and more efficient! Thank you!" Or, "Keep it up! I know you can continue to do this!"

Step #5 Re-teach the Behavior

As you may know, or have experienced, some children fail to deliver on the expected and taught behavior despite having gone through Steps #1 through #4. When confronted with this circumstance the child or children in question need to have the behavior re-taught to them. This re-teaching will take place at a time that is valued by the individual (i.e. play time, television viewing time, phone time, video game playing time, etc.).

In the process of establishing the time for this "remedial" session, the children need to know that you recognize that they are having difficulty with the desired behavior. As a result of this difficulty, you are going to assist them by re-teaching it so that they can be successful. In addition, the children need to clearly understand the fact that, if they do not get it during the first re-teaching session, you will continue to re-teach the behavior, on their valuable time, until they are successful. In other words, "I will continue to re-teach on your valued time each day for a short period until you get the behavior correct.

However, I know that it will not be necessary because you are capable and, as a result, will get it the first time."

By stating your objectives, you clearly identify for your children their need to be accountable and responsible and that you will be persistent with your expectations that all the children comply with the correct and consistent use of the expected behaviors. As an aside, we frequently call this re-teaching session a **seminar** in order to identify it as a learning opportunity and not a "punishment." We've also heard it referred to as a "camp" or a "clinic" or a "workshop." These terms assist in distinguishing the **seminar** from other consequences such as withholding or loss of a privilege, loss of certain decision-making freedoms, loss of free time, etc. You should not want your children to see the **seminar** as punishment. However, you do want your children to view the **seminar** as one of the pieces of the process the parent uses to hold children accountable for their home behaviors, and their behaviors in other important places such as church, other children's homes, the supermarket, the mall, restaurants, etc. It is important to note that parents should underscore this point (**seminar** is instructional not punitive) as you work through Steps #2, #3 and #4. For example, as part of Step #1, you might state: "As a part of teaching this specific behavior, I know that you will be able to successfully deliver on doing the dishes properly [or whatever behavior you're teaching]. However, on the off chance that you cannot, I am prepared to help you by re-teaching you on your valued time." **The re-teaching time should only be as long as it takes for the child to show you the behavior correctly -- probably only a few minutes.** Any time longer than that would appear as punishment to the child and could be lost as an instructional opportunity. Once the process is complete to your satisfaction, periodically thank your children for the good job they are doing and state how this contributes to keeping your and their home a more organized and pleasant place. This will underscore the importance and reinforce the desirable behavior. The frequency with which this is done will vary a bit depending upon the makeup of the specific child. Nonetheless, it needs to occur with regularity. On occasion, you may need to review the steps or content with the children. This is particularly true with younger or less motivated children. By revisiting Steps #2, #3 and #4, you will find that the children will tend to deliver the desired behavior in a consistent manner. Periodic review is essential to positively affect both accuracy and long-term memory. Just as in schools teachers systematically and periodically review content in the academic curriculum, parents should systematically review content from the home procedural and social skills arenas as well.

Next, we want to share some important information about using the **seminar** process.

Criteria for Getting Kids Ready

When deciding that children need a re-teaching session, it is important to keep the following ideas in mind.

1. **Be consistent** with the re-teaching sessions with all your children. Lack of consistency may appear to be favoritism and is the breeding ground for arguments.
2. **Be dispassionate**. It is important that you keep this businesslike and not make it personal by bringing in unproductive emotions and attitudes. This is not a time to lecture the child. The sole intent of the seminar is to re-teach the behavior.
3. **Never use sarcasm or ridicule** during this or any teaching session. Sarcasm and ridicule become weapons that injure the self-esteem of the person who becomes the target of the sarcasm or ridicule. It creates significant ill feelings and makes the entire behavior teaching process very difficult to manage.
4. **Be professional** by approaching the child who needs the re-teaching in private and telling her or him that because she/he has been unsuccessful in [name specific behavior here], he/she has earned a "seminar" at the following specific time. There is no need to humiliate the child by publicly announcing that he/she has "earned a seminar." We want to emphasize that the child **earned** the seminar by not complying with the behavioral objective; you did not **give** the seminar to her/him.
5. Remember that it is **the behavior that is bad, not the student**. Attack the behavior, not the child.
6. Once you've completed the "seminar," tell the child you will continue to re-teach him/her during **seminars over and over again until he/she gets the behavior correct**. We recommend the use of this statement: "If you have trouble getting it right again, don't worry, I'll help you get it right during the next seminar."

7. **Remain consistent** with your process. Develop a reputation with your children that you expect correct behavior and that you will always follow up inconsistent or incorrect behavior with a re-teaching **seminar**.

In the next section we will offer some advice to parents and teachers about the phenomenon of bullying at school.

Dealing with Bullying at School

The phenomenon of bullying, whether at school or elsewhere, has reached pandemic proportions. We have made an unfortunate discovery about bullying: in many if not most of the cases we've seen or of which we've heard, bullying has been so narrowly defined that most people believe bullying means only physical aggression. In our research into the phenomenon of bullying, the experts tell us otherwise. Bullying may be defined as any act of aggression, violence or the threat of violence – physical, verbal, non-verbal, emotional, mental, psychological, or social – where one person or a group of people attempts to dominate or control another person or group of people. Three types of behavioral phenomena exist in the bullying mix: bullies, victims and on-lookers. We must state additionally that it is not only kids who bully other kids, but sometimes adults bully kids and less frequently, kids bully adults and adults bully other adults. We've regretfully seen school venues where a kid or group of kids has taken control of a school, if not overtly, at least covertly. Since bullying in schools touches the lives of nearly every child in the school setting (approximately 14% are bullies, 16% or more are bullied and nearly 70% are witnesses or on-lookers), it also touches the lives of nearly every adult as well. Boys most commonly engage in physical bullying or taunting, while girls most commonly engage in what is termed "relational" bullying. We'd like to share some information here from two of the best sources we've discovered on this highly significant school issue. The first source is Dan Olweus, a researcher who describes the bullying phenomenon from his experiences as a psychologist in Sweden. The second is Stan Davis, a school counselor who, after becoming familiar with Olweus' work, decided to examine bullying from his own working experiences and design practical solutions to the bullying problem in schools. Both experts offer insightful and practical advice on dealing with the phenomenon of bullying in the school setting. Let's begin by looking at Olweus' research.

In his excellent and groundbreaking book ***Bullying in School*** (1993), Dan Olweus contributes the following facts from his research to the bullying dialogue:

1. Younger and weaker students are more often victims. Most bullies are older students.
2. A sharp drop in bullying occurs by 7th grade, reflecting the fact that 7th grade students being the youngest ones in the secondary/junior high school, have less "access" to "suitable victims" in lower grades to the same extent.
3. Almost twice as many students are bullied in school as on the way to and from school.
4. Nearly 14% of all students grades 2 though 9 report having bullied someone. Sixty to 70% of the students are not involved in bullying as targets or perpetrators, but they are bystanders.
5. Boys are more exposed to bullying than girls, and 80% of the bullying of boys is by boys.
6. When girls bully it is more frequently non-physical and primarily relational bullying, such as excluding others, starting rumors, extorting friendships, and severe ridicule.
7. Parents of students who are bullied or who are bullies are relatively unaware of the problem and seldom talk with their children about it.
8. School is without a doubt where most of the bullying occurs.
9. Teachers intervene to stop bullying only once in a while or almost never.
10. The greater the number of teachers actively supervising (during passing time, in hallways, restrooms, cafeterias and on playgrounds), the lower the level of bully/victim problems there are in a school.
11. Contrary to the myths commonly held, there is no evidence that aggressive behavior by boys is the result of poor performance / failure in school or low self-esteem.
12. Bullying can be viewed as a component of a more generally antisocial and rule-breaking (conduct-disordered) behavior pattern. From this perspective, it is

> natural to predict that youngsters who are aggressive and bully others run a clearly increased risk of later engaging in other problem behaviors such as criminal behavior and alcohol and drug abuse. Sixty percent of boys who characterized themselves as bullies in grades 6-9 had at least one conviction by the age of 24. Even more concerning is that 35 to 40% of former bullies had three or more convictions by age 24, compared to 10% of non-bullies.

Olweus concludes with this quote: "It is a fundamental democratic principle that every individual should have the right to be spared oppression and repeated, intentional humiliation in school and in society at large. No student should have to be afraid of going to school for fear of being harassed or degraded, and no parent should need to worry about such things happening to his or her child" (Olweus 1993).

The remaining question is what should be done about this systemic problem, which in some schools is epidemic. No school is truly without a bullying problem. The first step is to acknowledge what is actually happening in terms of how students treat each other. In the absence of a true sense of community in classrooms and schools where civility, caring, and advocating for each other exists, bullying will occur. The next step is to stop enabling or excusing this type of behavior by ceasing to give it one of the following familiar labels:

"It's a rite of passage -- everyone gets bullied."

"Boys will be boys." Or, "Girls will be girls."

"They're just having some fun. They don't mean anything by it."

"Bullying builds character."

"He's just asking for it by being such a wimp."

"I was bullied, and I turned out all right."

"Life isn't fair. The sooner kids learn that lesson, the better."

The final step is to develop a procedure to deal assertively with any act of aggression that occurs in your school. In turn, this makes your school a safe place, a place where people can be who they are and a place where people are free of ridicule and/or any type of harm.

In his book ***Schools Where Everyone Belongs*** (2005), educator Stan Davis offers several poignant recommendations regarding preventing the problem of bullying in schools (which includes places such as on the way to and from school, on school buses), and other venues where supervision is limited or non-existent.

1. **Establish clearly defined school-wide behavior expectations rather than rules that only describe general principles.** An example of a clearly defined rule: "No teasing. Teasing is name-calling, starting rumors, gestures, or other actions that are likely to make students feel badly about themselves." This is more effective than the general principle: "We will treat each other with respect." Clearly defined rules are more likely to lead to consistency among staff members as well.
2. **Use predictable and escalating consequences for aggression rather than creating a unique consequence for each student and each situation.** When there are inconsistent consequences for bullying, bullying is likely to continue. Planned, rubric-based consequences take much less time to administer and thus can be used more consistently. Predictable and consistent consequences help young people learn from each other's misdeeds. When two different students do exactly the same thing (referring here to aggressive or threatening behavior) yet receive consequences of different severity, cause and effect learning is jeopardized, not to mention a strong case of unfairness or showing partiality becoming an issue.
3. **Maintain a positive emotional tone between adults and youth rather than treating students with anger and frustration.** When consequences come from a rubric, when they are earned rather than given, and when there are planned next steps if the student continues to choose aggression, there is no need for adults to use anger as a behavior management tool. When adults monitor their own feelings of frustration (it's professional business – it's not personal), look for small signs of progress, and model friendly and respectful communication, they are more able to develop positive relationships with at-risk youth who are more likely to respond in kind.
4. **Acknowledge positive actions rather than ignoring positive behavior or use person-based praise.**

When school staff point out students' positive behavior using specific descriptive language, students are more likely to repeat this behavior. We may say, "I noticed that you walked away instead of hitting when you were out in the game." "I saw you sit with Susan when she was alone at lunch." Or, "You complimented Bobby." And more effectively, when we help students see the natural positive outcomes of their actions, we can be even more effective. We may say, "I noticed that you walked away instead of hitting when you were out in the game. You came back to the game and kept playing." Or, "I saw you sit with Susan when she was alone at lunch, and I saw her smiling." These types of feedback are very powerful reinforcers when used in a timely and appropriate manner.

5. **Provide structured opportunities for aggressive youth to think about their actions instead of using threats, lectures or anger.**
   When young people take responsibility for their actions and for hurting others, they strengthen conscience. When they realize what goals they were trying to reach by being aggressive and find other more appropriate ways to reach those goals, they learn to meet their needs in acceptable ways. They also learn the concept of cause and effect. My behavior (cause) has an effect on others and on me. Sometimes, that effect is not positive or acceptable.
6. **Work to develop a peer climate in which bystanders discourage bullying and in which peers befriend targets.**
   When the 60-85% of the school population – the bystanders – stop watching silently and start telling bullies to stop, inform adults about the problem, and reach out in friendship, bullying behavior becomes less damaging and less frequent. The best way to encourage youth to make these changes is for adults to model the behaviors for them by implementing effective discipline systems, recognizing positive behaviors, and spending time listening to, sharing enjoyment with, and validating all students. *[Note: **Informing** is not tattling. Informing is telling an adult something to help someone who is in trouble. **Tattling** is telling an adult something to get someone into trouble.]*

SECTION FIVE

7. **Protect targets and bystanders from repeated or retaliatory harassment.** Reducing the rate of bullying is the best support we can give targets. If we want young people to tell us about bullying, we have to make telling safe by using consequences for the harassment of youth who report bullying and who advocate for the victims.
8. **Help targets to reverse feelings of self-blame and to feel powerful.** "First they bully you, and then you bully yourself," a student told Stan Davis in Florida. Targets often begin to believe (a self-fulfilling prophecy) what the bullies say about them: that they are stupid, ugly, or fat, for instance. Helping targets to see themselves more positively often takes time. They need to feel included and find ways to experience their strengths. As targets learn to brainstorm and apply problem-solving steps, they feel more competent and less helpless.
9. **Help targets build friendships.** Youth have revealed that social isolation is the most painful part of being bullied. "If no one stands up for you, you feel like you don't exist," said one teenager in Ohio. We can encourage peers to reach out in friendship and help targets and other isolated youth participate in that friendship. Davis offers many excellent ideas in his book on how parents and teachers can help children build friendships.
10. **Recognize and build on the strengths and accomplishments of your school community.** When school administrators, school boards, parents and communities recognize the positive impacts of programs and practices being used to stop bullying in a school, teachers and other school staff members as well as students are more likely to continue using those strategies. When schools track improvements and show everyone involved that what they are doing is making a positive impact, it is more likely that people will stay committed to a bullying prevention program.

In addition to these two excellent studies on bullying and bully prevention ideas, we recommend the reading of two additional books. One is Barbara Coloroso's ***The Bully, the Bullied and the Bystander*** (2003) written more specifically for parents. Coloroso, a parent, an educator and a consultant, offers useful, honest, practical and applicable advice for dealing with the problem directly. The second is ***Bullying in American Schools*** by Anne G. Garrett. Garrett is a veteran school administrator with much professional experience and success in developing and ensuring safe schools for children, adolescents and school personnel. Along with the ideas of Olweus and Davis, these two books include specific and identifiable symptoms manifested by victims and bullies and offer hundreds of effective recommendations for both intervention and prevention. It is vital that parents and educators remain vigilant in watching for the signs that a child is being bullied. The most important intervention is to spend time with your child and really listen to what he/she is saying. You have to frequently "read between the lines" to identify trouble in the making or trouble existing. Don't give up on bullies either. Find out what is prompting their behavior and seek professional help to deal with the issues and problems that put young people in a position to be aggressive and seek out power over others. The primary reason that the existence of bullying is frequently denied by schools and school personnel is not because they don't want to deal with the issue, but because they don't know how to deal with it effectively. If schools admit bullying is taking place, they will have to deal with it in a direct fashion. The "how" to deal with bullying presents the greatest problem of all. Not knowing what to do is extremely frustrating. If more schools knew effective ways to intervene (such as those presented by the experts mentioned above), more schools would be stepping up to address the problem.

Final Thoughts on Bullying

Here are three final points on bullying. First, in the real world, adults are protected by law from assault, verbal harassment, sexual harassment, slander, libel and stalking. Perpetrators of these acts are dealt with through the criminal justice system. This begs the question: *Why then is it that society in general does not provide these same basic human rights to all children in schools?*

Second, if students who are bullied are not protected by the adults (administrators, teachers, parents) involved, the bullied person may have no other alternative but to resort to the use of bullying or other very aggressive behaviors in order to protect himself. When this happens, we have created another set of bullying problems.

Third, if you, as a parent, are not getting the school officials in your child's school to intervene to stop your child (and/or other children) from being bullied or being a bully, or you're being told that bullying doesn't occur when you know it is happening, or you are being told to move your child to another school, or you are being told that it's your child's fault, you may need to enlist the help of local law enforcement officials for a solution.

Tragically, physical bullying (direct bullying), when not stopped, can and has led to acts of violence and suicide. Also tragically, relationship bullying (indirect bullying), when not stopped, has led to victim drug and alcohol use, withdrawal, depression, promiscuity, eating disorders, and suicide. Solving this complex problem takes a coalition of adults and students who believe that schools do not have to mirror the ills of society in the interest of "toughening kids up" for the real world to come. School should be a safe haven for kids, away from the ills of society, where kids can learn in safety, believe that they belong, can make mistakes in a safe setting in order to grow, and can enjoy what it means to have high quality relationships with other children and with caring adults who are positive role models.

In Section Six we will examine some closing thoughts about teaching, learning, and classroom success.

Section Six: Closing Thoughts

Teaching is among the most rewarding of all occupations and one that is fraught with energy and excitement (and exhaustion!). It is an awesome responsibility and one that cannot ever be taken lightly. Most teachers we've met are more than ready and able for the intensities of the classroom and the stamina required for teaching. None of these specific characteristics needed by capable teachers are possessed by accident. Great teachers work at being great teachers all the time. It is ironic that many non-teachers view teaching as "something that anyone can do." In fact, most teachers feel both sadness and irritation when hearing or reading the quotation, "those that can – do; those that can't – teach." We only need to refer back to the *Public Agenda* survey of high school students (see Appendix E) to recall what teacher attributes high school students believe are positive. Teachers who exhibit those attributes consistently do so with a sense of mission and purpose – to make their students capable and successful. Those teachers are voracious readers who seek out ideas for improvement. They pay fees and expenses out of their own pockets to attend professional conferences to hear experts share ideas about all aspects of schooling. They attend classes and workshops for the purposes of growing their skills and dispositions for teaching and learning. They "talk shop" as often as possible to learn from the experiences of others. They listen to their students and legitimize student ideas by incorporating them into lessons as frequently as possible. We'd like to end using the same words of caution with which we began. As with any "how to" book, these ideas have worked extremely well in consistent practice for the authors, but there is no "magic" formula or prescription which takes the place of good practice built on techniques proven while working with learners of any age. We trust that you found some new ideas and had some of your own ideas about teaching and managing a classroom confirmed. Again, teachers must be **experts in the content they teach** and **in how teaching works**. This book is about encouraging positive change to achieve positive results. Remember: "if you always do what you've always done, you'll always get what you always got." Here's wishing you the results you want from teaching as well as the satisfaction of knowing that you are doing what is effective and efficient for each one of your students. You are a **Super Star Teacher**!

Section Seven: About the Authors

APL Associates

APL is an organization that has dedicated its focus and energies to working with professional educators. To this end we are committed to assisting educational organizations in planning and implementing a meaningful and ongoing staff development program. It is becoming increasingly evident that school districts and organizations that identify and implement comprehensive staff development programs are reaping some interesting and exciting dividends. Results include staff morale that is on the upswing, meaningful and positive communication, productive time on task management, improved planning and organization, consistent and positive classroom management, application of proven classroom instructional techniques and skills, and much more. Effective Schools research is clearly indicating that providing staff with a meaningful, practical and ongoing staff in-service is basic to realizing quality performance goals. APL not only develops and refines those skills that result in a more productive in-class program but also is committed to setting up and assisting in maintaining a follow-up process. APL Associates can provide an extensive listing of individuals and organizations that have had APL workshops.

We have had the pleasure of working with state organizations, regional education agencies, private schools, public schools, small rural school districts, and suburban and city districts. Our experiences have been extensive and wide-ranging. In each instance the feedback has been that APL is synonymous with quality. APL Associates has a wealth of experience in assisting districts in successfully planning for and realizing staff development goals, resulting in higher performance scores.

For more detailed information about APL and/or any of its exciting staff development/ in-service programs please contact:

APL ASSOCIATES
PO Box 250
Camillus, NY 13031
Telephone/Fax: (315) 672-5668
aplassociates@twcny.rr.com

The managing partners and key trainers for APL Associates have a rich background of experience that they bring to the sessions.

Jean T. Anastasio

Dr. Jean T. Anastasio has been a special education teacher and supervisor, regular education teacher, field coordinator of The Syracuse University Regional Resource Center, instructor for graduate and undergraduate programs at Syracuse University, Director of Pupil Personnel Services for a public school in New York state, and staff developer. Jean may be contacted through APL Associates or online at: http://www.aplassociates.com.

David J. Perry

David J. Perry has been a secondary classroom teacher of History, Department Chairman for social studies in the public schools, building principal at the middle school and junior high school levels, education professor in the State of New York University system, and staff developer. David may be contacted through APL Associates or online at: http://www.aplassociates.com.

Timothy J. Sharer

Timothy Sharer is a professor of education at Wayne State College in Nebraska. His teaching career spans four decades including 21 years as an educator at the K-12 level and 12 at the college level. For the last ten years, he has been working exclusively in teacher education. His higher education experiences include teaching undergraduate and graduate pedagogy courses in multicultural education, classroom management, instructional methods K-12, current issues and trends in education and serving as Director of the ***Northeast Nebraska Teacher Academy***. Contact information for Tim Sharer is:

Dr. Tim Sharer, Professor of Education
School of Education and Counseling
Wayne State College
1111 Main Street
Wayne, NE 68787
402.375.7380

The Northeast Nebraska Teacher Academy

The Northeast Nebraska Teacher Academy (***NENTA***) is a substitute teaching program built within a consortium of sixteen K-12 school districts, Wayne State College, Nebraska Educational Service Unit 1 and APL Associates. In this program, undergraduate juniors and seniors in the teacher education programs at Wayne State College are selected, prepared, certified and supported to serve as substitute teachers in the consortium school districts. Begun in the fall of 2000, this program has supplied over 450 substitute teaching days annually within those school district partners. Timothy Sharer serves as ***NENTA*** Director and was one of the two original designers of the program. Since the program's inception, APL Associates' Jean Anastasio and David Perry have served the ***NENTA*** as the primary staff development trainers for all the participants. Contact Tim Sharer for more information on the ***NENTA***.

Section Eight: Appendices

A: Instructional Skills

Name of Skill	*Outcome(s)*	*Definition*
Anticipatory Set	Focus Transfer	A mental process where the learner is asked to search his or her past for information that they have about that which is to be taught.
Active Participation	Rate & Degree	The consistent engagement of the minds of all the learners.
Checking for Understanding (CFU)	Retention	A mental process where the learner is asked to summarize his or her perception of what has been learned.
Feeling Tone	Focus	The psychological climate that the teacher creates.
Level of Concern	Focus	Increasing Anxiety or heightening the students' feelings to increase participation in a classroom activity.
Knowledge of Results	Focus	The immediate and specific feedback to the learner about his/her performance.
Interest	Focus	The activities that the teacher creates that are novel or vivid.
Practice	Retention Transfer	The consistent engagement of the learner in a repeated activity designed to correctly produce the desired outcome of product.
Modeling	Retention	The demonstration of a process or the examination of a product.
Reinforcement	Rate & Degree	A procedure using consequences to strengthen a desired behavior.
Shaping (Reinforcement Extended)	Retention	To positively reinforce successive approximations toward the new desired behavior.

Name of Skill	***Outcome(s)***	***Definition***
Closure	Retention	A mental process where the learner is asked to summarize his or her perception of what has been learned. Closure is the summative form of CFU.
If You Want It - Teach It!	Focus	A process designed to be successful by substituting self-control in place of teacher control.
Tell What and How	Focus Rate & Degree Transfer	A process of sharing instructional expectations or outcomes.
Manage Time to Facilitate Learning	Focus Rate & Degree	Strategies designed to facilitate the effective management of instructional time while assisting students in becoming better time managers.
Provide an Exit	Focus	A strategy designed to facilitate the human needs of youngsters in a structured instructional environment.
Clear Directions and Information	Focus	Strategies that address the question of how much information students can manage and the degree to which it is received accurately.
Classroom Conditions	Focus	Factors that we manage within the physical environment that impact instruction and learning.
Agenda	Focus Retention	A device used to inform learners of what concepts will be addressed during the lesson and how much time will be devoted to each concept.
Bell Ringer	Focus Retention	A strategy that asks the learners to recall information previously learned.

B: Four Basic Learner Outcomes of Instruction

1. ***Focus:*** *attending to the main idea(s)/concept(s)*

2. ***Rate & Degree****: pace & depth of content coverage*

3. ***Retention****: reliable recall of correct idea(s)/ concept(s)*

4. ***Transfer:*** *using knowledge/skills/attitudes in new context(s)*

C: Sample Lesson Plans for Teaching Behaviors

BEHAVIOR LESSON PLAN # 1: COMING PREPARED FOR CLASS

Behavior: Coming prepared for class

Brainstormed Elements: (samples)

- [ ] Textbook
- [ ] Textbook cover
- [ ] Notebook – type (spiral – 3 ring, etc.)
- [ ] Pen(s) – color ink
- [ ] Pencils:
    - [ ] type
    - [ ] sharpened
- [ ] Assignment book
- [ ] Paper
- [ ] Other related and relevant materials:
    - [ ] Hi-liters
    - [ ] Calculators
    - [ ] Trappers
    - [ ]
    - [ ]

Modeling: After previewing the elements of the behavior (verbally) the teacher can then model by holding up each required item for all to see. Following that demonstration the teacher can exit the room and then reenter with all the necessary materials so that all can again see.

Practice: Following the modeling of the behavior the teacher can then give a simple written quiz on the elements of coming prepared to class. At that point the teacher can indicate that the grade will be recorded as a regular test grade. The teacher should provide the opportunity for students to review for two minutes prior to the quiz. Following the in-class correction of the quiz the teacher can state that the quiz results clearly point out that each student has proven that they know what "coming to class prepared" means. Therefore there is no reason to think that each student cannot come prepared.

Further, the homework assignment for that night can be for the students to come prepared the next day with all the necessary materials. If the teacher should choose to take it a step further they can provide each student with a checklist to refer to as part of that assignment.

Reinforcement: For reinforcement purposes it would be desirable to make a comment or two the next day regarding how the students performed on the assignment of coming prepared to class. If there were students who failed to come to class with all the required materials, the teacher needs to privately communicate to those students that they need to see the teacher at the end of the class.

Reteaching / Retraining: For those students who did not comply, the teacher will provide a retraining session. During the session the teacher will go through step-by-step the exact same procedure that was followed when the behavior was taught originally in class.

The following guidelines for retraining must be followed:

[ ] Retraining must take place on the student's valued time (before school, after school, during recess, lunch, etc.)

[ ] Retraining should take only the time necessary to go through the behavior again step-by-step.

[ ] Retraining should occur as often as necessary with each student until the behavior is in place and then followed by some positive verbal feedback to the student individually.

[ ] This component of the teaching of a behavior process should be undertaken in an objective, non-confrontational manner. Remember: "It's business; it's not personal."

BEHAVIOR LESSON PLAN # 2: BE QUIET TRAINING (BQT)

Developed by Jeri C. Grant
General Brown Jr.-Sr. High School
Dexter, NY

In an effort to combat the increasing noise level and decreasing work ethic in my classroom, I created and implemented "BQT." "BQT" stands for "Be Quiet Training." The three steps in this process have aided me in the reduction of unnecessary noise as well as increasing productive class time.

The Three Stages are:

BQT Position # 1: Note Taking
Students are instructed to sit with their legs facing forward underneath their desks. Slouching is discouraged and good posture is recommended through demonstration. This position requires all students to write with one hand and raise the other hand to ask questions. This allows the student to keep taking notes. Their faces should alternate from the area that contains notes and back to their paper. This head movement eliminates many distractions from occurring in addition to any others being noticed.

BQT Position # 2: In Class Assignment
Because many students look at an in class assignment as a perfect opportunity to whisper to his/her neighbor, position of the body is once again reinforced. The head and eyes should be focused on the assignment while still maintain the posture recommended in BQT Position #1. Also, all work should be written using the dominant hand, while the other is raised for questions.

BQT Position # 2: Just Pay Attention
This behavior is called Just Pay Attention because that is the desired outcome. This should be used when the teacher is giving important information where not-taking is unnecessary. Once again, legs straight ahead and under the desk are a crucial detail that must be noted. Head up, shoulder back, and absolutely no slouching must be modeled and enforced. Hands may be clasped or flat on top of the desk. The mouth should be closed unless it is being used in direct communication with the teacher to ask or answer a question.

For each of these stages, the teacher must describe the action as well as model it. Being quiet and focused can be seen and NOT heard. After the students have been trained, it is important to remind them that this training never ends, and can be re-taught at any time.

D: Differential Reinforcement Matrix

Type	**Differential Reinforcement of Alternate Behavior DRA**	**Differential Reinforcement of Other Behavior DRO**	**Differential Reinforcement of Low Rate of Responding DRL**
Definition	The reinforcement of desirable behavior in order to increase the future likelihood that the desired behavior will continue to occur, and move the undesirable behavior to extinction.	Using a reinforcer when the problem behavior is absent to decrease the future likelihood that the undesirable behavior will continue.	Using a reinforcer when the rate of the problem behavior is reduced to a criterion level (an acceptable frequency).
Why Use It	To increase the frequency of desirable behavior and move undesirable behavior to extinction.	To decrease and ultimately eliminate the problem behavior through extinction.	To decrease an undesirable behavior to an acceptable limit (frequency).
When to Use It	When an undesirable behavior needs to be replaced by a desirable behavior.	After a specified interval of time in which the problem behavior does not occur, the reinforcer is delivered.	When a low rate of the problem behavior can be tolerated, or when the behavior is a problem only because of its high rate.
Key Questions	1. Do you want to increase the rate of desirable behavior? 2. Is the behavior already occurring at least occasionally?. 3. Do you have access to a reinforcer that you can deliver after the occurrence of the behavior?	1. Do you want to decrease to extinction the problem behavior? 2. Is the absence of the problem behavior occurring at least occasionally? 3. Do you have access to a reinforcer that you can deliver in the absence of the problem behavior?	1. Is DRL the appropriate type of Differential Reinforcement?
How to Use It	1. Define the desired behavior. 2. Define the undesirable behavior. 3. Identify the reinforcer. 4. Reinforce the desirable behavior immediately and consistently. 5. Eliminate reinforcement for the undesired behaviors. 6. Use intermittent reinforcement to maintain the target behavior. 7. Program for generalization (student use of the target behavior in all relevant situations.	1. Identify the reinforcer for the problem behavior. 2. Identify the reinforcer to use in the DRO procedure. 3. Choose the initial DRO Time Interval. 4. Eliminate the reinforcer for the problem behavior. DRO is similar to DRA except that no alternative behavior is identified and used to replace the problem behavior.	1. Identify the unacceptable target behavior. 2. Identify the acceptable level of the target behavior. 3. Choose the interval of time which should elapse between each occurrence of the behavior. 4. Decide whether to implement **full session** or **spaced responding** DRL. If timing is important then spaced responding DRL is most appropriate. 5. Inform the student of the procedure and the criterion of both time and acceptable frequency of the behavior. 6. Give feedback to the student on his/her performance. 7. Help the student learn strategies for self-monitoring.
Results	1. An increase in the future probability of the desirable behavior 2. A decrease in the future probability of undesired behavior.	Extinction of the problem behavior.	The undesirable behavior is reduced in frequency to a rate that is acceptable and tolerable.

E: *Public Agenda: What American Teenagers Think about Their Schools* (1996)

Public Agenda wanted to find out what characteristics students valued in teachers. The list includes the top ten characteristics that students identified as contributing "a lot" to their learning. In the A column are the percentages of the students surveyed who identified that characteristic as important. In the B column are the percentages of students who said the characteristics fit their own teachers.

Characteristic	A	B
Tries to make lessons fun and interesting.	78%	24%
Is enthusiastic about the subject they teach.	71%	29%
Knows a lot about the subject they teach.	71%	46%
Treats their students with respect.	69%	41%
Gives students a lot of individual help.	69%	41%
Uses hands-on and class discussion.	67%	22%
Explains lessons carefully.	66%	33%
Challenges students to do better.	66%	33%
Cares about students.	64%	30%
Knows how to handle disruptive students.	46%	29%

F: Course Goals Setting Framework

Student Name: **Course:**

Beginning of the Semester Goals and Strategies	
List the Grade You Intend to Earn in this Course.	
List Specifically What You Intend to Do in Order to Earn that Grade. (Examples are: attending class daily; completing your assignments with high quality; handing assignments in on time; fully participating in class activities and discussions, etc.)	
List Specifically What You Will Do to Help You Remember to Follow Your Plan. (Ex: include using the course syllabus/schedule; keeping a planner; plotting out assignments as to when due; when to begin; checkpoints, etc.)	
Select A Course Partner: The two of You Give Permission to each other to remind you of your Goals and encourage each other in your progress toward meeting them successfully.	**Name** **Email Address** **Phone Number(s)** **Best Time to Call You**

Mid-Term Self-Assessment of Goals and Strategies	
What is Your Current Grade in this Course?	
What Are You Currently Doing to Achieve the Grade You Want?	
What Behavior(s) Do You Need to Change or Add in Order to Achieve Your Goals? List them here.	
Has Your Course Partner Been Checking on Your Progress? How Frequently? Has it helped? How has it helped?	

End of Semester Self-Assessment of Goals and Strategies	
What Grade Did You Earn in this Course?	
What Did You Not Do or Think About that Kept You from Achieving the Grade You Originally Wanted?	
List the Behavior(s) You Will Need to Change in Order to Achieve Your Goals in the Future?	
How Has Your Course Partner Checking on Your Progress Been Helpful?	

SECTION EIGHT

G: Designing & Planning Effective Lessons: An APL Approach

Beginning Block (Prime Time 1)	**The first 7 to 10 minutes of a lesson which is the getting started part of any lesson. This may need to include roll taking and other "housekeeping" actions as necessary to keep the class organized.**
Bell Ringer Activity (1:00-2:00)	A job the teacher gives students to do immediately upon arriving in the classroom. This job (task) should be based on objectives learned either yesterday, or in the immediate past (last ten days).
Sharing the Agenda (0:30)	A posted schedule for that lesson. The order of topics and, if appropriate, the amount of time allotted for each topic/activity. This should be shared with students at the beginning of class.
Homework (5:00-7:00)	If homework is assigned and has an impact on today's lesson, it should be gone over as a class. Notice the abbreviated amount of time devoted to this activity. The amount of time available to go over homework will impact the amount of homework assigned.
Stating the Objectives (0:30)	The teacher must tell the students two important features of the lesson to follow: 1) What the students will know after the lesson 2) How the students will need to prove they learned it.
Middle Block	**This is where the majority of teaching and learning occurs in any lesson. This part varies in length but common ranges are somewhere between 15 to 70 minutes.**
Focus Activity (1:00-3:00)	This is designed to move students to a place mentally where they can eliminate distractions and begin the process of learning. The key strategy that works here is called Anticipatory Set. This strategy fosters student focus as they search their past for information that is relevant to this lesson.
Input: The Instructional Procedure (5:00 to 10:00 increments. It is recommended that this part be divided into segments of 3 to 10 minutes based on the students focus duration abilities)	Input Activities– may include a variety of processes such as teacher lecture and student note taking; viewing a video; listening to a sound recording; reading; researching; computer and other media sources; discovery, etc. During Input teachers must be aware of students' abilities to maintain focus based on students' developmental levels. Here is a basic rule of thumb in determining focus durations: o Kindergartners maximum focus time is about two to three minutes. o Grades 1-6 focus time gradually increases from three minutes to a maximum of about six or seven minutes by upper elementary. o Middle school (grades 6-8) focus time increases from six or seven minutes to a maximum of about nine or ten minutes by grade 8. o High school students focus duration increases from about nine to ten minutes to a maximum of about 12 minutes for the most capable students. These durations are estimates based on research. An individual's ability to maintain focus is based on his/her individual maturity and developmental level. It is extremely important that teachers implement the strategy of **Serial Positioning** requiring the application of the **10-2** or **5-1 Rules** in order to most positively influence *focus* and *retention.*
Checking for Understanding CFU	A process that teachers must use to determine what are the students' perceptions of what has just been taught and learned. For ***High School*** students this strategy should be employed at least once every 10 minutes using the **10-2 Rule**: teach no longer than 10 minutes and CFU for 2 minutes. Then resume the Input Activity. For ***Elementary School*** students this strategy should be employed at least once every 3 to 5 minutes using the **5-1 Rule**: teach no longer than 5 minutes and CFU for 1 minute. Then resume the Input Activity.
Interactive Strategies	This works in two ways. 1) The teacher interacts with individuals or groups to facilitate learning, or 2) Students interact with each other in small groups or full group to facilitate learning. Cooperative Learning, Teacher-Led Full Class Discussion; Leaderless Discussion; Think-Pair-Share; and Hands-On, and the **Interaction Sequence** are examples of Interactive Strategies.
Using On-the-Clock	Assigning and monitoring a specific amount of time that students have to perform a task or think about and respond to a question. On-the-Clock fosters better time management by teachers and reduces student procrastination and boredom. Using a timing device is the most accurate monitoring strategy.

Designing & Planning Effective Lessons: An APL Approach

Ending Block (Prime Time 2)	**The last 7 to 10 minutes of a lesson divided into two parts. During the first part the teacher asks each student to think about and summarize what he/she has learned in the lesson, and to share his/her responses (closure). During the second part the teacher guides the students in getting their homework started.**
Closure (1:00-4:00)	A student-centered process whereby the students are asked to summarize in their own words what they have learned during this lesson. Closure allows the teacher to determine what students have learned and to what extent they have learned it (Rate & Degree of Learning). Closure allows teachers to then determine whether to move on to the next objective or to reteach. Closure allows students to function metacognitively: What do I know? What do I still need to learn? How can I learn it?
Getting Homework Started (6-8:00)	It is important to get homework started before leaving class to 1) ensure student understanding of the task, and how to do it; and 2) make sure everyone gets started so that you can identify and address problems before students leave for the day.
Learning Assessment Formative Summative	Assessments are the formal means of evaluating what students have learned and the degree to which they've learned it. **Formative** is on-going and occurs within and at the end of every lesson. Quizzes, Bell Ringers, Checking for Understanding, Closure and Homework are Formative Assessments. **Summative** Assessments occur at the end of a major activity such as the end of a unit, at midterm, end of a semester, end of the school year, etc. Examples may include tests, projects, papers, presentations, portfolios, performances, etc.

SECTION EIGHT

H: References

Active Participation

Anderson, L.M. & Evertson C. (1978). Classroom organization at the beginning of school: Two case studies. Paper presented at American Association of Colleges for Teacher Education. Chicago.

Ausubel, D.P. (1960). The Use of Advanced Organizers in the Learning and Retention of Meaningful Material. *Journal of General Psychology.* 51: 267-272.

Bellack, A.A. (1966). *The Language of the Classroom.* New York: Teachers College Press.

Borg, W. (1969). The Minicourse as a Vehicle for Changing Behavior: The Research Evidence. San Francisco: Far West Laboratory for Educational Research and Development.

Brophy, J. (1979). Teacher Behavior and Student Learning. *Educational Leadership.* 37: 33-38.

Campbell, J. (1973). Pattern Analysis – A Macroscopic Development for Interaction Analysis. Paper presented at National Association for Research in Science Teaching. Chicago.

Crawford, W., King, C., Brophy, J., & Evertson, C. (1975). Error Rates and Question Difficulty Related to Elementary Children's Learning. Paper presented at American Educational Research Association. Washington, D.C.

Dalton, W. (1969). The Relationships between Classroom Interactions and Teacher Ratings of Pupils: An Exploration of One Means by Which a Teacher may Communicate Her Expectations. *Peobody Papers in Human Development.* 7: 6.

Dunkin, M. & Biddle, B. (1974). *The Study of Teaching.* New York: Holt, Rinehart and Winston.

Fagan, E., Hassler, D., & Szabo, M. (1981). Evaluation of Questioning Strategies in Language Arts Instruction. *Research in the Teaching of English.* 15 (3): 267-273.

Fredrick, W. (1977). The Use of Classroom Time in high Schools Above or Below the Median Reading Score. *Urban Education.* 1977: 459-464.

Hunter, Madeline. (1994). Mastery Teaching: Increasing Instructional Effectiveness in Elementary and Secondary Schools, Colleges and Universities. (Reprint). Thousand Oaks, CA: Corwin Press.

Kounin, J. (1970). *Discipline and Group Management in Classrooms.* New York: Holt, Rinehart & Winston.

Leinhardt, G., Zigmond, N., & Cooley, W. (1981). Reading Instruction and Its Effects. *American Educational Research Journal.* 18.

Melton, R.F. (1978). The Resolution of Conflicting Claims Concerning the Effect of Behavioral Objectives on Student Learning. *Review of Educational Research.* 48: 291-302.

Mills, S. R. et. al. (1980). The correspondence between teacher questions and student answers in classroom discourse. *Journal of Experimental Education.* 48: 194-204.

Pankratz, R. (1967). Verbal Interaction Patterns in the Classrooms of Selected Physics Teachers. In Amidon, E., & Hough, J. (eds) *Interaction Analysis: Theory, Research and Application.* Reading, PA: Addison Wesley.

Powell, D. & Eash, M. (1974). Secondary School Cases. In Walberg, H (ed). *Evaluating Educational Performance.* Berkeley, CA: McCutchan Publishing Corporation. 277-293.

Redfield, R. & Rousseau, E. (1981). A Meta-Analysis of Research on Teacher Questioning Behavior. *Review of Educational Research.* 51: 237-245.

Rosenshine, B. (1979). Content, Time and Direct Instruction. In Peterson and Walberg. *Research on Teaching: Concepts, Findings and Implications.* Berkeley, CA: McCutchan Publishing Corporation.

Rowe, M. (1974). Wait-Time and Rewards as Instructional Variables, Their Influence on Language, Logic and Fate Control: Part One Wait-Time. *Journal of Research in Science Teaching.* 11: 81-94.

Rutter, M., Maughan, B., Mortimore, P., Ouston, J., & Smith A. (1979). *Fifteen Thousand Hours.* Cambridge, MA: Harvard University Press.

Springer, L., Stanne, M., & Donovan, S. (1999). Effects of small-group learning on undergraduates in science, mathematics, engineering, and technology: A meta-analysis. *Review of Educational Research*, 69 (1), 21-51.

Squire, J. (1999). Language Arts. In Calwelti, G. (Ed.), *Handbook of Research on Improving Student Achievement.* Arlington, VA: Educational Research Service.

Stallings, J. & Robertson, A. (1979). *Factors Influencing Women's Decisions to Enroll in Elective Mathematics Classes in High School. Final Report to National Institute of Education.* Menlo Park, CA: SRI International.

Tobin, K., & Capie, W. (1982). Relationships Between Classroom Process Variables and Middle School Science Achievement. *Journal of Educational Psychology.* 74: 441-454.

Yelon, S.L. & Schmidt, W.H. (1971). The Effective of Objectives and Instructions on the Learning of a Complex Cognitive Task. Paper presented at the annual meeting of the American Educational Research Association, New York, 1971.

Wahlberg, H. (1988). Synthesis of research on time and learning. *Educational Leadership*, 45, 76-85.

Wahlberg, H. (1999). Generic practices. In Calwelti, G. (Ed.), *Handbook of Research on Improving Student Achievement.* Arlington, VA: Educational Research Service.

Wang, M., Haertel, G., & Wahlberg, H. (1994). What helps students learn? *Educational Leadership*, 51 (4), 74-79.

Winne, P.H. (1979). Experiments Relating Teachers' use of Higher Cognitive Questions to Student Achievement. Review of Educational Research (Winter). 13: 50

Wittrock, M. (1986). Students' thought processes. In M. Wittrock (Ed.), *Handbook of Research on Teaching.* New York: Macmillan Publishing, Co.

Wright, C. & Nuthall, G. (1970). Relationships Between Teacher Behaviors and Pupil Achievement in Three Experimental Elementary Science Lessons. *American Educational Research Journal.* 7: 477-491.

Yair, G. (2000). Not just about time: Instructional practices and productive time in school. *Educational Administration Quarterly*, 36 (4), 485-512.

Zahorik, J. (1968). Classroom Feedback Behavior of Teachers. *Journal of Educational Research.* 62: 147-150.

Alignment
Carr, J., & Harris, D. (2001). *Succeeding with Standards*. Alexandria, VA: ASCD

Anticipatory Set
Ausubel, D.P. (1960). The Use of Advanced Organizers in the Learning and Retention of Meaningful Material. *Journal of General Psychology*. 51: 267-272.

Bellack, A.A. (1966). *The Language of the Classroom*. New York: Teachers College Press.

Duchastel, P.C. & Merrill, P.F. (1973). The Effects of Behavioral Objectives on Learning: A Review of Empirical Studies. *Review of Educational Research*. 43: 53-69.

Hunter, Madeline. (1994). Mastery Teaching: Increasing Instructional Effectiveness in Elementary and Secondary Schools, Colleges and Universities. (Reprint). Thousand Oaks, CA: Corwin Press.

Luiten, J., Ames, W., & Ackerson, G. (1980). Meta-Analysis of the Effects of Advanced Organizers on Learning and Retention. *American Educational Research Journal*. 17: 211-218.

Mayer, R. (1983). Can You Repeat That? Qualitative Effects of Repetition and Advanced Organizers from Science Prose. *Journal of Educational Psychology*. 75: 40-49.

Melton, R.F. (1978). The Resolution of Conflicting Claims Concerning the Effect of Behavioral Objectives on Student Learning. *Review of Educational Research*. 48: 291-302.

Soar, R. S. & Soar, R.M. (1980). Setting Variables, Classroom Interaction, and Multiple Pupil Outcomes. *JSAS Catalog of Selected Documents in Psychology*. 10: 2110.

Wright, C. & Nuthall, G. (1970). Relationships Between Teacher Behaviors and Pupil Achievement in Three Experimental Elementary Science Lessons. *American Educational Research Journal*. 7: 477-491.

Yelon, S.L. & Schmidt, W.H. (1971). The Effective of Objectives and Instructions on the Learning of a Complex Cognitive Task. Paper presented at the annual meeting of the American Educational Research Association, New York, 1971.

Bullying in Schools
Coloroso, B. (2003). *The Bully, the Bullied and the Bystander*. New York: Harper-Collins Publishers.

Davis, S. (2005). *Schools Where Everyone Belongs*. Champaign: IL: Research Press.

Garrett, A. (2003). *Bullying in American Schools*. Jefferson, NC: McFarland & Co.

Olweus, D. (1993). *Bullying in School*. Malden, MA: Blackwell Publishing.

Checking for Understanding
Hunter, Madeline. (1994). Mastery Teaching: Increasing Instructional Effectiveness in Elementary and Secondary Schools, Colleges and Universities. (Reprint). Thousand Oaks, CA: Corwin Press.

Miller, G. A. (1956). The magical number seven, plus-or-minus two: Some limits on our capacity for processing information. *Psychological Review*. 101, 343-352.

Russell, P. (1979). *The brain book*. New York: E.P. Dutton.

Sousa, D. (2006). *How the Brain Learns*. 3rd ed. Thousand Oaks, CA: Corwin Press.

Classroom Conditions

Addington, D. W. (1971). The Effect of Vocal Variations on Ratings of Source Credibility. *Speech Monographs.* 38: 242-247.

Bangert-Drowns, R., Kulik, C., Kulik, J., & Morgan, M. (1991). The instructional effect of feedback in test-like events. *Review of Educational Research.* 61. (2), 213-238

Carver R. (1973). Effect of Increasing the Rate of Speech Presentation Upon Comprehension. *Journal of Educational Psychology.* 65: 118-126.

D'Arcangelo, M. (2000). How does the brain develop? A conversations with Steven Peterson. Educational Leadership, 58 (3), 68-71.

Diehl, C.F. & McDonald, E. T. (1956). Effect of Voice Quality on Communication. *Journal of Speech and Hearing* Disorders. 21: 233-237.

Diehl, C.F., White, R. C. & Satz, P.H. (1961). Pitch Change and Comprehension. *Speech Monographs.* 28: 65-68.

Kounin, J. (1970). *Discipline and Group Management in Classrooms.* New York: Holt, Rinehart & Winston.

Leeper, H. & Thomas, C. (1978). Young Children's Preferences for Listening Rates. *Perceptual and Motor Skills.* 47: 891-898.

McCoard, W.B. (1944). Speech Factors as Related to Teaching Efficiency. *Speech Monographs.* 11: 53-64.

Osterman, K. (2000). Students' need for belonging in the school community. *Review of Educational Research.* 70 (3), 323-367.

Pert, C. (1997). Molecules of Emotion: Why You Feel the Way You Feel. New York: Scribner.

Wang, M., Haertel, G., & Wahlberg, H. (1994). What helps students learn? *Educational Leadership*, 51 (4), 74-79.

Clear Directions and Understanding

Anderson, L., Evertson, C. & and Brophy, J. (1979). An experimental study of effective teaching in first grade reading groups. *Elementary School Journal.* 79: 193-223.

Ausubel, D.P. (1960). The Use of Advanced Organizers in the Learning and Retention of Meaningful Material. *Journal of General Psychology.* 51: 267-272.

Bellack, A.A. (1966). *The Language of the Classroom.* New York: Teachers College Press.

Bloom, B. (1976). *Human Characteristics and School Learning.* New York: McGraw-Hill.

Brophy, J. (1981). Teacher Praise: A Functional Analysis. *Review of Educational Research.* 51: 5-32.

Duchastel, P.C. & Merrill, P.F. (1973). The Effects of Behavioral Objectives on Learning: A Review of Empirical Studies. *Review of Educational Research.* 43: 53-69.

Dunkin, M. & Biddle, B. (1974). *The Study of Teaching.* New York: Holt, Rinehart and Winston.

Martin, J, Veldman, D. & Anderson, L. (1980). Within-Class Relationships between Student Achievement and Teacher Behaviors. *American Educational Research Journal.* 17: 479-490.

Melton, R.F. (1978). The Resolution of Conflicting Claims Concerning the Effect of Behavioral Objectives on Student Learning. *Review of Educational Research.* 48: 291-302.

Peterson, P. & Walberg, H. (Eds.). (1979). *Research on Teaching: Concepts, Findings and Implications.* Berkeley, CA: McCutchan Publishing Corporation.

Rosenshine, B.(1971). *Teaching Behaviors and Student Achievement.* London: International Association for the Evaluation of Educational Achievement.

Sousa, D. (2006). *How the Brain Learns.* 3rd ed. Thousand Oaks, CA: Corwin Press.

Stallings, J. & Kaskowitz, D. (1974). *Follow Through Classroom Observation Evaluation, 1972-1973: A Study of Implementation.* Menlo Park, CA: Stanford University Research Institute.

Stallings, J., Needels, M. & Stayrook, N. (1979). *How to Change the Process of Teaching Basic Reading Skills in Secondary Schools.* Menlo Park, CA: SRI International.

Yelon, S.L. & Schmidt, W.H. (1971). The Effective of Objectives and Instructions on the Learning of a Complex Cognitive Task. Paper presented at the annual meeting of the American Educational Research Association, New York, 1971.

Clear Directions – Three Step Maximum

Crawford, W. (1975). An Examination of the Effect of Error Rates and Grade Point Averages on Learning Gains. Paper presented at Southwest Psychological Association. Houston.

DeVilliers, P.A. (1974). Imagery and Theme in Recall of Connected Discourse. *Journal of Experimental Psychology.* 103 (2): 263-268.

Dunkin, M. & Biddle, B. (1974). *The Study of Teaching.* New York: Holt, Rinehart and Winston.

Evans, W.E. & Guyman, R.E. (1978). Clarity of Explanation: A Powerful Indicator of Teacher Effectiveness. Paper presented at American Educational Research Association. Toronto.

Hiller, J.H. et.al. (1969). A computer investigation of verbal characteristics of effective classroom lecturing. *American Educational Research Journal.* 6: 661-675.

Hiller, J.H. (1971). Verbal Response Indicators of Conceptual Vagueness. *American Educational Research Journal.* 8: 151-162.

Hines, C.V. (1981). A Further investigation of Teacher Clarity: The Relationship Between Observed and perceived Clarity and Student Achievement and Satisfaction. *Dissertation Abstracts International.*

Land, M.L. & Smith, L.R. (1979). Effect of Teacher Clarity Variable on Student Achievement. *Journal of Educational research.* 72: 196-198.

Medley, D.M. (1977). *Teacher Competence and Teacher Effectiveness: A Review of Process-Product Research.* Washington, D.C.: American Association of Colleges for Teacher Education.

Mills, S. R. et. al. (1980). The correspondence between teacher questions and student answers in classroom discourse. *Journal of Experimental Education.* 48: 194-204.

Pompi, K.F. & Lachman, R. (1967). Surrogate Processes in the Short-Term Retention of Connected Discourse. *Journal of Experimental Psychology.* 35: 143-150.

Redfield, D.R. & Rousseau, E.W. (1981). A Meta-analysis of Research on Teacher Questioning Behavior. *Review of Educational Research.* 51: 237-245.

Rosenshine, B. (1979). Content, Time and Direct Instruction. In Peterson and Walberg. *Research on Teaching: Concepts, Findings and Implications.* Berkeley, CA: McCutchan.

Smith, L.R. (1977). Aspects of Teacher Discourse and student Achievement in Mathematics. *Journal of Research in Mathematics Education.* 8: 195-204.

Smith, L.R. & Edmonds, E.M. (1978). Teacher Vagueness and Pupil Participation in Mathematics Learning. *Journal for Research in Mathematics Education.* 9: 228-232.

Smith, L.R. & Cotton, M.L. (1980). Effect of Lesson Vagueness and Discontinuity on Student Achievement and Attitudes. *Journal of Educational Psychology.* 72: 670-675.

Smith, L.R. & Land, M.L. (1980). Student Perception of Teacher Clarity in Mathematics. *Journal of Research in Mathematics Education.* 11: 137-146.

Solomon, D. Rosenberg, L. & Bezdek, W. (1964). Teacher Behavior and Student Learning. *Journal of Educational Psychology.* 55: 23-30.

Sousa, D. (2006). *How the Brain Learns.* 3rd ed. Thousand Oaks, CA: Corwin Press.

Thompson, E. (1960). An Experimental Investigation of the Relative Effectiveness of Organizational Structure in Oral Communication. *Southern Speech Journal.* 26: 50-69.

Winne, P.H. (1979). Experiments Relating Teachers' use of Higher Cognitive Questions to Student Achievement. Review of Educational Research (Winter). 13: 50

Wright, C. & Nuthall, G. (1970). Relationships Between Teacher Behaviors and Pupil Achievement in Three Experimental Elementary Science Lessons. *American Educational Research Journal.* 7: 477-491.

Closure

Ausubel, D.P. (1960). The Use of Advanced Organizers in the Learning and Retention of Meaningful Material. *Journal of General Psychology.* 51: 267-272.

Ausubel, D.P. & Youssef, M. (1965). The Effect of Spaced Repetition on Meaningful Retention. *Journal of Educational Psychology..* 73: 147-150

Bellack, A.A. (1966). *The Language of the Classroom.* New York: Teachers College Press.

Duchastel, P.C. & Merrill, P.F. (1973). The Effects of Behavioral Objectives on Learning: A Review of Empirical Studies. *Review of Educational Research.* 43: 53-69.

Gay, L.R. (1973). Temporal Position of Reviews and Its Effect on the Retention of Mathematical Rules. *Journal of Educational Psychology.* 26: 65-72.

Good, T. (1979). Teacher Effectiveness in the Elementary School: What We Know about It Now. *Journal of Teacher Education.* 30: 52-64.

Hunter, Madeline. (1994). Mastery Teaching: Increasing Instructional Effectiveness in Elementary and Secondary Schools, Colleges and Universities. (Reprint). Thousand Oaks, CA: Corwin Press.

Medley, D.M. (1977). *Teacher Competence and Teacher Effectiveness: A Review of Process-Product Research.* Washington, D.C.: American Association of Colleges for Teacher Education.

Melton, R.F. (1978). The Resolution of Conflicting Claims Concerning the Effect of Behavioral Objectives on Student Learning. *Review of Educational Research.* 48: 291-302.

Peterson, H.A. et. al. (1935). Some Measurements of the Effects of Reviews. *Journal of Educational Psychology*. 23: 65-72.

Petros, T. & Hoving, K. (1980). The Effects of Review of Young Children's Memory for Prose. *Journal of Experimental Child Psychology*. 30: 33-43.

Spitzer, H.F. (1939). Studies in Retention. *Journal of Educational Psychology*. 30: 641-656.

Wright, C. & Nuthall, G. (1970). Relationships Between Teacher Behaviors and Pupil Achievement in Three Experimental Elementary Science Lessons. *American Educational Research Journal*. 7: 477-491.

Yelon, S.L. & Schmidt, W.H. (1971). The Effective of Objectives and Instructions on the Learning of a Complex Cognitive Task. Paper presented at the annual meeting of the American Educational Research Association, New York, 1971.

Construction of the Objective

Anderson, L.M. & Evertson, C.M. (1978). Classroom organization at the beginning of school: Two case studies. Paper presented to the American Association of Colleges for Teacher Education. Chicago.

Buckley, P.K. & Cooper J.M. (1978). A ethnographic study of an elementary school teacher's establishment and maintenance of group norms. Paper presented to the American Educational Research Association. Toronto.

Clark, C.M. & Yinger, R.J. (1979). Three studies of teacher planning. *Research Series No. 55*. East Lansing, MI: Institute for Research on Teaching.

Duchastel, P.C. & Merrill, P.F. (1973). The Effects of Behavioral Objectives on Learning. A Review of Empirical Studies. *Review of Educational Research*. 43: 53-69.

Goodlad, J.I., Klein, M.F. & associates. (1974). *Looking Behind the Classroom Door*. Worthington, OH: Charles A. Jones Publishing Co.

Joyce, B.R. & Harootunion, B. (1964). Teaching as problem solving. *Journal of Teacher Education*. 15: 420-427.

MacDonald, J.B. (1965). Myths about instruction. *Educational Leadership*. 22: 571-576; 609-617.

Mager, R.F. (1962). *Preparing Instructional Objectives*. Palo Alto, CA: Pearson Publishers.

Mann, T.R. (1975). The Practice of planning: The impact of elementary school on teachers' curriculum planning. *Dissertation Abstracts International* 35.

McCutcheon, G. (1980). How do elementary school teachers plan their courses? *Elementary School Journal*. 81: 4-23.

Melton, R.F. (1978). Resolution of Conflicting Claims Concerning the Effect of Behavioral Objectives on Student Learning. *Review of Educational Research*. 48: 291-302.

Merriman, E.L. (1975). Considerations identified by elementary teachers as elements of their planning for instructional activities. *Dissertation Abstracts International.*

Mintz, A.L. (1979). Teacher Planning: A simulation study. *Dissertation Abstracts International.*

Morine, G. (1976). *A Study of Teacher Planning.* Special Study C BTES Technical Report 76-3-1. San Francisco, CA: West Laboratory for Educational Research and Development.

Peterson, P.L., Marx R.W. & Clark, C.M. (1978). Teaching planning, teacher behavior and students' achievement. *American Educational Research Journal.* 15: 417-432.

Schultz, J. & Florio, S. (1979). Stop and Freeze: The Negotiation of Social and Physical Space in a Kindergarten/First Grade Classroom. *Anthropology and Education Quarterly.* 10: (3).

Taylor, P.H. (1970). *How teachers plan their course.* National Foundation for Educational Research.

Tikunoff, W.J. & Ward, B.A. (1978). *A naturalistic study of the initiation of students into three classroom social systems Report A-78-11.* San Francisco, CA: West Laboratory for Educational Research and Development.

Yinger, R.J. (1977). A study of teacher planning: Description and theory development using ethnographic and information processing methods. *Dissertation Abstracts International.*

Zahorik, J.A. (1970). The effect of planning on teaching. *Elementary School Journal.* December.

Zahorik, J.A. (1975). Teachers' planning models. Paper presented at American Educational Research Association. Washington, D.C.

Feeling Tone

Addington, D. W. (1971). The Effect of Vocal Variations on Ratings of Source Credibility. *Speech Monographs.* 38: 242-247.

Allen, E.K. (1981). A Study of the Relationships Between Teacher Enthusiasm and Selected Student Variables in Area Vocational-Technical Schools. *Dissertation Abstracts International.* 42 (3): 1114A.

Becker, W.C. & others. (1968). Production and elimination of disruptive classroom behavior by systematically varying teacher's behavior. *Journal of Applied Behavior Analysis.* 1: 35-45.

Bettencourt, E.M. (1979). Effects of Training Teachers in Enthusiasm on Student Achievement and Attitudes. *Dissertation Abstracts International.* 40: 3237A.

Bracey, G. W. (1999). *Reducing Class Size*: The Findings, the Controversy. *Phi Delta Kappan.* 81 (3): 246-247.

Brophy, J. (1981). Teacher Praise: A Functional Analysis. *Review of Educational Research.* 51: 5-32.

Burgoon, J.K. (1979). Attributes of the Newscaster's Voice as Predictors of His Credibility. *Journalism Quarterly.* 55: 276-281.

Carver R. (1973). Effect of Increasing the Rate of Speech Presentation Upon Comprehension. *Journal of Educational Psychology.* 65: 118-126.

Charles, C. M. (1999). *Building Classroom Discipline.* New York: Longman Press.

Coats, W. & Smidchens, U. (1966). Audience recall as a Function of Speaker Dynamism. *Journal of Educational Psychology.* 57: 189-191.

Darling-Hammond, L. et.al.(1996). What Matters Most. *Phi Delta Kappan.* 78, 193-200.

Diehl, C.F. & McDonald, E. T. (1956). Effect of Voice Quality on Communication. *Journal of Speech and Hearing* Disorders. 21: 233-237.

Diehl, C.F., White, R. C. & Satz, P.H. (1961). Pitch Change and Comprehension. *Speech Monographs.* 28: 65-68.

Gillett, M.H. (1980). Effects of Teacher Enthusiasm on At-Task Behavior of Students in Elementary Classes. *Dissertation Abstracts International.* 41 (5): 1919A.

Gollnick, D., & Chinn, P. (2005). *Multicultural Education in a Pluralistic Society.* 7th ed. New York: Prentice Hall.

Gunderson, D.F. & Hopper, R. (1976). Relationship Between Speech Delivery and Speech Effectiveness. *Communication Monographs.* 43: 158-165.

Hunter, Madeline. (1994). Mastery Teaching: Increasing Instructional Effectiveness in Elementary and Secondary Schools, Colleges and Universities. (Reprint). Thousand Oaks, CA: Corwin Press.

Kounin, J. (1970). *Discipline and Group Management in Classrooms.* New York: Holt, Rinehart & Winston.

Leeper, H. & Thomas, C. (1978). Young Children's Preferences for Listening Rates. *Perceptual and Motor Skills.* 47: 891-898.

McCoard, W.B. (1944). Speech Factors as Related to Teaching Efficiency. *Speech Monographs.* 11: 53-64.

Minton, Elaine, (1999). Extreme experiences and asking the unaskable: An interview with Ted Sizer. *Active Learner: A Foxfire Journal for Teachers.* 1 (1): 12-15.

Wessler, S. (2003). It's Hard to Learn When You're Scared. *Educational Leadership* 61 (1), 40-43

Group Work

Louisell, R & Descamps, J. (2001). *Developing a Teaching Style.* Prospect Heights, IL: Waveland Press, Inc.

Sawyer, R. (1999). Health Education. In Calwelti, G. (Ed.), *Handbook of Research on Improving Student Achievement.* Arlington, VA: Educational Research Service.

Springer, L., Stanne, M., & Donovan, S. (1999). Effects of small-group learning on undergraduates in science, mathematics, engineering, and technology: A meta-analysis. *Review of Educational Research*, 69 (1), 21-51.

Steinberg, L. (1996). *Beyond the Classroom: Why School Reform Has Failed and What parents Need to Do.* New York: Simon & Schuster.

Wahlberg, H. (1999). Productive Teaching. In H. Waxman & H. Wahlberg (Ed.), *New Directions for Teaching Practice and Research.* Berkeley, CA: McCutchen Publishing.

Homework

Cooper, H. (2001). Homework for all – in moderation. *Educational Leadership*, 58 (7), 34-38.

Interest

Addington, D. W. (1971). The Effect of Vocal Variations on Ratings of Source Credibility. *Speech Monographs.* 38: 242-247.

Burgoon, J.K. (1979). Attributes of the Newscaster's Voice as Predictors of His Credibility. *Journalism Quarterly.* 55: 276-281.

Carver R. (1973). Effect of Increasing the Rate of Speech Presentation Upon Comprehension. *Journal of Educational Psychology.* 65: 118-126.

Diehl, C.F. & McDonald, E. T. (1956). Effect of Voice Quality on Communication. *Journal of Speech and Hearing* Disorders. 21: 233-237.

Diehl, C.F., White, R. C. & Satz, P.H. (1961). Pitch Change and Comprehension. *Speech Monographs.* 28: 65-68.

Haberman, M. (1991). The pedagogy of poverty versus good teaching. *Kappan.* 73 (4), 290-294.

Hidi, S., & Harackiewicz, J. (2000). Motivating the academically unmotivated: A critical issue for the 21st century. *Review of Educational Research.* 70 (2), 151-179.

Hunter, Madeline. (1994). Mastery Teaching: Increasing Instructional Effectiveness in Elementary and Secondary Schools, Colleges and Universities. (Reprint). Thousand Oaks, CA: Corwin Press.

Kounin, J. (1970). *Discipline and Group Management in Classrooms.* New York: Holt, Rinehart & Winston.

Leeper, H. & Thomas, C. (1978). Young Children's Preferences for Listening Rates. *Perceptual and Motor Skills.* 47: 891-898.

McCoard, W.B. (1944). Speech Factors as Related to Teaching Efficiency. *Speech Monographs.* 11: 53-64.

Wahlberg, H. (1999). Productive Teaching. In H. Waxman & H. Wahlberg (Ed.), *New Directions for Teaching Practice and Research.* Berkeley, CA: McCutchen Publishing.

Knowledge of Results/Feedback

Addington, D. W. (1971). The Effect of Vocal Variations on Ratings of Source Credibility. *Speech Monographs.* 38: 242-247.

Allen, E.K. (1981). A Study of the Relationships Between Teacher Enthusiasm and Selected Student Variables in Area Vocational-Technical Schools. *Dissertation Abstracts International.* 42 (3): 1114A.

Anderson, L.M. & Evertson C. (1978). Classroom organization at the beginning of school: Two case studies. Paper presented at American Association of Colleges for Teacher Education. Chicago.

Anderson, L., Evertson, C. & and Brophy, J. (1979). An experimental study of effective teaching in first grade reading groups. *Elementary School Journal.* 79: 193-223.

Austin, J. (1976). Do Comments on Mathematics Homework Affect Student Achievement? *School Science and Mathematics.* 76: 159-164.

Bangert-Drowns, R., Kulik, C., Kulik, J., & Morgan, M. (1991). The instructional effect of feedback in test-like events. *Review of Educational Research.* 61. (2), 213-238

Barringer, C. & Gholson, B. (1979). Effects of Type and Combination of Feedback upon Conceptual Learning by Children: Implications for Research in Academic Learning. *Review of Educational Research.* 49: 459-478.

Bettencourt, E.M. (1979). Effects of Training Teachers in Enthusiasm on Student Achievement and Attitudes. *Dissertation Abstracts International.* 40: 3237A.

Bloom, B. (1976). *Human Characteristics and School Learning.* New York: McGraw-Hill.

Brackbill, Y. & Kappy, M. (1962). Delay of Reinforcement and Retention. *Journal of comparative and Physiological Psychology.* 55: 14-18.

Bridgement B. (1974). Effects of Test Score Feedback on Immediately Subsequent Test Performance. *Journal of Educational Psychology.* 66: 62-66.

Brophy, J. (1979). Teacher Behavior and Student Learning. *Educational Leadership*. 37: 33-38.

Brophy, J. (1981). Teacher praise: A functional analysis. *Review of Educational Research*, 51, 5-32.

Brophy, J. & Evertson, C. (1974). Teachers' Communication of Differential Expectations for Children's Classroom Performance: Some Behavioral Data. *Journal of Educational Psychology.* 61: 365-374.

Brophy, J. & Good, T. (1986). Teacher behavior and student achievement. In M. Wittrock (Ed.), *Handbook of Research on Teaching.* New York: Macmillan Publishing Co.

Burgoon, J.K. (1979). Attributes of the Newscaster's Voice as Predictors of His Credibility. *Journalism Quarterly*. 55: 276-281.

Carver R. (1973). Effect of Increasing the Rate of Speech Presentation Upon Comprehension. *Journal of Educational Psychology.* 65: 118-126.

Coats, W. & Smidchens, U. (1966). Audience recall as a Function of Speaker Dynamism. *Journal of Educational Psychology.* 57: 189-191.

Collins, M. (1977). The Effects of Training for Enthusiasm on the Enthusiasm Displayed by Preservice Elementary Teachers. *Dissertation Abstracts International*. 37A: 7083-7084A.

Coker, H., Lorenz, J. & Coker, J. (1976). *Interim Report on County CBTC Project, Fall, 1976.* Atlanta: Georgia Department of Education.

Cooke, D. & Brown G. (1935). Home Study Has Many Angles. *Journal of Education.* 118: 409-410

Cooper, H.M. & Baron, R. (1977). Academic expectations and attributed responsibility as predictors of teachers' reinforcement behavior. *Journal of Educational Psychology*. 69: 409-418.

Dalton, W. (1969). The Relationships between Classroom Interactions and Teacher Ratings of Pupils: An Exploration of One Means by Which a Teacher may Communicate Her Expectations. *Peobody Papers in Human Development.* 7: 6.

Diehl, C.F. & McDonald, E. T. (1956). Effect of Voice Quality on Communication. *Journal of Speech and Hearing* Disorders. 21: 233-237.

Diehl, C.F., White, R. C. & Satz, P.H. (1961). Pitch Change and Comprehension. *Speech Monographs.* 28: 65-68.

Di Napoli, P. (1937). *Homework in the New York City Schools.* New York: Bureau of Publication: Teacher's College.

Dunkin, M. & Biddle, B. (1974). *The Study of Teaching*. New York: Holt, Rinehart and Winston.

Evertson, C. (1980). Differences in Instructional Activities in High and Low Achieving Junior High Classes. Paper presented at American Educational Research Association. Boston.

Evertson, C., Anderson, C., Anderson, L., & Brophy, J. (1980). Relationships between Classroom Behaviors and Student Outcomes in Junior High Mathematics and English Classes. *American Educational Research.* 17: 43-60.

Flanders, N. (1970). *Analyzing Teacher Behavior*. Reading, PA: Addison Wesley.

Gillett, M.H. (1980). Effects of Teacher Enthusiasm on At-Task Behavior of Students in Elementary Classes. *Dissertation Abstracts International.* 41 (5): 1919A.

Good, T., & Grouws, D. (1975). *Process-Product Relationship in Fourth Grade Mathematics Classroom.* Columbia, MO: University of Missouri Press.

Good, T., & Grouws, D. (1975). *Teacher's Manual: Missouri Mathematics Effectiveness Project.* Columbia, MO: Center for Research in Social Behavior. University of Missouri Press.

Gunderson, D.F. & Hopper, R. (1976). Relationship Between Speech Delivery and Speech Effectiveness.

Heines, B. & Hawthorne, R. (1978). *Sibling-Related Teacher Expectancies and Their Possible Influence on Classroom Behaviors and Achievement Levels in Seventh Grade English Classes.* Paper presented at American Educational Research Association.

Hughes, D. (1973). An Experimental Investigation of the Effects of Pupil Responding and Teacher Reacting on Pupil Achievement. *American Educational Research Journal.* 10: 21-38.

Hunter, Madeline. (1994). Mastery Teaching: Increasing Instructional Effectiveness in Elementary and Secondary Schools, Colleges and Universities. (Reprint). Thousand Oaks, CA: Corwin Press.

Kounin, J. (1970). *Discipline and Group Management in Classrooms.* New York: Holt, Rinehart & Winston.

Leeper, H. & Thomas, C. (1978). Young Children's Preferences for Listening Rates. *Perceptual and Motor Skills.* 47: 891-898.

Lysakowski, R. & Walberg, H. (1981). Classroom Reinforcement and Learning: A Quantitative Synthesis. *Journal of Educational Research.* 75: 69-77.

Mahaffey, L., Brophy, J. & Evertson, C. (1975). Teacher Feedback to Children's Answers: Process-Product Relationships. Paper presented to Research Association. Washington, D.C.

Martin, J, Veldman, D. & Anderson, L. (1980). Within-Class Relationships between Student Achievement and Teacher Behaviors. *American Educational Research Journal.* 17: 479-490.

Marzano, R., Pickering, D., & Pollock, J. (2001). *Classroom Instruction that Works.* Alexandria, VA: ASCD.

Mastin, V. (1963). Teacher Enthusiasm. *Journal of Educational Research.* 56: 385-386.

McCoard, W.B. (1944). Speech Factors as Related to Teaching Efficiency. *Speech Monographs.* 11: 53-64.

Mims, M. & Gholson, B. (1977). Effects of Type and Amount of Feedback upon Hypothesis Sampling Among 7-8 Year Old Children. *Journal of Experimental child Psychology.* 24: 358-371.

Page, E. (1958). Teacher comments and Student Performance: A Seventy-Four Classroom Experiment in School Motivation. *Journal of Educational Psychology.* 49: 173-181.

Pankratz, R. (1967). Verbal Interaction Patterns in the Classrooms of Selected Physics Teachers. In Amidon, E., & Hough, J. (eds) *Interaction Analysis: Theory, Research and Application.* Reading, PA: Addison Wesley.

Ratliff, R. (1972). Two-Choice Discrimination Learning in Children as a Function of Punishment Modality and Reinforcement Combination. *Journal of Experimental Child Psychology.* 14: 365-371.

Rosenshine, B.(1971). *Teaching Behaviors and Student Achievement.* London: International Association for the Evaluation of Educational Achievement.

Rosenthal, R. (1971). Teacher Expectation and Pupil Learning. In Strom, R. (ed). *Teachers and the Learning Process.* Englewood Cliffs, NJ: Prentice-Hall.

Rowe, M. (1974). Wait-Time and Rewards as Instructional Variables, Their Influence on Language, Logic and Fate Control: Part One Wait-Time. *Journal of Research in Science Teaching.* 11: 81-94.

Saigh, P. (1981). The Effects of Positive Examiner Verbal Comments on the Total WISC-R Performance of Institutionalized EMR Students. *Journal of School Psychology.* 19: 86-91.

Schoen, H. & Kreye, B. (1974). Five Forms of Written Feedback to Homework in a Mathematics Course for Elementary Teachers. *Journal for Research in Mathematics Education.* 5: 140-145.

Soar, R. (1966). *An Integrative Approach to Classroom Learning.* Philadelphia: Temple University Press.

Soar, R. (1973). *Follow-Through Classroom Process Measurement and Pupil Growth: Final Report.* Gainesville, FL: College of Education. University of Florida.

Spence, J. (1970). The Distraction Effects of Material Reinforcers in the Discrimination Learning of Lower and Middle Class Children. *Child Development.* 41: 103-111.

Stallings, J. & Kaskowitz, D. (1974). *Follow Through Classroom Observation Evaluation, 1972-1973: A Study of Implementation.* Menlo Park, CA: Stanford University Research Institute.

Stallings, J., Needels, M. & Stayrook, N. (1979). *How to Change the Process of Teaching Basic Reading Skills in Secondary Schools.* Menlo Park, CA: SRI International.

Steinberg, L. (1996). *Beyond the Classroom: Why School Reform Has Failed and What parents Need to Do.* New York: Simon & Schuster.

Surber, J. & Anderson, R. (1975). Delay-Retention Effect in Natural Classroom Settings. *Journal of Educational Psychology.* 67 (2): 170-173.

Teahan, G. (1935). Required Homework is Unwise. *American School Board Journal.* 91: 41.

Terrill, R, Terrill, S. & Taylor, J. (1980). Effects of Race of Examiner and Type of Reinforcement on the Intelligence Test Performance of Lower-Class Blacks. *Psychology in the Schools.* 17: 270-272.

Wang, M., Haertel, G., & Wahlberg, H. (1994). What helps students learn? *Educational Leadership*, 51 (4), 74-79.

Zahorik, J. (1968). Classroom Feedback Behavior of Teachers. *Journal of Educational Research.* 62: 147-150.

Lesson Design

Anderson, R. (1972). Learning Concepts from Definitions. *American Journal of Educational Research.* 7: 385-390.

Ausubel, D.P. (1960). The Use of Advanced Organizers in the Learning and Retention of Meaningful Material. *Journal of General Psychology.* 51: 267-272.

Bartov, H. (1978). Can Students Be Taught to Distinguish Between Teleological and Causal Explanations? *Journal of Research in Science Education.* 15: 567-572.

Beck, D., Sullivan, E. & Taylor, N. (1972). Stimulating Transition to Post-Conventional Morality: The Pickering High School Study. *Interchange*. 3: 28-37.

Bellack, A.A. (1966). *The Language of the Classroom*. New York: Teachers College Press.

Blatt, M. & Kohlberg, L. (1975). The Effects of Classroom Moral Discussion Upon Children's Level of Moral Judgment. *Journal of Moral Education.* 4: 129-161.

Clark, D. (1971). Teaching Concepts in the Classroom. *Educational Psychology Monograph*. 62: 253-273.

Ennis, R. (1969). *Logic in Teaching*. Englewood Cliffs, NJ: Prentice-Hall.

Feldman, K. (1980). The Effects of Number of Positive and Negative Instances, Concept Definition and of Mathematical Concepts. *Review of Educational Research*. 50: 33-67.

Frayer, D. (1970). *The Effect of Number of Instances and Emphasis of Relevant Attribute Values on Mastery of Geometric Concepts by Fourth and Sixth Grade Children. Technical Report 116.* Research and Development Center for Cognitive Learning.

Jungwirth, E. (1975). The Problem of Teleology in Biology as a Problem of Biology-Teacher Education. *Journal of Biological Education*. 9: 243-246.

Jungwirth, E. (1979). Do Students Accept Anthropomorphic and Teleological Formulations as Scientific Explanations?. *Journal of Biological Education.* 12: 152-155.

Klausmeier, H. (1976). Instructional Design and the Teaching of Concepts. In Levin, J. & Allen, V. (ed). *Cognitive Learning in Children*. New York: Academic Press.

Kohlberg, L. & Turiel, E., (1971). Moral Development and Moral Education. In Lesser, G. (ed). *Psychology and Educational Practice*. Chicago: Scott & Foresman.

Lookwood, A. (1978). The Effects of Values Clarification and Morals Development Curricula on School Age-Subjects. A Critical Review of Recent Research. *Review of Educational Research.* 48: 325-364.

Luiten, J., Ames, W., & Ackerson, G. (1980). Meta-Analysis of the Effects of Advanced Organizers on Learning and Retention. *American Educational Research Journal*. 17: 211-218.

Markle, S. (1980). Teaching Conceptual Networks. Paper presented at Educational Communications and Technology Convention 1977. Miami, FL. *Review of Educational Research.* 50: 55-67.

Mayer, R. (1983). Can You Repeat That? Qualitative Effects of Repetition and Advanced Organizers from Science Prose. *Journal of Educational Psychology*. 75: 40-49.

Medley, D.M. (1977). *Teacher Competence and Teacher Effectiveness: A Review of Process-Product Research*. Washington, D.C.: American Association of Colleges for Teacher Education.

Metcalf, L. (ed). (1971). *Values Education*. 41st Yearbook. National Council for the Social Studies. Washington, D.C.: National Education Association.

Piaget, J. (1951). *The Child's Conception of Physical Reality*. New York: Humanities Press.

Raths, L., Harmin, M., & Simon S. (1966). *Values and Teaching*. Columbus, OH: Charles E. Merrill.

Rosenshine, B.(1971). *Teaching Behaviors and Student Achievement*. London: International Association for the Evaluation of Educational Achievement.

Smith, B. & Meux, M. et.al. (1967). *A Study of the Strategies of Teaching.* Urbana, IL: Bureau of Educational Research. University of Illinois.

Smith. B. et.al. (1970). *A Study of the Logic of Teaching.* Urbana, IL: University of Illinois Press.

Soar, R. S. & Soar, R.M. (1979). Emotional Climate and Management. In Peterson, P. & Walberg, H. (eds). *Research on Teaching.* Berkeley, CA: McCutchan Publishing Corporation. 97-119.

Tennyson, R. (1972). Exemplar and Non-Exemplar Variables Which Produce Correct Concept Classification Behavior and Specified Classification Errors. *Journal of Educational Psychology.* 63: 144-152.

Tennyson, R. (1973). Effects of Negative Instances in Concept Acquisitions Using a Verbal-Learning Task. *Journal of Educational Psychology.* 64: 247-260.

Wright, C. & Nuthall, G. (1970). Relationships Between Teacher Behaviors and Pupil Achievement in Three Experimental Elementary Science Lessons. *American Educational Research Journal.* 7: 477-491.

Level of Concern

Addington, D. W. (1971). The Effect of Vocal Variations on Ratings of Source Credibility. *Speech Monographs.* 38: 242-247.

Allen, E.K. (1981). A Study of the Relationships Between Teacher Enthusiasm and Selected Student Variables in Area Vocational-Technical Schools. *Dissertation Abstracts International.* 42 (3): 1114A.

Bates, J. (1979). Extrinsic reward and intrinsic motivation: A review with implications for the classroom. *Review of Educational Research.* 49: 557-576.

Becker, W.C. & others. (1968). Production and elimination of disruptive classroom behavior by systematically varying teacher's behavior. *Journal of Applied Behavior Analysis.* 1: 35-45.

Bettencourt, E.M. (1979). Effects of Training Teachers in Enthusiasm on Student Achievement and Attitudes. *Dissertation Abstracts International.* 40: 3237A.

Blanck, P. & others. (1970). *The Effects of Verbal Reinforcement on Intrinsic Motivation for Sex-Linked Tasks.* Paper presented at American Psychological Association.

Brophy, J. (1981). Teacher praise: A functional analysis. *Review of Educational Research*, 51, 5-32.

Burgoon, J.K. (1979). Attributes of the Newscaster's Voice as Predictors of His Credibility. *Journalism Quarterly.* 55: 276-281.

Carver R. (1973). Effect of Increasing the Rate of Speech Presentation Upon Comprehension. *Journal of Educational Psychology.* 65: 118-126.

Coats, W. & Smidchens, U. (1966). Audience recall as a Function of Speaker Dynamism. *Journal of Educational Psychology.* 57: 189-191.

Collins, M. (1977). The Effects of Training for Enthusiasm on the Enthusiasm Displayed by Preservice Elementary Teachers. *Dissertation Abstracts International.* 37A: 7083-7084A.

Cooper, H. & others. (1979*). Gender differences in the academic locus of control beliefs of young children.* Columbia, MO: Center for the Study of Behavior: University of Missouri.

Diehl, C.F. & McDonald, E. T. (1956). Effect of Voice Quality on Communication. *Journal of Speech and Hearing* Disorders. 21: 233-237.

Diehl, C.F., White, R. C. & Satz, P.H. (1961). Pitch Change and Comprehension. *Speech Monographs.* 28: 65-68.

Dweck, C. & others. (1978). Sex differences in learned helplessness: II. The Contingencies of evaluative feedback in the classroom. III. An Experimental Analysis. *Developmental Psychology.* 14: 268-276.

Gillett, M.H. (1980). Effects of Teacher Enthusiasm on At-Task Behavior of Students in Elementary Classes. *Dissertation Abstracts International.* 41 (5): 1919A.

Gunderson, D.F. & Hopper, R. (1976). Relationship Between Speech Delivery and Speech Effectiveness.

Hidi, S., & Harackiewicz, J. (2000). Motivating the academically unmotivated: A critical issue for the 21st century. *Review of Educational Research.* 70 (2), 151-179.

Hunter, Madeline. (1994). Mastery Teaching: Increasing Instructional Effectiveness in Elementary and Secondary Schools, Colleges and Universities. (Reprint). Thousand Oaks, CA: Corwin Press.

Kounin, J. (1970). *Discipline and Group Management in Classrooms.* New York: Holt, Rinehart & Winston.

Kruglanski, A. (1978). Endogenous attribution and intrinsic motivation. In Lepper & Greene (eds). *The Hidden Costs of Reward: A New Perspective on the Psychology of Human Motivation.* Hillsdale, NJ: Lawrence Erlbaum & Associates.

LeDoux, J. (1996). *The Emotional Brain.* New York: Simon & Schuster.

Leeper, M. & Dafoe, J. (1979). Incentives, constraints, and motivation in the classroom. In Frieze, I. & others. *New Approaches to Social Problems.* San Francisco, CA: Jossey-Bass.

Leeper, H. & Thomas, C. (1978). Young Children's Preferences for Listening Rates. *Perceptual and Motor Skills.* 47: 891-898.

Maehr, M. & Stallings, W. (1972). Freedom form external evaluation. *Child Development.* 43: 177-185.

Mastin, V. (1963). Teacher Enthusiasm. *Journal of Educational Research.* 56: 385-386.

McCoard, W.B. (1944). Speech Factors as Related to Teaching Efficiency. *Speech Monographs.* 11: 53-64.

Meyer, W. & others. (1979). The informational value of evaluative behavior: influences of praise and blame on perceptions of ability. *Journal of Educational Psychology.* 71: 259-268.

Nichols, J. (1978). The Development of the concept of effort and Ability, Perception of Academic Attainment, and the Understanding that Difficult Tasks Require More Ability. *Child Development.* 49: 800-814.

Nichols, J. (1979). The Development of Perception of Own Attainment and Causal Attributions for Success and Failure in Reading. *Journal of Educational Psychology.* 71: 94-99.

Pert, C. (1997). Molecules of Emotion: Why You Feel the Way You Feel. New York: Scribner.

Piaget, J. (1970). Piaget's Theory. In Mussen. P. (ed). *Carmichael's Manual of Child Psychology 3rd ed. Volume 1.* New York: Wiley.

Pittman, T. & others. (1980). Informational vs. controlling rewards, levels of surveillance and intrinsic motivation. *Personality and Social Psychology Bulletin.* 6: 228-233.

Rosswork, S. (1977). Goal Setting: The effects on an academic task with varying magnitudes of incentive. *Journal of Educational Psychology*. 69: 710-715.

Ruble, D. & others. (1979). *Rewards and Extrinsic Motivation in Children: An examination of competence and complexity preference*. Paper presented at conference on Teacher and Student Perceptions of Success and Failure and Applications for Learning and Instruction. University of Pittsburg.

Stewart, L., & White, M. (1976). Teacher comments, letter grades, and student performance: what do we really know? *Journal of Educational Psychology*. 68: 488-500.

Sylwester, R. (2000). *A Biological Brain in a Cultural Classroom*. Thousand Oaks, CA: Corwin Press.

Weiner, B. (1979). A theory of motivation for some classroom experiences. *Journal of Educational Psychology*. 71: 3-25.

Mastery
Springer, L., Stanne, M., & Donovan, S. (1999). Effects of small-group learning on undergraduates in science, mathematics, engineering, and technology: A meta-analysis. *Review of Educational Research*, 69 (1), 21-51.

Meaning
Kounin, J. (1970). *Discipline and Group Management in Classrooms*. New York: Holt, Rinehart & Winston.

Memory
Steinberg, L. (1996). *Beyond the Classroom: Why School Reform Has Failed and What parents Need to Do*. New York: Simon & Schuster.

Wahlberg, H. (1999). Generic practices. In Calwelti, G. (Ed.), *Handbook of Research on Improving Student Achievement*. Arlington, VA: Educational Research Service.

Modeling
Anderson, R. (1972). Learning Concepts from Definitions. *American Journal of Educational Research*. 7: 385-390.

Atkinson, R., Derry, S., Renkl, A. & Wortham, D. (2000). Learning from examples: Instructional principles from the worked examples research. Review of Educational Research, 70 (2), 181-214.

Bauer, D. (1975). The Effects of Instructions, Anxiety and Locus of Control on Intelligence Test Scores. *Measurement and Evaluation in Guidance*. 8: 12-19.

Bligh, H.F. (1965). Trends in the Measurement of Educational Achievement. *Review of Educational Research*. 35: 34-49.

Brophy, J., & Evertson, C. (1976). *Learning from Teaching: A Developmental Perspective*. Boston: Allyn & Bacon.

Burr, W.L. (1963). Empirical Relationships Among Modes of Testing, Modes of Instruction and Reading Levels: In Sixth Grade Social Studies. *Journal of Experimental Education*. 31: 433-435.

Bushway, A., & Nash, W.R. (1977). School cheating Behavior. *Review of Educational Research*. 147: 623-632.

Clark, D. (1971). Teaching Concepts in the Classroom. *Educational Psychology Monograph*. 62: 253-273.

Clawson, T.W., Firment, C.K., & Tower, T.L. (1981). Test Anxiety: Another Origin for Racial Bias in Standardized Testing. *Measurement and Evaluation in Guidance.* 13: 210-215.

Coker, H., Lorenz, J. & Coker, J. (1976). *Interim Report on County CBTC Project, Fall, 1976.* Atlanta: Georgia Department of Education.

Cotler, S.& Palmer, R. (1970). The Effects of Test Anxiety, Sex of Subject, and Type of Verbal Reinforcement on Maze Performance of Elementary School Children. *Journal of Personality.* 38: 216-234.

Culler, R.E., & Holohan, C.G. (1980). Test Anxiety and Academic Performance: The Effects of Study-Related Behaviors. *Journal of Educational Psychology.* 72: 16-20

Curtis, H.A., & Kropp, R.P. (1961). A Comparison of Scores Obtained by Administering a Test Normally and Visually. *Journal of Experimental Education.* 29: 249-260.

Ehrensberger, B. (1945). An Experimental Study of the Relations Effectiveness of Certain Forma of Emphasis in Public Speaking. *Speech Monographs.* 12: 94-111.

Feldman, K. (1980). The Effects of Number of Positive and Negative Instances, Concept Definition and of Mathematical Concepts. *Review of Educational Research.* 50: 33-67.

Fischer, C.T. Levels of Cheating under Conditions on Informative Appeal to Honest, Public Affirmation of Value and Threats of Punishment. *Journal of Educational Psychology.*

Frayer, D. (1970). *The Effect of Number of Instances and Emphasis of Relevant Attribute Values on Mastery of Geometric Concepts by Fourth and Sixth Grade Children. Technical Report 116.* Research and Development Center for Cognitive Learning.

French, J.W. (1962). Effect of Anxiety on Verbal and Mathematical Examination Scores. *Educational and Psychological Measurement.* 22: 553-564.

Good, T., & Grouws, D. (1975). *Teacher's Manual: Missouri Mathematics Effectiveness Project.* Columbia, MO: Center for Research in Social Behavior. University of Missouri Press.

Green, K. (1981). Item-Response changes on Multiple-Choice Tests as a Function of Text Anxiety. *Journal of Experimental Education.* 49: 225-228.

Hunter, Madeline. (1994). Mastery Teaching: Increasing Instructional Effectiveness in Elementary and Secondary Schools, Colleges and Universities. (Reprint). Thousand Oaks, CA: Corwin Press.

Ingle, B., & DeAmica, G. (1969). Effect of Physical Conditions of the Test Room on Standardized Achievement Test Scores. *Journal of Educational Measurement.* 6: 237-240.

Jersild, A. (1928). Modes of Emphasis in Public Speaking. *Journal of Applied Psychology.* 12: 611-620.

Johnson, R.E., & Klores, M.S. (1968). Attitudes Toward Cheating as a Function of Classroom Dissatisfaction and Peer Norms. *Journal of Educational Research.* 62: 60-64.

Johnson, D., & Stratton, R. (1966). Evaluation of Five Methods of Teaching Concepts. *Journal of Educational Psychology.* 57: 48-53.

Keith, L., Tornatzky, L., & Pettigrew, L. (1974). An Analysis of Verbal and Nonverbal Classroom Teaching Behavior. *Journal of Experimental Education.* 42: 30-38.

Kirkland, K. & Hollandsworth, J.G. Jr. (1979). Test Anxiety, Study Skills, and Academic Performance. *Journal of College Student Personnel.* 20: 431-436.

Klausmeier, J. et.al. (1976). *Conceptual Learning and Development.* New York: Academic Press.

Kounin, J. (1970). *Discipline and Group Management in Classrooms.* New York: Holt, Rinehart & Winston.

Maddox, H. & Hoole, E. (1975).Performance Decrement in the Lecture. *Educational Review.* 28: 17-30.

Markle, S. (1980). Teaching Conceptual Networks. Paper presented at Educational Communications and Technology Convention 1977. Miami, FL. *Review of Educational Research.* 50: 55-67.

Mayer, R. (1983). Can You Repeat That? Qualitative Effects of Repetition and Advanced Organizers from Science Prose. *Journal of Educational Psychology.* 75: 40-49.

McQueen, R. (1957). Examination Deception as a Function of Residual Background and Immediate Stimulus Factors. *Journal of Personality.* 25: 643-650.

Medley, D.M. (1977). *Teacher Competence and Teacher Effectiveness: A Review of Process-Product Research.* Washington, D.C.: American Association of Colleges for Teacher Education.

Nottelman, E.D. & Hill, K.T. (1977). Test Anxiety and Off-Task Behavior in Evaluative Situations. *Child Development.* 48: 225-231.

Petrie, C.R. (1963). Informative Speaking: A Summary and Bibliography of Related Research. *Speech Monographs.* 30: 79-91.

Pinney, R.H. (1969). *Presentational Behavior Related to Success in Teaching.* Doctoral Dissertation. Stanford, CA: Stanford University.

Rogosin, H. (1951). What About "Cheating" on Examinations and Honesty? *School and Society.* 74: 402.403.

Schwarz, J.C. (1967). A New Procedure for Administering Objective Tests to Large Classes. *Journal of Educational Measurement.* 4: 167-168.

Shirk, E., & Hoffman, R.W. (1961). The Academic Setting of the Dishonest Student. *Improving College and University Teaching* 9: 130-134.

Steiniger, J, Johnson, R.E., & Kirts, D.K. 1964). Cheating on College Examinations as a Function of Situationality Aroused Anxiety and Hostility. *Journal of Educational Psychology.* 55: 317-324.

Super, D.E., Braasch, W.F. Jr., & Shay, J.B. (1947). The Effects of Distractions on Test Results. *Journal of Educational Psychology.* 38: 373-377.

Tennyson, R. (1972). Exemplar and Non-Exemplar Variables Which Produce Correct Concept Classification Behavior and Specified Classification Errors. *Journal of Educational Psychology.* 63: 144-152.

Tennyson, R. (1973). Effects of Negative Instances in Concept Acquisitions Using a Verbal-Learning Task. *Journal of Educational Psychology.* 64: 247-260.

Traxler, A.E., & Hilkert, R.N. (1942). Effect of Type of Desk on Results of Machine-Scored Tests. *School and Society.* 56: 277-296.

Trentham, L.L. (1979). Anxiety and Instruction Effects on Sixth-Grade Students in A Testing Situation. *Psychology in the Schools.* 16: 439-443.

Trentham, L.L. (1975). The Effect of Distractions on Sixth-Grade Students in a Testing Situation. *Journal of Educational Measurement.* 12: 13-18.

Uhlig, G.E., & Howes, B. (1967). Attitude Toward Cheating and Opportunistic Behavior. *Journal of Educational Research.* 60: 411-412.

Vitro, F.T., & Schoer, L.A. (1972). The Effects of Probability of Test Success, Test Importance, and Risk of Detection on the Incidence of Cheating. *Journal of School Psychology.* 10: 269-277.

Wahlberg, H. (1999). Generic practices. In Calwelti, G. (Ed.), *Handbook of Research on Improving Student Achievement.* Arlington, VA: Educational Research Service.

Walker R.E., Sannito, T.C., & Firetto, A.C. (1970). The Effect of Subjectively Reported Anxiety on Intelligence Test Performance. *Psychology in the Schools.* 7: 241-243.

Wine, J. (1971). Test Anxiety and Direction of Attention. *Psychological Bulletin.* 76: 92-104.

Wrightsman, L.S. Jr., (1962). The Effects of Anxiety, Achievement Motivation, and Task Importance upon Performance on an Intelligence Test. *Journal of Educational Psychology.* 53: 150-156.

Modes of Learning

Anderson, R. (1972). Learning Concepts from Definitions. *American Journal of Educational Research.* 7: 385-390.

Clark, D. (1971). Teaching Concepts in the Classroom. *Educational Psychology Monograph.* 62: 253-273.

Feldman, K. (1980). The Effects of Number of Positive and Negative Instances, Concept Definition and of Mathematical Concepts. *Review of Educational Research.* 50: 33-67.

Frayer, D. (1970). *The Effect of Number of Instances and Emphasis of Relevant Attribute Values on Mastery of Geometric Concepts by Fourth and Sixth Grade Children. Technical Report 116.* Research and Development Center for Cognitive Learning.

Johnson, D., & Stratton, R. (1966). Evaluation of Five Methods of Teaching Concepts. *Journal of Educational Psychology.* 57: 48-53.

lausmeier, J. et.al. (1976). *Conceptual Learning and Development.* New York: Academic Press.

Medley, D.M. (1977). *Teacher Competence and Teacher Effectiveness: A Review of Process-Product Research.* Washington, D.C.: American Association of Colleges for Teacher Education.

Tennyson, R. (1972). Exemplar and Non-Exemplar Variables Which Produce Correct Concept Classification Behavior and Specified Classification Errors. *Journal of Educational Psychology.* 63: 144-152.

Tennyson, R. (1973). Effects of Negative Instances in Concept Acquisitions Using a Verbal-Learning Task. *Journal of Educational Psychology.* 64: 247-260.

Monitor & Adjust

Cruickshank, D., & Haefele, D. (2001). Good teachers, plural. *Educational Leadership*, 58 (5), 26-30.

Motivation

Bloom, B. (1984). The search for methods of group instruction as effective as one-to-one tutoring. *Educational Leadership*, 45, 40-48.

Brophy, J. (1987). Synthesis of research on strategies for motivating students to learn. Educational Leadership, 45, 40-48

D'Arcangelo, M. (2000). How does the brain develop? A conversations with Steven Peterson. Educational Leadership, 58 (3), 68-71.

Goleman, D. (1995). *Emotional Intelligence.* New York: Bantam Books.

Pert, C. (1997). Molecules of Emotion: Why You Feel the Way You Feel. New York: Scribner.

Steinberg, L. (1996). *Beyond the Classroom: Why School Reform Has Failed and What parents Need to Do.* New York: Simon & Schuster.

Pass Option

Abraham, E., Nelson, M., & Reynolds, W. (1971). Discussion Strategies and Student Cognitive Skills. Paper presented at American Educational Research Association. New York.

Brophy, J. & Evertson, C. (1974). *Process-Product Correlations in the Texas Teacher Effectiveness Study: Final Report.* Austin: University of Texas.

Mahaffey, L., Brophy, J. & Evertson, C. (1975). Teacher Feedback to Children's Answers: Process-Product Relationships. Paper presented to Research Association. Washington, D.C.

Rowe, M. (1974). Wait-Time and Rewards as Instructional Variables, Their Influence on Language, Logic and Fate Control: Part One Wait-Time. *Journal of Research in Science Teaching.* 11: 81-94.

Positive Teacher Attributes

Glasser, W. (1998). *Choice Theory: A New Psychology for a New Century.* New York: Harper Collins.

Powell, McLaughlin, Savage & Zehm. (2001). *Classroom Management: Perspectives on the Social Curriculum.* New York: Merrill Prentice Hall.

Sousa, D. (2006). *How the Brain Learns.* 3rd ed. Thousand Oaks, CA: Corwin Press.

Practice

Austin, J. (1976). Do Comments on Mathematics Homework Affect Student Achievement? *School Science and Mathematics.* 76: 159-164.

Ausubel, D.P. & Youssef, M. (1965). The Effect of Spaced Repetition on Meaningful Retention. *Journal of Educational Psychology.*. 73: 147-150

Brophy, J., & Alleman, J. (1991). Activities as instructional tools: A framework for analysis and evaluation. Educational Researcher, 20 (4), 9-23.

Brophy, J., & Evertson, C. (1976). *Learning from Teaching: A Developmental Perspective.* Boston: Allyn & Bacon.

Coker, H., Lorenz, J. & Coker, J. (1976). *Interim Report on County CBTC Project, Fall, 1976.* Atlanta: Georgia Department of Education.
Cooke, D. & Brown G. (1935). Home Study Has Many Angles. *Journal of Education.* 118: 409-410

Crawford, W., King, C., Brophy, J., & Evertson, C. (1975). Error Rates and Question Difficulty Related to Elementary Children's Learning. Paper presented at American Educational Research Association. Washington, D.C.

Dunkin, M. & Biddle, B. (1974). *The Study of Teaching.* New York: Holt, Rinehart and Winston.

Gay, L.R. (1973). Temporal Position of Reviews and Its Effect on the Retention of Mathematical Rules. *Journal of Educational Psychology*. 26: 65-72.

Good, T. & Grouws, D.A. (1979). The Missouri Mathematics Effectiveness Project: An Experimental Study in Fourth-Grade Classrooms. *Journal of Educational Psychology*. 71: 355-362.

Good, T. & Grouws, D.A. (1977). *Teachers Manual: Missouri Mathematics Effectiveness Project.* Columbia, MO: University of Missouri.

Hovland, C.I. (1938). Experimental Studies in Rote-Learning Theory: III. Distribution of Practice with Varying Speech of Syllable Presentation. *Journal of Experimental Psychology*. 23: 172-190.

Hunter, Madeline. (1994). Mastery Teaching: Increasing Instructional Effectiveness in Elementary and Secondary Schools, Colleges and Universities. (Reprint). Thousand Oaks, CA: Corwin Press.

Johnson, K. (1996) *Language teaching and skill learning*. Oxford: Oxford University Press.

Keppel, G. 1964). Facilitation in Short- and Long-Term Retention of Paired Associates Following distributed Practice in learning. *Journal of Verbal Learning*. 3: 90-111.

Medley, D.M. (1977). *Teacher Competence and Teacher Effectiveness: A Review of Process-Product Research.* Washington, D.C.: American Association of Colleges for Teacher Education.

Peterson, H.A. et. al. (1935). Some Measurements of the Effects of Reviews. *Journal of Educational Psychology*. 23: 65-72.

Petros, T. & Hoving, K. (1980). The Effects of Review of Young Children's Memory for Prose. *Journal of Experimental Child Psychology*. 30: 33-43.

Pyle, W. H. (1913). Economical Learning. *Journal of Educational Psychology*. 4: 148-158.

Rosenshine, B. (1983). Teaching Functions in Instructional Programs. *The Elementary School Journal*. 83 (4): 335-353.
Spitzer, H.F. (1939). Studies in Retention. *Journal of Educational Psychology*. 30: 641-656.

Schoen, H. & Kreye, B. (1974). Five Forms of Written Feedback to Homework in a Mathematics Course for Elementary Teachers. *Journal for Research in Mathematics Education*. 5: 140-145.

Sullivan, H.G. et al. (1971). Effects of Systematic Practice on the Composition Skills of First Graders. *Elementary English*. 51: 635-641.

Teahan, G. (1935). Required Homework is Unwise. *American School Board Journal*. 91: 41.

Underwood, B.J. (1961). Ten Years of Massed Practice on Distributed Practice. *Psychological Review*. 68: 229-247.

Wahlberg, H. (1999). Generic practices. In Calwelti, G. (Ed.), *Handbook of Research on Improving Student Achievement*. Arlington, VA: Educational Research Service.

Wright, C. & Nuthall, G. (1970). Relationships Between Teacher Behaviors and Pupil Achievement in Three Experimental Elementary Science Lessons. *American Educational Research Journal*. 7: 477-491.

Primacy-Recency/Prime Time

Buzan, T. (1989). *Use Both Sides of Your Brain*. 3rd ed. New York: Penguin.

Thomas, E. (1972). The variation of memory with time for information appearing during a lecture. *Studies in Adult Education.* April: 57-62.

Reinforcement

Anderson, L., Evertson, C. & and Brophy, J. (1979). An experimental study of effective teaching in first grade reading groups. *Elementary School Journal*. 79: 193-223.

Bates, J. (1979). Extrinsic reward and intrinsic motivation: A review with implications for the classroom. *Review of Educational Research*. 49: 557-576.

Becker, W.C. & others. (1968). Production and elimination of disruptive classroom behavior by systematically varying teacher's behavior. *Journal of Applied Behavior Analysis.* 1: 35-45.

Bennett, S. (1978). Recent Research on Teaching: A Dream, A Belief, and a Model. *British Journal of Educational Psychology*. 48: 127-147.

Blanck, P. & others. (1970). *The Effects of Verbal Reinforcement on Intrinsic Motivation for Sex-Linked Tasks*. Paper presented at American Psychological Association.

Bloom, B. (1976). *Human Characteristics and School Learning*. New York: McGraw-Hill.

Borg, W.R & Ascione, F. R. (1982). Classroom Management in Elementary Mainstreaming Classrooms. *Journal of Educational Psychology*. 74: 85-95.

Borg, W. R. (1975). Protocol materials as related to teacher performance and pupil achievement. *Journal of Educational Research*. 69: 23-30.

Borg, W.R. & others. (1975a). Teacher classroom management skills and pupil behavior. *Journal of Experimental Education*. 44: 52-58.

Brackbill, Y. & Kappy, M. (1962). Delay of Reinforcement and Retention. *Journal of comparative and Physiological Psychology*. 55: 14-18.

Brophy, J. (1981). Teacher praise: A functional analysis. *Review of Educational Research*, 51: 5-32.

Brophy, J. (1979). Teacher Behavior and Student Learning. *Educational Leadership*. 37: 33-38.

Brophy, J. & Evertson, C. (1974). *The Texas Teacher Effectiveness Project: Presentation of Non-Linear Relationships and Summary Discussion, Report No. 74-6*. Austin: University of Texas R & D Center for Teacher Education.

Cooper, H.M. & Baron, R. (1977). Academic expectations and attributed responsibility as predictors of teachers' reinforcement behavior. *Journal of Educational Psychology*. 69: 409-418.

Deci, E., Koestner, R., & Ryan, R. (2001). Extrinsic rewards and intrinsic motivation in education: Reconsidered once again. *Review of Educational Research*, 71 (1), 1-27.

Dunkin, M. & Biddle, B. (1974). *The Study of Teaching*. New York: Holt, Rinehart and Winston.

Dweck, C. & others. (1978). Sex differences in learned helplessness: II. The Contingencies of evaluative feedback in the classroom. III. An Experimental Analysis. *Developmental Psychology*. 14: 268-276.

Fischer, C.W., Filby, N.A., Marliave, R., Cahen, L.S., Dishaw, M.M., Moore, J.E. & Berliner, D.C. (1978). Technical Report V-1: Teaching Behaviors, Academic Learning Time and Student Achievement: Final report of phase III-B, Beginning Teacher Evaluation Study. San Francisco: Far West Laboratory.

Good, T., & Beckerman, T. (1978). Time on Task: A Naturalistic Study in Sixth Grade Classrooms. *Elementary School Journal*. 73: 193-201.

Gump, P. (1974). Operating Environments in Schools of Open or Traditional Design. *School Review*. 82: 575-594.

Hunter, Madeline. (1994). Mastery Teaching: Increasing Instructional Effectiveness in Elementary and Secondary Schools, Colleges and Universities. (Reprint). Thousand Oaks, CA: Corwin Press.

Kohlbert, L. (1969). State and sequence: the cognitive development approach to socialization. In D. Goslin (Ed.) *Handbook of Socialization Theory and Research*. Chicago: Rand McNally.

Kounin, J. (1970). *Discipline and Group Management in Classrooms*. New York: Holt, Rinehart & Winston.

Kounin, J.S. & others. (1966). Managing emotionally disturbed children in regular classrooms. *Journal of Educational Psychology*. 57: 1-13.

Kruglanski, A. (1978). Endogenous attribution and intrinsic motivation. In Lepper & Greene (eds). *The Hidden Costs of Reward: A New Perspective on the Psychology of Human Motivation*. Hillsdale, NJ: Lawrence Erlbaum & Associates.

Leeper, M. & Dafoe, J. (1979). Incentives, constraints, and motivation in the classroom. In Frieze, I. & others. *New Approaches to Social Problems*. San Francisco, CA: Jossey-Bass.

Maehr, M. & Stallings, W. (1972). Freedom form external evaluation. *Child Development*. 43: 177-185.
Marzano, R., Pickering, D., & Pollock, J. (2001). *Classroom Instruction that Works*. Alexandria, VA: ASCD.

Martin, J, Veldman, D. & Anderson, L. (1980). Within-Class Relationships between Student Achievement and Teacher Behaviors. *American Educational Research Journal*. 17: 479-490.

Meyer, W. & others. (1979). The informational value of evaluative behavior: influences of praise and blame on perceptions of ability. *Journal of Educational Psychology*. 71: 259-268.

Nichols, J. (1979). The Development of Perception of Own Attainment and Causal Attributions for Success and Failure in Reading. *Journal of Educational Psychology*. 71: 94-99.

Nichols, J. (1978). The Development of the concept of effort and Ability, Perception of Academic Attainment, and the Understanding that Difficult Tasks Require More Ability. *Child Development*. 49: 800-814.

O'Leary, K.D. & others. (1970). The effects of loud and soft reprimands on the behavior of disruptive students. *Exceptional Children*. 37: 145-155.

Oliver, J.K., & Taylor, B.L. (1970). The Effects of teaching Social Studies on Immediate Retention. *Journal of Educational Research*. 63: 198-200.

Peterson, P. & Walberg, H. (Eds.). (1979). *Research on Teaching: Concepts, Findings and Implications*. Berkeley, CA: McCutchan Publishing Corporation.

Piaget, J. (1970). Piaget's Theory. In Mussen. P. (ed). *Carmichael's Manual of Child Psychology 3rd ed. Volume 1*. New York: Wiley.

Pittman, T.S. & others. (1980). Informational vs. controlling rewards, levels of surveillance and intrinsic motivation. *Personality and Social Psychology Bulletin*. 6: 228-233.

Rosenshine, B.(1971). *Teaching Behaviors and Student Achievement.* London: International Association for the Evaluation of Educational Achievement.

Rosswork, S. (1977). Goal Setting: The effects on an academic task with varying magnitudes of incentive. *Journal of Educational Psychology.* 69: 710-715.

Ruble, D. & others. (1979). *Rewards and Extrinsic Motivation in Children: An examination of competence and complexity preference.* Paper presented at conference on Teacher and Student Perceptions of Success and Failure and Applications for Learning and Instruction. University of Pittsburg.

Rutter, M., Maughan, B., Mortimore, P., Ouston, J., & Smith A. (1979). *Fifteen Thousand Hours.* Cambridge, MA: Harvard University Press.

Saigh, P. (1981). The Effects of Positive Examiner Verbal Comments on the Total WISC-R Performance of Institutionalized EMR Students. *Journal of School Psychology.* 19: 86-91.

Stallings, J. & Kaskowitz, D. (1974). *Follow Through Classroom Observation Evaluation, 1972-1973: A Study of Implementation.* Menlo Park, CA: Stanford University Research Institute.

Stallings, J. & Robertson, A. (1979). *Factors Influencing Women's Decisions to Enroll in Elective Mathematics Classes in High School. Final Report to National Institute of Education.* Menlo Park, CA: SRI International.

Stewart, L., & White, M. (1976). Teacher comments, letter grades, and student performance: what do we really know? *Journal of Educational Psychology.* 68: 488-500.

Surber, J. & Anderson, R. (1975). Delay-Retention Effect in Natural Classroom Settings. *Journal of Educational Psychology.* 67 (2): 170-173.

Terrill, R, Terrill, S. & Taylor, J. (1980). Effects of Race of Examiner and Type of Reinforcement on the Intelligence Test Performance of Lower-Class Blacks. *Psychology in the Schools.* 17: 270-272.

Weiner, B. (1979). A theory of motivation for some classroom experiences. *Journal of Educational Psychology.* 71: 3-25.

Sharing the Objective

Ausubel, D.P. (1960). The Use of Advanced Organizers in the Learning and Retention of Meaningful Material. *Journal of General Psychology.* 51: 267-272.

Bellack, A.A. (1966). *The Language of the Classroom.* New York: Teachers College Press.

Bloom, B. (1956). *Taxonomy of Educational Objectives: Handbook I: Cognitive Domain.* New York: McKay.

Hunter, Madeline. (1994). Mastery Teaching: Increasing Instructional Effectiveness in Elementary and Secondary Schools, Colleges and Universities. (Reprint). Thousand Oaks, CA: Corwin Press.

Luiten, J., Ames, W., & Ackerson, G. (1980). Meta-Analysis of the Effects of Advanced Organizers on Learning and Retention. *American Educational Research Journal.* 17: 211-218.

Mager, R.F. (1962). *Preparing Instructional Objectives.* Palo Alto, CA: Pearson Publishers.

Mayer, R. (1983). Can You Repeat That? Qualitative Effects of Repetition and Advanced Organizers from Science Prose. *Journal of Educational Psychology.* 75: 40-49.

Melton, R.F. (1978). The Resolution of Conflicting Claims Concerning the Effect of Behavioral Objectives on Student Learning. *Review of Educational Research.* 48: 291-302.

Schonfeld, I., Rasmussen, E., Nieto, R., and Sims, C. (1988). Enhancing Undergraduate Achievement in Educational Psychology with Instruction Objectives. Education 109 (2), 165-169.

Soar, R. S. & Soar, R.M. (1979). Emotional Climate and Management. In Peterson, P. & Walberg, H. (eds). *Research on Teaching.* Berkeley, CA: McCutchan Publishing Corporation. 97-119.

Veronin, M., and Patry, R. (2002). Instructional Objectives: What They Are, What They Aren't. *Pharmacy Education.* 1 (4), 207-213.

Wahlberg, H. (1999). Productive Teaching. In H. Waxman & H. Wahlberg (Ed.), *New Directions for Teaching Practice and Research.* Berkeley, CA: McCutchen Publishing.

Wright, C. & Nuthall, G. (1970). Relationships Between Teacher Behaviors and Pupil Achievement in Three Experimental Elementary Science Lessons. *American Educational Research Journal.* 7: 477-491.

Specificity

Brophy, J. & Good, T. (1986). Teacher behavior and student achievement. In M. Wittrock (Ed.), *Handbook of Research on Teaching.* New York: Macmillan Publishing Co.

DeVilliers, P.A. (1974). Imagery and Theme in Recall of Connected Discourse. *Journal of Experimental Psychology.* 103 (2): 263-268.

Evans, W.E. & Guyman, R.E. (1978). Clarity of Explanation: A Powerful Indicator of Teacher Effectiveness. Paper presented at American Educational Research Association. Toronto.

Hiller, J.H. (1971). Verbal Response Indicators of Conceptual Vagueness. *American Educational Research Journal.* 8: 151-162.

Hiller, J.H. et.al. (1969). A computer investigation of verbal characteristics of effective classroom lecturing. *American Educational Research Journal.* 6: 661-675.

Hines, C.V. (1981). A Further investigation of Teacher Clarity: The Relationship Between Observed and perceived Clarity and Student Achievement and Satisfaction. *Dissertation Abstracts International.*

Kennedy, J.J., Cruickshank, D.R., Bush, A.J. & Myers, B. (1979). Additional Investigations into the Nature of Teacher Clarity. *Journal of Educational Research.* 72: 3-10.

Land, M.L. & Smith, L.R. (1979). Effect of Teacher Clarity Variable on Student Achievement. *Journal of Educational research.* 72: 196-198.

Pompi, K.F. & Lachman, R. (1967). Surrogate Processes in the Short-Term Retention of Connected Discourse. *Journal of Experimental Psychology.* 35: 143-150.

Smith, L.R. (1977). Aspects of Teacher Discourse and student Achievement in Mathematics. *Journal of Research in Mathematics Education.* 8: 195-204.

Smith, L.R. & Edmonds, E.M. (1978). Teacher Vagueness and Pupil Participation in Mathematics Learning. *Journal for Research in Mathematics Education.* 9: 228-232.

Smith, L.R. & Cotton, M.L. (1980). Effect of Lesson Vagueness and Discontinuity on Student Achievement and Attitudes. *Journal of Educational Psychology.* 72: 670-675.

Smith, L.R. & Land, M.L. (1980). Student Perception of Teacher Clarity in Mathematics. *Journal of Research in Mathematics Education.* 11: 137-146.

Solomon, D. Rosenberg, L. & Bezdek, W. (1964). Teacher Behavior and Student Learning. *Journal of Educational Psychology.* 55: 23-30.

Thompson, E. (1960). An Experimental Investigation of the Relative Effectiveness of Organizational Structure in Oral Communication. *Southern Speech Journal.* 26: 50-69.

Wright, C. & Nuthall, G. (1970). Relationships Between Teacher Behaviors and Pupil Achievement in Three Experimental Elementary Science Lessons. *American Educational Research Journal.* 7: 477-491.

Sticking with the Objective

Anderson, L., Evertson, C. & and Brophy, J. (1979). An experimental study of effective teaching in first grade reading groups. *Elementary School Journal.* 79: 193-223.

Bennett, S. (1978). Recent Research on Teaching: A Dream, A Belief, and a Model. *British Journal of Educational Psychology.* 48: 127-147.

Bloom, B. (1976). *Human Characteristics and School Learning.* New York: McGraw-Hill.

Brophy, J., & Evertson, C. (1976). *Learning from Teaching: A Developmental Perspective.* Boston: Allyn & Bacon.

Coker, H., Lorenz, J. & Coker, J. (1976). *Interim Report on County CBTC Project, Fall, 1976.* Atlanta: Georgia Department of Education.

Dunkin, M. & Biddle, B. (1974). *The Study of Teaching.* New York: Holt, Rinehart and Winston.

Evertson, C., Anderson, C., Anderson, L., & Brophy, J. (1980). Relationships between Classroom Behaviors and Student Outcomes in Junior High Mathematics and English Classes. *American Educational Research.* 17: 43-60.

Fisher, C., Berliner, D., Filby, N. Marliave, R., Cahen, L., & Dishaw, M. (1980). *Teaching Behaviors, Academic Learning Time and Student Achievement: An Overview.* In Denham, C., & Lieberman, A. (eds). *Time to Learn.*. Washington, D.C.: National Institute of Education: U.S. Department of Education.

Fisher, C., Filby, N. Marliave, R., Cahen, L. Dishaw, M., Moore, J. & Berliner, D. (1978). *Technical Report V-1: Teaching Behaviors, Academic Learning Time and Student Achievement: Final report of phase III-B, Beginning Teacher Evaluation Study.* San Francisco, CA: Far West Laboratory.

Fredrick, W. (1977). The Use of Classroom Time in High Schools Above or Below the Median Reading Score. *Urban Education.* 1977: 459-464.

Good, T. & Beckerman, T. (1978). *The Effect of Classroom Context on Student Achievement: Technical Report No. 145.* Columbia, MO: Center for Research in Social Behavior.

Gump, P. (1974). Operating Environments in Schools of Open or Traditional Design. *School Review.* 82: 575-594.

Kounin, J. (1970). *Discipline and Group Management in Classrooms.* New York: Holt, Rinehart & Winston.

Leinhardt, G., Zigmond, N., & Cooley, W. (1981). Reading Instruction and Its Effects. *American Educational Research Journal.* 18.

Medley, D.M. (1977). *Teacher Competence and Teacher Effectiveness: A Review of Process-Product Research.* Washington, D.C.: American Association of Colleges for Teacher Education.

Powell, D. & Eash, M. (1974). Secondary School Cases. In Walberg, H (ed). *Evaluating Educational Performance.* Berkeley, CA: McCutchan Publishing Corporation. 277-293.

Rosenshine, B.(1971). *Teaching Behaviors and Student Achievement.* London: International Association for the Evaluation of Educational Achievement.

Rutter, M., Maughan, B., Mortimore, P., Ouston, J., & Smith A. (1979). *Fifteen Thousand Hours.* Cambridge, MA: Harvard University Press.

Stallings, J. (1981). Testing Teachers' In-Class Instruction and Measuring Change Resulting from Staff Development. Paper presented at National Teacher Examinations Policy Council. Princeton, NJ.

Stallings, J. & Kaskowitz, D. (1974). *Follow Through Classroom Observation Evaluation, 1972-1973: A Study of Implementation.* Menlo Park, CA: Stanford University Research Institute.

Stallings, J., Needels, M. & Stayrook, N. (1979). *How to Change the Process of Teaching Basic Reading Skills in Secondary Schools.* Menlo Park, CA: SRI International.

Stallings, J. & Robertson, A. (1979). *Factors Influencing Women's Decisions to Enroll in Elective Mathematics Classes in High School. Final Report to National Institute of Education.* Menlo Park, CA: SRI International.

Success/Sharing the Objective

Bloom, B. (1956). *Taxonomy of Educational Objectives: Handbook I: Cognitive Domain.* New York: McKay.

Wahlberg, H. (1999). Productive Teaching. In H. Waxman & H. Wahlberg (Ed.), *New Directions for Teaching Practice and Research.* Berkeley, CA: McCutchen Publishing.

Task Analysis/Sequencing

Anderson, R. & Faust, G. (1973). *Educational Psychology.* New York: Harper & Row.

Ennis, C. (1999). Physical Education. In Calwelti, G. (Ed.), *Handbook of Research on Improving Student Achievement.* Arlington, VA: Educational Research Service.

Hunter, Madeline. (1994). Mastery Teaching: Increasing Instructional Effectiveness in Elementary and Secondary Schools, Colleges and Universities. (Reprint). Thousand Oaks, CA: Corwin Press.

Wahlberg, H. (1999). Productive Teaching. In H. Waxman & H. Wahlberg (Ed.), *New Directions for Teaching Practice and Research.* Berkeley, CA: McCutchen Publishing.

Teaching Behaviors

Advani, K. & Beaumaster, E. (1973). *The Rise of Behavior Modification Techniques in a Class of Slow Learners.* Kingston, Ontario: Frontenac County Board of Education.

Anderson, L., Evertson, C. & and Brophy, J. (1979). An experimental study of effective teaching in first grade reading groups. *Elementary School Journal.* 79: 193-223.

Bennett, S. (1978). Recent Research on Teaching: A Dream, A Belief, and a Model. *British Journal of Educational Psychology.* 48: 127-147.

Bloom, B. (1976). *Human Characteristics and School Learning.* New York: McGraw-Hill.

Borg, W.R & Ascione, F. R. (1982). Classroom Management in Elementary Mainstreaming Classrooms. *Journal of Educational Psychology*. 74: 85-95.

Borg, W.R. & others. (1975a). Teacher classroom management skills and pupil behavior. *Journal of Experimental Education*. 44: 52-58.

Brophy, J. & Evertson, C. (1974). *The Texas Teacher Effectiveness Project: Presentation of Non-Linear Relationships and Summary Discussion, Report No. 74-6.* Austin: University of Texas R & D Center for Teacher Education.

Brophy, J. & Putnam, J. (1978). *Classroom Management in the Elementary Grades.* East Lansing, MI: Institute for Research on Teaching.

Coker, H., Lorenz, J. & Coker, J. (1976). *Interim Report on County CBTC Project, Fall, 1976.* Atlanta: Georgia Department of Education.

Cummings, C. (2002). *Teaching Makes a Difference*. Seattle, WA: Teaching, Inc.

Darling-Hammond, L. et.al.(1996). What Matters Most. *Phi Delta Kappan*. 78, 193-200.

Emmer, E.T., Evertson, C.M. & Anderson, L.M. (1980). Effective classroom management at the beginning of the school year. *Elementary School Journal*. 80: 219-231.

Fischer, C., Berliner, D., Filby, N., Marliave, R., Cahen, L. & Dishaw, M. (1980). Teaching Behaviors, Academic Learning Time and Student Achievement: An Overview. In C. Denhan and A. Lieberman (Eds.) *Time to Learn*. Washington, D.C.: The National Institute of Education, U.S. Department of Education.

Fisher, C., Filby, N. Marliave, R., Cahen, L. Dishaw, M., Moore, J. & Berliner, D. (1978). *Technical Report V-1: Teaching Behaviors, Academic Learning Time and Student Achievement: Final report of phase III-B, Beginning Teacher Evaluation Study.* San Francisco, CA: Far West Laboratory.

Fredrick, W. (1977). The Use of Classroom Time in High Schools Above or Below the Median Reading Score. *Urban Education.* 1977: 459-464.

Fisher, C., Filby, N. Marliave, R., Cahen, L. Dishaw, M., Moore, J. & Berliner, D. (1978). *Technical Report V-1: Teaching Behaviors, Academic Learning Time and Student Achievement: Final report of phase III-B, Beginning Teacher Evaluation Study.* San Francisco, CA: Far West Laboratory.

Greenwood, C.R. & others. (1974). Group contingencies for group consequences in classroom management: A further analysis. *Journal of Applied Behavior Analysis*. 7: 413-425.

Gump, P. (1974). Operating Environments in Schools of Open or Traditional Design. *School Review.* 82: 575-594.

Herman, S.H. & Traymontana, J. (1971). Instructions and group versus individual reinforcement in modifying disruptive behavior. *Journal of Applied Behavior Analysis*. 4: 113-119

Kounin, J. (1970). *Discipline and Group Management in Classrooms.* New York: Holt, Rinehart & Winston.

Kounin, J.S. & others. (1966). Managing emotionally disturbed children in regular classrooms. *Journal of Educational Psychology*. 57: 1-13.

Leinhardt, G., Zigmond, N., & Cooley, W. (1981). Reading Instruction and Its Effects. *American Educational Research Journal*. 18.

Madsen, C.H. & others. (1968). Rules, praise, and ignoring elements of elementary classroom control. *Journal of Applied Behavior Analysis*. 1: 139-150.

Marzano, R., Pickering, D., & Pollock, J. (2001). *Classroom Instruction that Works*. Alexandria, VA: ASCD.

Medley, D.M. (1977). *Teacher Competence and Teacher Effectiveness: A Review of Process-Product Research*. Washington, D.C.: American Association of Colleges for Teacher Education.

Moskovitz, G. & Hayman, J.L. (1969). Success strategies of inner-city teachers: a year-long study. *Journal of Educational Research*. 69: 283-289.

O'Leary, K.D. & Becker, W.C. (1968). The effects of a teacher's reprimands on children's behavior. *Journal of School Psychology*. 7: 8-11.

O'Leary, K.D. & others. (1970). The effects of loud and soft reprimands on the behavior of disruptive students. *Exceptional Children*. 37: 145-155.

Porter, A., & Brophy, J. (1988). Synthesis of research on good teaching: Insights from the work of the Institute of Research on Teaching. *Educational Leadership,* 45, 74-85.

Powell, D. & Eash, M. (1974). Secondary School Cases. In Walberg, H (ed). *Evaluating Educational Performance.* Berkeley, CA: McCutchan Publishing Corporation. 277-293.

Rutter, M., Maughan, B., Mortimore, P., Ouston, J., & Smith A. (1979). *Fifteen Thousand Hours.* Cambridge, MA: Harvard University Press.

Sanford, J.P. & Evertson, C.M. (1981). Classroom management in a low SES junior high: three case studies. *Journal of Teacher Education*. 38: 34-38.

Smith, J., Lee, V., & Newmann, F. (2001). Instruction and achievement in Chicago elementary schools. Chicago: Consortium on Chicago School Research. (interactive teaching)

Stallings, J. (1981). Testing Teachers' In-Class Instruction and Measuring Change Resulting from Staff Development. Paper presented at National Teacher Examinations Policy Council. Princeton, NJ.

Stallings, J., Needels, M. & Stayrook, N. (1979). *How to Change the Process of Teaching Basic Reading Skills in Secondary Schools*. Menlo Park, CA: SRI International.

Stallings, J. & Kaskowitz, D. (1974). *Follow Through Classroom Observation Evaluation, 1972-1973: A Study of Implementation.* Menlo Park, CA: Stanford University Research Institute.

Thomas, D.R. & others. (1968). Production and elimination of disruptive classroom behavior by systematically varying teacher's behavior. *Journal of Applied Behavior Analysis*. 1 35-45.

Wang, M., Haertel, G., & Wahlberg, H. (1994). What helps students learn? *Educational Leadership*, 51 (4), 74-79.

Wright, S., Horn, S., & Sanders, W. (1997). Teacher and classroom context effects on student achievement: Implications for teacher education. *Journal of Personnel Evaluation in Education*, 11, 57-67.

Time Management/On the Clock

Bennett, S. (1978). Recent Research on Teaching: A Dream, A Belief, and a Model. *British Journal of Educational Psychology*. 48: 127-147.

Bloom, B. (1976). *Human Characteristics and School Learning*. New York: McGraw-Hill.

Brophy, J., & Evertson, C. (1976). *Learning from Teaching: A Developmental Perspective.* Boston: Allyn & Bacon.

Coker, H., Lorenz, J. & Coker, J. (1976). *Interim Report on County CBTC Project, Fall, 1976.* Atlanta: Georgia Department of Education.

Evertson, C. (1980). Differences in Instructional Activities in High and Low Achieving Junior High Classes. Paper presented at American Educational Research Association. Boston.

Fisher, C., Filby, N. Marliave, R., Cahen, L. Dishaw, M., Moore, J. & Berliner, D. (1978). *Technical Report V-1: Teaching Behaviors, Academic Learning Time and Student Achievement: Final report of phase III-B, Beginning Teacher Evaluation Study.* San Francisco, CA: Far West Laboratory.

Fredrick, W. (1977). The Use of Classroom Time in High Schools Above or Below the Median Reading Score. *Urban Education.* 1977: 459-464.

Good, T. & Beckerman, T. (1978). *The Effect of Classroom Context on Student Achievement: Technical Report No. 145.* Columbia, MO: Center for Research in Social Behavior.

Gump, P. (1974). Operating Environments in Schools of Open or Traditional Design. *School Review.* 82: 575-594.

Medley, D.M. (1977). *Teacher Competence and Teacher Effectiveness: A Review of Process-Product Research.* Washington, D.C.: American Association of Colleges for Teacher Education.

Rutter, M., Maughan, B., Mortimore, P., Ouston, J., & Smith A. (1979). *Fifteen Thousand Hours.* Cambridge, MA: Harvard University Press.

Stallings, J. (1981). Testing Teachers' In-Class Instruction and Measuring Change Resulting from Staff Development. Paper presented at National Teacher Examinations Policy Council. Princeton, NJ.

Stallings, J. & Kaskowitz, D. (1974). *Follow Through Classroom Observation Evaluation, 1972-1973: A Study of Implementation.* Menlo Park, CA: Stanford University Research Institute.

Stallings, J. & Robertson, A. (1979). *Factors Influencing Women's Decisions to Enroll in Elective Mathematics Classes in High School. Final Report to National Institute of Education.* Menlo Park, CA: SRI International.

Time Management/Wait Time

Abraham, E., Nelson, M., & Reynolds, W. (1971). Discussion Strategies and Student Cognitive Skills. Paper presented at American Educational Research Association. New York.

Bloom, B. (1976). *Human Characteristics and School Learning.* New York: McGraw-Hill.

Borg, W.R & Ascione, F. R. (1982). Classroom Management in Elementary Mainstreaming Classrooms. *Journal of Educational Psychology.* 74: 85-95.

Brophy, J. & Evertson, C. (1974). *Process-Product Correlations in the Texas Teacher Effectiveness Study: Final Report.* Austin: University of Texas.

Brophy, J. & Evertson, C. (1974). *The Texas Teacher Effectiveness Project: Presentation of Non-Linear Relationships and Summary Discussion, Report No. 74-6.* Austin: University of Texas R & D Center for Teacher Education.

Brophy, J. & Putnam, J. (1978). *Classroom Management in the Elementary Grades.* East Lansing, MI: Institute for Research on Teaching.

Campbell, J. (1973). Pattern Analysis – A Macroscopic Development for Interaction Analysis. Paper presented at National Association for Research in Science Teaching. Chicago.

Coker, H., Lorenz, J. & Coker, J. (1976). *Interim Report on County CBTC Project, Fall, 1976.* Atlanta: Georgia Department of Education.

Fagan, E., Hassler, D., & Szabo, M. (1981). Evaluation of Questioning Strategies in Language Arts Instruction. *Research in the Teaching of English.* 15 (3): 267-273.

Fisher, C., Filby, N. Marliave, R., Cahen, L. Dishaw, M., Moore, J. & Berliner, D. (1978). *Technical Report V-1: Teaching Behaviors, Academic Learning Time and Student Achievement: Final report of phase III-B, Beginning Teacher Evaluation Study.* San Francisco, CA: Far West Laboratory.

Gabel, D. (1999). Science. In Calwelti, G. (Ed.), *Handbook of Research on Improving Student Achievement.* Arlington, VA: Educational Research Service.

Good, T. & Beckerman, T. (1978). *The Effect of Classroom Context on Student Achievement: Technical Report No. 145.* Columbia, MO: Center for Research in Social Behavior.

Grouws, D., & Cebulla, J. (1999). Mathematics. In Calwelti, G. (Ed.), *Handbook of Research on Improving Student Achievement.* Arlington, VA: Educational Research Service.

Kounin, J. (1970). *Discipline and Group Management in Classrooms.* New York: Holt, Rinehart & Winston.

Mahaffey, L., Brophy, J. & Evertson, C. (1975). Teacher Feedback to Children's Answers: Process-Product Relationships. Paper presented to Research Association. Washington, D.C.

Medley, D.M. (1977). *Teacher Competence and Teacher Effectiveness: A Review of Process-Product Research.* Washington, D.C.: American Association of Colleges for Teacher Education.

Rowe, M. (1974). Wait-Time and Rewards as Instructional Variables, Their Influence on Language, Logic and Fate Control: Part One Wait-Time. *Journal of Research in Science Teaching.* 11: 81-94.

Rowe, M. (1987). Wait time: slowing down may be a way of speeding up. *American Educator*, Spring, 38-47.

Scherer, M. (2001). How and why standards can improve student achievement. *Educational Leadership*, 59 (1), 14-18.

Stallings, J. & Kaskowitz, D. (1974). *Follow Through Classroom Observation Evaluation, 1972-1973: A Study of Implementation.* Menlo Park, CA: Stanford University Research Institute.
Steinberg, L. (1996). *Beyond the Classroom: Why School Reform Has Failed and What parents Need to Do.* New York: Simon & Schuster.

Wahlberg, H. (1988). Synthesis of research on time and learning. *Educational Leadership*, 45, 76-85.
Yair, G. (2000). Not just about time: Instructional practices and productive time in school. *Educational Administration Quarterly*, 36 (4), 485-512.

General References

Charles, C. M. (1999). *Building Classroom Discipline.* New York: Longman Press.

Cooper, H. (2001). *The Battle Over Homework: Common Ground for Administrators, Teachers, and Parents* 2nd edition. Corwin Press.

Curwin, Richard L., Mendler, Allen N. and Mendler, Brian D. (2008). *Discipline with Dignity: New Challenges, New Solutions.* Alexandria, VA: ASCD.

Darling-Hammond, L. (2002). "The Research and Rhetoric On Teacher Certification: A Response To 'Teacher Certification Reconsidered.'" *Education Policy Analysis Archives* 9 (1). http://epaa.asa.edu/epaa/v10n36.html.

Dweck, Carol S. (2008). *Mindset: The New Psychology of Success: How We Can Lead to Fulfill Our Potential.* New York: Ballantine Books/Random House Publishing.

Fay & Funk. (1997). *Teaching with Love and Logic*. Golden, CO: Love and Logic Press.

Garrett, A. (2003). *Bullying in American Schools*. Jefferson, NC: McFarland Publishing.

Glasser, W. (1997). *Choice Theory: A New Psychology for a New Century*. New York: Harper Collins.

Goldhaber, D. and Brewer, D. (2000). "Does Teacher Certification Matter? High School Teacher Certification Status and Student Achievement." *Educational Evaluation and Policy Analysis* 22:129-145.

Hanushek, E., Kain, J. and Rivkin, S. (1999). *Do Higher Salaries Buy Better Teachers?* Working Paper No 7082. Cambridge: National Bureau of Economic Research.

Himmele, Pérsida, and Himmele, William. (2011). *Total Participation Techniques: Making Every Student an Active Learner.* Alexandria, VA: ASCD.

Hunter, Madeline. (1994). Mastery Teaching: Increasing Instructional Effectiveness in Elementary and Secondary Schools, Colleges and Universities. (Reprint). Thousand Oaks, CA: Corwin Press.

Hyatt, C. & Gottlieb, L. (1987). *Why Smart People Fail.* New York: Simon and Schuster.

Jensen, E. (1998). *Teaching with the Brain in Mind.* Alexandria, VA: Association for Supervision and Curriculum Development.

Lezotte, L. (1997). *Learning for All.* Okemus, MI: Effective Schools Products.

Louisell, R & Descamps, J. (2001). *Developing a Teaching Style.* Prospect Heights, IL: Waveland Press, Inc.

Maslow, Abraham. (1998). *Toward a Psychology of Being. 3rd ed.* Hoboken, NJ: Wiley Publishing.

Minton, Elaine, (1999). Extreme experiences and asking the unaskable: An interview with Ted Sizer. *Active Learner: A Foxfire Journal for Teachers.* 1 (1): 12-15.

Molloy, John T.. (1988). *New Dress for Success.* Lebanon, IN: Warner Books.

Oettinger, G. (1999). Does High School Employment Affect High School Academic Performance? Industrial and Labor Relations Review. 53 (1). 136-151.

Pink, Daniel H. (2005-2006). *A Whole New Mind: Why Right-Brainers Will Rule the Future.* New York: Riverhead Books / Penguin Group.

Pink, Daniel H. (2009). *Drive: The Surprising Truth About What Motivates Us.* New York: Riverhead Books / Penguin Group.

Powell, McLaughlin, Savage & Zehm. (2001). *Classroom Management: Perspectives on the Social Curriculum.* New York: Merrill Prentice Hall.

Schmoker, Michael J. (2011). *Focus: Elevating the Essentials to Radically Improve Student Learning.* Alexandria, VA: ASCD.

Schmoker, Michael J. (2006). *Results Now: How We Can Achieve Unprecedented Improvements in Teaching and Learning.* Alexandria, VA: ASCD.

Schmoker, Michael J. (1999). *Results Now: The Key to Continuous School Improvement.* Alexandria, VA: ASCD.

Schmoker, Michael J. (2001-2002). *The Results Fieldbook: Practical Strategies from Dramatically Improved Schools.* Alexandria, VA: ASCD.

Vatterott, Cathy. (2009). *Rethinking Homework: Best Practices that Support Diverse Needs.* Alexandria, VA: ASCD.

Willingham, Daniel T. (2009). *Why Don't Students Like School?: A Cognitive Scientist Answers Questions About How the Mind Works and What it Means for the Classroom.* San Francisco, CA: Josey-Bass Books.

Wixted, J. & Ebbesen, E. (1997). Genuine power curves in forgetting: A quantitative analysis of individual subject forgetting. *Memory & Cognition.* 25 (5): 731-740.

Wong, H. and Wong, R. (1998). *The First Days of School.* Mountain View, CA: Wong and Wong

Wessler, S. (2003). It's Hard to Learn When You're Scared. *Educational Leadership* 61 (1), 40-43.

Section Nine: Index of Subjects

A

B

C

D

E

F

G

H

I

N

O

P

Q

R

S

T

U

V

W

X-Y-Z